YOUTH IN REVOLT

◊

Critical Interventions: Politics, Culture, and the Promise of Democracy

Edited by Henry A. Giroux, Susan Searls Giroux, and Kenneth J. Saltman

YOUTH IN REVOLT
Reclaiming a Democratic Future

HENRY A. GIROUX

PARADIGM PUBLISHERS
Boulder • London

Copyright © 2013 Paradigm Publishers

Published in the United States by Paradigm Publishers, 5589 Arapahoe Avenue, Boulder, CO 80303 USA.

Paradigm Publishers is the trade name of Birkenkamp & Company, LLC, Dean Birkenkamp, President and Publisher.

Library of Congress Cataloging-in-Publication Data

Giroux, Henry A.
  Youth in revolt : reclaiming a democratic future / Henry A. Giroux.
     p. cm.
  Includes bibliographical references and index.
  ISBN 978-1-61205-264-9 (pbk. : alk. paper)
  1. Youth—Political activity—United States.   2. Youth movements—United States.   3. Political violence—United States.   4. Democracy—United States.   I. Title.
  HQ799.2.P6G57 2013
  305.235—dc23

                                                              2012026108

Printed and bound in the United States of America on acid-free paper that meets the standards of the American National Standard for Permanence of Paper for Printed Library Materials.

Designed and Typeset by Straight Creek Bookmakers.

17   16   15   14   13   1   2   3   4   5

For Roger Simon:
my dear friend and brother for over thirty years

◆

Contents

◇

Acknowledgments

I want to thank Susan Searls Giroux for her enormous insights in helping me think critically about many of the ideas in this book. Susan always took the conversation to a place I could never have reached alone. I cannot imagine thinking through and writing a book without her. As usual, my colleague Grace Pollock was indispensable in bringing her formidable editorial skills to this book. My administrative assistant, Maya Sabados, was incalculably helpful in gathering and reading research for the book. She was also hugely proficient in correcting the text for technical and stylistic errors. Her contribution was invaluable. Victoria Harper, my editor at *Truthout,* is my guardian angel and has provided me with unwavering support in publishing my work there, some of which is included in this book. I would also like to thank Dr. Mo Elbestawi and Dr. Fiona E. McNeill for supporting, with great conviction and ethical courage, my research at McMaster University. Patrick Deane, the president of McMaster University, has renewed my faith in academic leadership and the democratic mission of the university, and has been a source of great intellectual insight and hope for many students and faculty. My colleague David Clark was enormously generous with his time and thoughts in reading many of the chapters in this book while offering a number of invaluable critical insights. I want to thank Tyler Pollard and Jennifer Fisher, my two brilliant graduate students, for exhibiting great patience, intelligence, moral courage, and leadership while writing their dissertations and sharing their insights with me. I want to thank Gottfried and Renate Helnwein for their generosity in allowing me, once again, to grace the cover of my book with Gottfried's haunting, inimitable, and provocative images. I want to thank my dear friend Subhash Dighe, whose sense of curiosity, spirit of generosity, and sheer humanity never fail to inspire me. Finally, I would also like to thank the Social Sciences and Humanities Research Council of Canada for their generous support. Highly modified versions of some of these chapters have been published in *Third Text*, *JAC*, and *Policy Futures in Education.*

◆

Introduction

Criminalizing Dissent and Punishing the Occupy Movement Protesters

> Military-style command and control systems are now be-
> ing established to support "zero tolerance" policing and
> urban surveillance practices designed to exclude failed
> consumers or undesirable persons from the new enclaves
> of urban consumption and leisure.
>
> —*Stephen Graham*

Young people are demonstrating all over the world against a
variety of issues ranging from economic injustice and massive
inequality to drastic cuts in education and public services.[1] In
the fall of 2011, on the tenth anniversary of September 11, as
the United States revisited the tragic loss and celebrated the
courage displayed on that torturous day, another kind of commemoration took place. The Occupy movement shone out like
a flame in the darkness—a beacon of the irrepressible spirit of
democracy and a humane desire for justice. Unfortunately, the
peacefully organized protests across America have often been
met with derogatory commentaries in the mainstream media
and, increasingly, state-sanctioned violence. The war against
society has become a war against youthful protesters and increasingly bears a striking resemblance to the violence waged
against Occupy movement protesters and the violence associated with the contemporary war zone.[2] Missing from both the
dominant media and state and national politics is an attempt

to critically engage the issues the protesters are raising, not to mention any attempt to dialogue with them over their strategies, tactics, and political concerns. That many young people have become "a new class of stateless individuals ... cast into a threatening and faceless mass whose identities collapse into the language of debt, survival, and disposability" appears to have escaped the attention of the mainstream media.[3] Matters of justice, human dignity, and social responsibility have given way to a double gesture that seeks to undercut democratic public spheres through the criminalization of dissent while also resorting to crude and violent forms of punishment as the only mediating tools to use with young people who are attempting to open a new conversation about politics, inequality, and social justice.

In the United States, the state monopoly on the use of violence has intensified since the 1980s and in the process has been directed disproportionately against young people, poor minorities, immigrants, women, and the elderly. Guided by the notion that unregulated, market-driven values and relations should shape every domain of human life, a business model of governance has eviscerated any viable notion of social responsibility and conscience, thereby furthering the dismissal of social problems and expanding cutbacks in basic social services.[4] The examples are endless, but one in particular stands out. In March 2012, Texas governor Rick Perry joined eight other states in passing legislation to ban funding for clinics, including Planned Parenthood facilities, affiliated with abortion services for women.[5] As a result, the federal government has stopped funding the Texas Women's Health Program. Unfortunately, this attempt by Perry to punish all women because of his antiabortion stance means that more than 130,000 women in Texas will not have access to vital services ranging from mammograms to health care for their children. There is more at work here than a resurgent war on women and their children or "an insane bout of mass misogyny."[6] There is also a deep-seated religious and political authoritarianism that has become one of the fundamental pillars of what I call a neoliberal culture of cruelty. As the welfare state is hollowed out, a culture of compassion is replaced by a culture of violence, cruelty, waste, and disposability.[7] Banks, hedge funds, and finance capital as the contemporary registers of class power have a new visibility, and their spokespersons are unabashedly blunt in supporting a corporate culture in which "ruthlessness is prized and money is the ultimate measure."[8] Collective insurance policies and social protections have given way to the forces of economic deregulation, the transformation of the welfare state into punitive workfare programs, the privatization of public goods, and an appeal to individual culpability as a substitute for civic responsibility. At the same time, violence—or what Anne-Marie Cusac calls "American punishment"—travels from our prisons and schools to various aspects of our daily lives, "becoming omnipresent ... [from] the shows we watch on television, [to] the way many of us treat children [to] some influential religious practices."[9]

David Harvey has argued that neoliberalism is "a political project to re-establish the conditions for capital accumulation and to restore the power of economic elites" through the implementation of "an institutional framework characterized by strong private property rights, free markets, and free trade."[10] Neoliberalism is also a pedagogical project designed to create particular subjects, desires, and values defined largely by market considerations. National destiny becomes linked to a market-driven logic in which freedom is stripped down to freedom from government regulation, freedom to consume, and freedom to say anything one wants, regardless of how racist or toxic the consequences might be. This neoliberal notion of freedom is abstracted from any sense of civic responsibility or social cost. In fact, "neoliberalism is grounded in the idea of the 'free, possessive individual,'" with the state cast "as tyrannical and oppressive."[11] The welfare state, in particular, becomes the archenemy of freedom. As Stuart Hall points out, according to apostles of free-market fundamentalism, "The state must never govern society, dictate to free individuals how to dispose of their private property, regulate a free-market economy or interfere with the God-given right to make profits and amass personal wealth."[12]

Paradoxically, neoliberalism severely proscribes any vestige of social and civic agency through the figure of the isolated automaton for whom choice is reduced to the practice of endless shopping, fleeing from any sense of civic obligation, and safeguarding a radically individualized existence. Neoliberal governance translates into a state that attempts to substitute individual security for social welfare but in doing so offers only the protection of gated communities for the privileged and incarceration for those considered flawed consumers or threats to the mythic ideal of a white Christian nation. Neoliberalism refuses to recognize how private troubles are connected to broader systemic issues, legitimating instead an ode to self-reliance in which the experience of personal misfortune becomes merely the just desserts delivered by the righteous hand of the free market—not a pernicious outcome of the social order being hijacked by an antisocial ruling elite and forced to serve a narrow set of interests. Critical thought and human agency are rendered impotent as neoliberal rationality "substitutes emotional and personal vocabularies for political ones in formulating solutions to political problems."[13] Within such a depoliticized discourse, youths are told that there is no dream of the collective, no viable social bonds, only the actions of autonomous individuals who must rely on their own resources and who bear sole responsibility for the effects of larger systemic political and economic problems.

Under the regime of neoliberalism, no claims are recognized that call for compassion, justice, and social responsibility. No claims are recognized that demand youths have a future better than the present, and no claims are recognized in which young people assert the need to narrate themselves as part of a broader struggle for global justice and radical democracy. Parading as a species of democracy, neoliberal economics and ideology cancel out democracy "as the incommensurable sharing of existence that makes the political possible."[14] Symptoms of ethical, political, and economic impoverishment are all around us. And, as if that were not enough, at the current moment in history we are witnessing the merging of violence and governance along with a systemic disinvestment in and breakdown of institutions and public spheres that have provided the minimal conditions for democracy and the principles of communal responsibility. Young people are particularly vulnerable. As Jean-Marie Durand points out, "Youth is no longer considered the world's future, but as a threat to its present. [For] youth, there is no longer any political discourse except for a disciplinary one."[15]

As young people make diverse claims on the promise of a radical democracy in the streets, on campuses, and at other occupied sites, articulating what a fair and just world might be, they are treated as criminal populations—rogue groups incapable of toeing the line, "prone to irrational, intemperate and unpredictable" behavior.[16] Moreover, they are increasingly subjected to orchestrated modes of control and containment, if not police violence. Such youths are now viewed as the enemy by the political and corporate establishment because they make visible the repressed images of the common good and the impor-tance of democratic public spheres, public services, the social state, and a society shaped by democratic values rather than market values. Youthful protesters and others are reclaiming the repressed memories of the Good Society and a social state that once, as Zygmunt Bauman has pointed out, "endorsed collective insurance against individual misfortune and its consequences."[17] Bauman explains that such a state "lifts members of society to the status of citizens—that is, makes them stake-holders in addition to being stock-holders, beneficiaries but also actors responsible for the benefits' creation and availability, individuals with acute interest in the common good understood as the shared institutions that can be trusted to assure solidity and reliability of the state-issued 'collective insurance policy.'"[18] In an attempt to excavate the repressed memories of the welfare state, David Theo Goldberg spells out in detail the specific mechanisms and policies it produced in the name of the general welfare between the 1930s and 1970s in the United States. He writes,

> From the 1930s through the 1970s, the liberal democratic state had offered a more or less robust set of institutional appara-tuses concerned in principle at least to advance the welfare of its citizens. This was the period of advancing social security, welfare safety nets, various forms of national health system, the expansion of and investment in public education, including higher education, in some states to the exclusion of private and religiously sponsored educational institutions. It saw the emer-gence of state bureaucracies as major employers especially in later years of historically excluded groups. And all this, in turn, offered optimism among a growing proportion of the populace for access to middle-class amenities, including those previously racially excluded within the state and new immigrants from the global south.[19]

Young people today are protesting against a strengthening global capitalist project that erases the benefits of the welfare state and the possibility of a radical notion of democracy. They are protesting against a neoliberal project of accumulation, dispossession, deregulation, privatization, and commodification that leaves them out of any viable notion of the future. They are rejecting and resisting a form of casino capitalism that has ushered in a permanent revolution marked by a massive project of depoliticization, on the one hand, and an aggressive, if not savage, practice of distributing upward wealth, income, and opportunity for the 1 percent on the other. Under neoliberalism, every moment, space, practice, and social relation offers the possibility of financial investment, or what Ernst Bloch once called the "swindle of fulfillment."[20] Goods, services, and targeted human beings are ingested into its waste machine and dismissed and disposed of as excess. Flawed consumers are now assigned the status of damaged and defective human beings. Resistance to such oppressive policies and practices does not come easily, and many young people are paying a price for such resistance. According to OccupyArrests.com, "there have been at least 6705 arrests in over 112 different cities as of March 6, 2012."[21]

Occupy movement protests and state-sponsored violence "have become a mirror"—and I would add a defining feature—"of the contemporary state."[22] Abandoned by the existing political system, young people in Oakland, California, New York City, and numerous other cities have placed their bodies on the line, protesting peacefully while trying to produce a new language, politics, and "community that manifests the values of equality and mutual respect that they see missing in a world that is structured by neoliberal principles."[23] Well aware that the spaces, sites, and spheres for the representation of their voices, desires, and concerns have collapsed, they have occupied a number of spaces ranging from public parks to college campuses in an effort to create a public forum where they can narrate themselves and their visions of the future while representing the misfortunes, suffering, and hopes of the unemployed, poor, incarcerated, and marginalized. This movement is not simply about reclaiming space but also about producing new ideas, generating a new conversation, and introducing a new political language.

Rejecting the notion that democracy and markets are the same, young people are calling for the termination of corporate control over the commanding institutions of politics, culture, and economics, an end to the suppression of dissent, and a shutting down of the permanent warfare state. Richard Lichtman is right to insist that the Occupy movement should be praised for its embrace of communal democracy as well as an emerging set of shared concerns, principles, and values articulated "by a demand for equality, or, at the very least, for a significant lessening of the horrid extent of inequality; for a working democracy; for the elimination of the moneyed foundation of politics; for the abolition of political domination by a dehumanized plutocracy; for the replacement of ubiquitous commodification by the reciprocal recognition of humanity in the actions of its agents."[24] As Arundhati Roy points out, what connects the protests in the United States to resistance movements all over the globe is that young people "know that their being excluded from the obscene amassing of wealth of U.S. corporations is part of the same system of the exclusion and war that is being waged by these corporations in places like India, Africa, and the Middle East."[25] Of course, Lichtman, Roy, and others believe that this is just the beginning of a movement and that much needs to be done, as Staughton Lynd argues, to build new strategies, a vast network of new institutions and public spheres, a community of trust, and political organization that invites poor people into its ranks.[26] Stanley Aronowitz goes further and insists that the Occupy movement needs to bring together the fight for economic equality and security with the task of reshaping American institutions along genuinely democratic lines.[27]

All of these issues are important, but what must be addressed in the most immediate sense is the danger the emerging police state in the United States poses not just to the young protesters occupying a number of American cities but to democracy itself. This threat is particularly evident in the results of a merging of neoliberal modes of discipline and education with a warlike mentality in which it becomes nearly impossible to reclaim the language of obligation, compassion, community, social responsibility, and civic engagement. And unless the actions of young protesters, however diverse they may be, are understood alongside a robust notion of the social, civic courage, communal bonds, and the imperatives of a vital democracy, it will be difficult for the American public to challenge state violence and the framing of protest, dissent, and civic engagement as un-American or, worse, as a species of criminal behavior.

Although considerable coverage has been given in the progressive media to the violence being waged against the Occupy protesters, these analyses rarely go far enough. I want to build on these critiques by arguing that it is important to situate the growing police violence within a broader set of categories that both enables a critical understanding of the underlying social, economic, and political forces at work in such assaults and allows us to reflect critically on the distinctiveness of the current historical period in which they are taking place. For example, it is difficult to address such state-sponsored violence against young people and the Occupy movement without analyzing the devolution of the social state and the corresponding rise of the warfare and punishing state.[28] The notion of historical conjuncture is important here because it both provides an opening into the diverse forces shaping a particular moment and allows for a productive balance of theory and strategy to inform future interventions. That is, it helps us to address theoretically how youth protests are largely related to and might resist a historically specific neoliberal project that promotes vast inequalities in income and wealth, creates the student-loan debt bomb, eliminates much-needed social programs, privileges profits and commodities over people, and eviscerates the social wage.

Within the United States, the often violent response to nonviolent forms of youth protest must also be analyzed within the framework of a mammoth military-industrial state and its commitment to war and the militarization of the entire society. The merging of the military-industrial complex and unchecked finance capital points to the need for strategies that address what is specific about the current warfare state and the neoliberal project that legitimates it. That is, what are the diverse practices, interests, modes of power, social relations, public pedagogies, and economic configurations that shape the politics of the punishing state? Focusing on the specifics of the current historical conjuncture is invaluable politically in that such an approach makes visible the ideologies, policies, and modes of governance produced by the neoliberal warfare state. When neoliberal mechanisms of power and ideology are made visible, it becomes easier for the American public to challenge the common assumptions that legitimate these apparatuses of power. This type of interrogative strategy also reclaims the necessity of critical thought, civic engagement, and democratic politics by invoking the pedagogical imperative that humans not only make history but can alter its course and future direction.

For many young people today, human agency is defined as a mode of self-reflection and critical social engagement rather than a surrender to a paralyzing and unchallengeable fate. Likewise, democratic expression has become fundamental to their existence. Many young people are embracing democracy not merely as a mode of governance, but more importantly, as Bill Moyers points out, as a means of dignifying people "so they become fully free to claim their moral and political agency."[29] Human agency has become a vital force to struggle over as part of an ongoing project in which the future remains an open horizon that cannot be dismissed through appeals to the end of history or end of ideology.[30] But to understand how politics refuses any guarantees and resistance becomes possible, we must first understand the present. Following Stuart Hall, I want to argue that the current historical moment, or what he calls the "long march of the Neoliberal Revolution,"[31] has to be understood not only through the emergent power of finance capital and its institutions but also in terms of the growing forms of authoritarian violence that it deploys and reinforces. I want to address these antidemocratic pressures and their relationship to the rising protests of young people in the United States and abroad through the lens of two interrelated crises: the crisis of governing through violence and the crisis of what Alex Honneth has called "a failed sociality"[32]—which currently conjoin as a driving force to dismantle any viable notion of public pedagogy and civic education. If we are not to fall prey to a third crisis—"the crisis of negation"[33]—then it is imperative that we recognize the hope symbolized and embodied by young people across America and their attempt to remake society in order to ensure a better, more democratic future for us all.

The Crisis of Governing through Violence

The United States is addicted to violence, and this dependency is fueled increasingly by its willingness to wage war at home and abroad.[34] As Andrew Bacevich rightly argues, "war has become a normal condition [matched by] Washington's seemingly irrevocable abandonment of any semblance of self-restraint regarding the use of violence as an instrument of statecraft."[35] But war in this instance is not merely the outgrowth of policies designed to protect the security and well-being of the United States. It is also, as C. Wright Mills pointed out, part of a "military metaphysics"[36]—a complex of forces that includes corporations, defense industries, politicians, financial institutions, and universities. The culture of war provides jobs, profits, political payoffs, research funds, and forms of political and economic power that reach into every aspect of society. War is also one of the nation's most honored virtues. Its militaristic values now bear down on almost every aspect of American life.[37] Similarly, as the governing-through-violence complex becomes normalized in the broader society, it continually works in a variety of ways to erode any distinction between war and peace.

Increasingly stoked by a moral and political hysteria, war-like values produce and endorse shared fears and organized violence as the primary registers of social relations. The conceptual merging of war and violence is evident in the ways in which the language of militarization is now used by politicians to address a range of policies as if they are operating on a battlefield or in a war zone. War becomes the adjective of choice as policymakers talk about waging war on drugs, poverty, and the underclass. There is more at work here than the prevalence of armed knowledge and a militarized discourse; there is also the emergence of a militarized society in which "the range of acceptable opinion inevitably shrinks."[38] And this choice of vocabulary and slow narrowing of democratic vision further enable the use of violence as an instrument of domestic policy.

How else to explain that the United States has become the punishing state par excellence, as indicated by the hideous fact that while it contains "5 percent of the Earth's population, it is home to nearly a quarter of its prisoners"?[39] Senator Lindsay Graham made this very clear in his rhetorical justification of the 2012 National Defense Authorization Act by stating "that under this Act the U.S. homeland is considered a 'battlefield.'"[40] The ominous implications behind this statement, especially for Occupy movement protesters, became obvious in light of the fact that the act gives the US government the right to detain "U.S. citizens indefinitely without charge or trial if deemed necessary by the president.... Detentions can follow mere membership, past or present, in 'suspect organizations.'"[41]

Since 9/11, the war on terror and the campaign for homeland security have increasingly mimicked the tactics of the enemies they sought to crush and as such have become a war on democracy. A new military urbanism has taken root in the United States as state surveillance projects proliferate, signaling what Stephen Graham calls "the startling militarization of civil society—the extension of military ideas of tracking, identification, and targeting into the quotidian spaces and circulations of everyday life."[42] This is partly evident in the ongoing militarization of police departments throughout the United States. Baton-wielding cops are now being supplied with the latest military equipment imported straight from the war zones of Iraq and Afghanistan. Military technologies once used exclusively on the battlefield are now being supplied to police units across the nation: drones, machine-gun-equipped armored trucks, SWAT-type vehicles, "digital communications equipment, and Kevlar helmets, like those used by soldiers used in foreign wars."[43] The domestic war against "terrorists" (code for young protesters) provides new opportunities for major defense contractors and corporations to become "more a part of our domestic lives."[44] As Glenn Greenwald points out, the United States since 9/11

> has aggressively paramilitarized the nation's domestic police forces by lavishing them with countless military-style weapons and other war-like technologies, training them in war-zone military tactics, and generally imposing a war mentality on them. Arming domestic police forces with paramilitary weaponry will ensure their systematic use even in the absence of a terrorist attack on U.S. soil; they will simply find other, increasingly permissive uses for those weapons.[45]

These domestic paramilitary forces also undermine free speech and dissent through the sheer threat of violence while often wielding power that runs roughshod over civil liberties, human rights, and civic responsibilities.[46] Given that "by age 23, almost a third of Americans are arrested for a crime," it is not unreasonable to assume that in the new militarized state the perception of young people as predators, threats to corporate governance, and disposable objects will intensify, as will the growth of a punishing state that acts out against young protesters in increasingly unrestrained and savage ways.[47] Young people, particularly poor minorities of color, have already become the targets of what David Theo Goldberg calls "extraordinary power in the name of securitization ... [viewed as] unruly populations ... [who] are to be subjected to necropolitical discipline through the threat of imprisonment or death, physical or social."[48]

Shared fears and the media hysteria that promotes them produce more than a culture of suspects and unbridled intimidation. Fear on a broad public scale serves the interests of policymakers who support a growing militarization of the police along with the corporations that supply high-tech scanners, surveillance cameras, riot extinguishers, and toxic chemicals—all of which are increasingly used with impunity on anyone who engages in peaceful protests against the warfare and corporate state.[49] Images abound in the mainstream media of such abuses. There is the now famous image of an eighty-four-year-old woman looking straight into a camera, her face drenched in a liquid spray used by the police after attending a protest rally. There is the image of a woman who is two months pregnant being carried to safety after being pepper-sprayed by the police. By now, the images of young people being dragged by their hair across a street to a waiting police van have become all too familiar.[50] Some protesters have been seriously hurt, as in the case of Scott Olsen, an Iraq War veteran who was critically injured in a protest in Oakland in October 2011. Too much of this violence is reminiscent of the violence used against civil rights demonstrators by the enforcers of Jim Crow in the 1950s and 1960s.[51]

No longer restricted to a particular military ideology, the celebration and permeation of warlike values throughout the culture have hastened the militarization of the entire society. As Michael Geyer points out, militarization can be defined as "the contradictory and tense social process in which civil society organizes itself for the production of violence."[52] As the late Tony Judt put it, "The United States is becoming not just a militarized state but a military society: a country where armed power is the measure of national greatness, and war, or planning for war, is the exemplary (and only) common project."[53] But the prevailing intensification of American society's permanent war status does more than embrace a set of unifying symbols that promote a survival-of-the-fittest ethic, conformity over dissent, the strong over the weak, and fear over responsibility. Such a move also gives rise to a "failed sociality" in which violence becomes the most important tool of power and the mediating force in shaping social relationships.

The Crisis of Sociality

A state that embraces a policy of permanent war needs willing subjects to abide by its values, ideology, and narratives of fear and violence. Such legitimation is largely provided through people's immersion in a market-driven society that appears increasingly addicted to consumerism, militarism, and the spectacles of violence endlessly circulated through popular culture.[54] Examples of the violent fare on offer extend from the realm of high fashion and Hollywood movies to extreme sports, video games, and music concerts sponsored by the Pentagon.[55] The market-driven celebration of a militaristic mind-set demands a culture of conformity, quiet intellectuals, and a largely passive republic of consumers. It also needs subjects who find intense pleasure in spectacles of violence.[56]

In a society saturated with hyperviolence and spectacular representations of cruelty, it becomes more difficult for the American public to respond politically and ethically to the violence as it is actually happening on the ground. In this instance, previously unfamiliar violence such as extreme images of torture and death become banally familiar, while familiar violence that occurs daily is barely recognized, relegated to the realm of the unnoticed and unnoticeable. How else to explain the public indifference to the violence inflicted on nonviolent youth protesters who are raising their voices against a state in which they have been excluded from any claim on hope, prosperity, and democracy? While an increasing volume of brutality is pumped into the culture, yesterday's spine-chilling and nerve-wrenching displays of violence lose their shock value. As the demand for more intense images of violence accumulates, the moral indifference and desensitization to violence grow, while matters of savage cruelty and suffering are offered up as fodder for sports, entertainment, news media, and other pleasure-seeking outlets.

As American culture is more and more marked by exaggerated aggression and a virulent notion of hard masculinity, state violence—particularly the use of torture, abductions, and targeted assassinations—wins public support and requires little or no justification as US exceptionalism becomes accepted by many Americans as a matter of common sense.[57] The social impacts of a "political culture of hyper punitiveness"[58] can be seen in how structures of discipline and punishment have infiltrated the social order like a highly charged electric current. For example, the growing taste for violence can be seen in the criminalization of behaviors such as homelessness that once elicited compassion and social protection. We throw the homeless in jail instead of building houses, just as we increasingly send poor, semiliterate students to jail instead of providing them with a decent education. Similarly, instead of creating jobs for the unemployed, we allow banks to foreclose on their mortgages and in some cases put jobless people in debtors' prisons. The prison in the twenty-first century becomes a way of making the effects of ruthless power invisible by making the victims of such power disappear. As Angela Davis points out, "According to this logic the prison becomes a way of disappearing people in the false hope of disappearing the underlying social problems they represent."[59] As the notion of the social is emptied out, criminality is now defined as an essential part of a person's identity. As a rhetoric of punishment gains ground in American society, social problems are reduced to character flaws, insufficient morality, or a eugenicist notion of being "born evil."[60]

Another symptomatic example of the way in which violence has saturated everyday life and produced a "failed sociality" can be seen in the growing acceptance by the American public of modeling public schools after prisons and criminalizing the behavior of young people in public schools. Incidents that were traditionally handled by teachers, guidance counselors, and school administrators are now dealt with by the police and the criminal justice system. The consequences have been disastrous for young people. Not only do schools increasingly resemble the culture of prisons, but young children are being arrested and subjected to court appearances for behaviors that can only be called trivial. How else to explain the case of the five-year-old student in Florida who was put in handcuffs and taken to the local jail because she had a temper tantrum, or the case of Alexa Gonzales in New York, who was arrested for doodling on her desk? Or twelve-year-old Sarah Bustamatenes, who was pulled from a Texas classroom, charged with a criminal misdemeanor, and hauled into court because she sprayed perfume on herself?[61] How do we explain the arrest of a thirteen-year-old student in a Maryland school for refusing to say the pledge of allegiance?[62] Or the case of a sixteen-year-old student with an IQ below 70 being pepper-sprayed because he did not understand a question asked by the police officer in his school? After being pepper-sprayed, the startled youth started swinging his arms and for that was charged with two counts of assault on a public servant and faces a possible prison sentence.[63] In the most extreme cases, children have been beaten, Tasered, and killed by the police.

These examples may still be unusual enough to shock, though they are becoming more commonplace. What must be recognized is that too many schools have become combat zones in which students are routinely subjected to metal detectors, surveillance cameras, uniformed security guards, weapons searches, and in some cases SWAT raids and police dogs sniffing for drugs.[64] Under such circumstances, the purpose of schooling becomes to contain and punish young people, especially those marginalized by race and class, rather than educate them. "Arrests and police interactions ... disproportionately affect low-income schools with large African-American and Latino populations."[65] For the many disadvantaged students being funnelled into the "school-to-prison pipeline," schools ensure that their futures look grim indeed as their educational experiences acclimatize them to forms of carceral treatment.[66] There is more at work here than a flight from responsibility on the part of educators, parents, and politicians who support and maintain policies that fuel this expanding edifice of law enforcement against youth. Underlying the repeated decisions to turn away from helping young people is the growing sentiment that youths, particularly minorities of color and class, constitute a threat to adults and the only effective way to deal with them is to subject them to mind-crushing punishment. Students being miseducated, criminalized, and arrested through a form of penal pedagogy in prison-type schools provides a grave reminder of the degree to which the ethos of containment and punishment now creeps into spheres of everyday life that were largely immune in the past to this type of state and institutional violence.

The era of failed sociality that Americans now inhabit reminds us that we live in a time that breaks young people, devalues justice, and saturates the minute details of everyday life with the constant threat, if not reality, of violence. The medieval turn to embracing forms of punishment that inflict pain on the psyches and bodies of young people is part of a larger immersion of society in public spectacles of violence. The control society[67] is now the ultimate form of entertainment in America, as the pain of others, especially those considered disposable and powerless, is no longer a subject of compassion but one of ridicule and amusement. High-octane violence and human suffering are now considered consumer entertainment products designed to raise the collective pleasure quotient. Brute force and savage killing replayed over and over in the culture function as part of an anti-immune system that turns the economy of genuine pleasure into a mode of sadism that saps democracy of any political substance and moral vitality, even as the body politic appears engaged in a process of cannibalizing its own young. It is perhaps not far-fetched to imagine a reality TV show in which millions tune in to watch young kids being handcuffed, arrested, tried in the courts, and sent to juvenile detention centers. No society can make a claim to being a democracy as long as it defines itself through shared hatred and fears rather than shared responsibilities.

In the United States, society has been reconfigured to eliminate many young people's access to the minimal conditions required for living a full, dignified, and productive life as well as the conditions necessary for sustaining and nurturing democratic structures and ideologies. The cruelty and violence infecting the culture are both a symptom and a cause of our collective failure to mobilize large-scale collective resistance against a growing police state and the massive suffering caused by the savagery of neoliberal capitalism. Unfortunately, even as expressions of authentic rage against Wall Street continue in the Occupy movement, the widespread hardship that young people and other marginalized populations face today "has not found resonance in the public space of articulation."[68] With the collapse of a market economy into a market society, democracy no longer makes a claim on the importance of the common good. As a mode of diseased sociality, the current version of market fundamentalism has turned the principle of freedom against itself, deforming a collective vision of democracy and social justice that once made equality a viable economic idea and political goal in the pursuit of one's own freedom and civil liberties. As Zygmunt Bauman insists, one of the consequences of this market-driven sovereignty is "the progressive decomposition and crumbling of social bonds and communal cohesion."[69]

Neoliberalism creates a language of social magic in which the social either vaporizes into thin air or is utterly pathologized. Shared realities and effects of poverty, racism, inequality, and financial corruption disappear, but not the ideological and institutional mechanisms that make such scourges possible.[70] And when the social is invoked favorably, the invocation is only ever used to recognize the claims and values of corporations, the ultrarich, bankers, hedge fund managers, and other privileged groups comprising the 1 percent. Self-reliance and the image of the self-made man cancel out any viable notion of social relations, the common good, public values, and collective struggle.

The Occupy movements have recognized that what erodes under such conditions is not only an acknowledgment of the historical contexts, social and economic formations, relations of power, and systemic forms of discrimination that have produced massive inequalities in wealth, income, and opportunity but also any claim to the promise of a substantive democracy. Increasingly, as both the public pedagogy and economic dictates of neoliberalism are contested by the Occupiers, the state responds with violence. But the challenges to militarism, inequality, and political corruption with which young people have confronted American society are being met with a violence that encompasses more than isolated incidents of police brutality. It is a violence emanating from an ongoing wholesale transformation of the United States into a warfare state, from a state that once embraced the social contract—at least minimally—to one that no longer has even a language for community, a state in which the bonds of fear and commodification have replaced the bonds of civic responsibility and democratic commitment. As a result, violence on the part of the state and corporations is not aimed just at youthful protesters. Through a range of visible and invisible mechanisms, an ever-expanding multitude of individuals and populations has been caught in a web of cruelty, dispossession, exclusion, and exploitation.

The predominance of violence in all aspects of social life suggests that young people and others marginalized by class, race, and ethnicity have been abandoned as American society's claim on democracy gives way to the forces of militarism, market fundamentalism, and state terrorism. We must address how a metaphysics of war and violence has taken hold of American society, and the savage social costs it has entailed.

It is these very forms of social, political, and economic violence that young people have recognized and endured against their own minds and bodies, but they are using their indignation to inspire action rather than despair. The spreading imprint of violence throughout society suggests the need for a politics that not only critiques the established order but imagines a new one—one informed by a radical vision in which the future does not imitate the present. Critique must emerge alongside a sense of realistic hope, and individual struggles must merge into larger social movements.

Occupy Wall Street surfaced in the wake of the 9/11 memorials and global economic devastation rooted in market deregulation and financial corruption. It also developed in response to atrocities committed by the US military in the name of the war on terror, violent and racist extremism spreading through US politics and popular culture, a growing regime of discipline and punishment aimed at marginalized youth, retrograde education policies destructive of knowledge and critical learning, and the enactment of ruthless austerity policies that serve only to increase human suffering. With the democratic horizon in the United States increasingly darkened by the shadows of a looming authoritarianism and unprecedented levels of social and economic inequality, the Occupy movement and other global movements signify hope and renewal. The power of these movements to educate and act for change should not be underestimated, particularly among youths, even as we collectively bear witness to the violent retaliation of official power against democratic protesters and the growing fury of the punishing state. In the book that follows, I present chapters that move from negation to hope, from critique to imagining otherwise in order to act otherwise.

The first chapter provides a retrospective on 9/11 that acknowledges the way in which the tragic events of 2001 were used to unleash brutal violence on a global scale and legitimate the expansion of the warfare state and unthinkable forms of torture against populations increasingly deemed disposable. In particular, the traumatic aftermath of 9/11 in the United States was distorted into a culture of fear; heightened domestic security; and accelerated disciplinary forces that targeted youth, particularly the most vulnerable marginalized by race and class, as potential threats to the social order. This chapter exposes some of the widespread impacts of an unchecked punishing state and its apparatuses—most notably the escalating war on youth, the attack on the social state, and the growth of a "governing through crime" complex—while also paying tribute to the resilience and humanity of the victims of the 9/11 attacks and their families. It asserts that public recollection in the aftermath of those traumatic events—particularly the sense of common purpose and civic commitment that ensued—should serve as a source of collective hope for a different future than the one we have seen on display since September 2001.[71]

Chapter 2 discusses in further detail the cultural shift in the United States that has led to the inscription and normalization of cruelty and violence. In spring 2011, the role of the dominant media in sanctioning this culture of cruelty extended to its failure to provide a critical response when the "Kill Team" photographs were released. Even as young people around the world demonstrated against military power and authoritarian regimes, soldiers in the US military fighting in the "war on terror" gleefully participated in horrifying injustices inflicted upon helpless others. The "Kill Team" photos—images of US soldiers smiling and posing with dead Afghan civilians and their desecrated bodies—serve as but one example signaling a broader shift in American culture away from compassion for the suffering of other human beings toward a militarization of the culture and a sadistic pleasure in violent spectacles of pain and torture. Further discussion of American popular culture demonstrates how US society increasingly manifests a "depravity of aesthetics" through eagerly consuming displays of aggression, brutality, and death. Connecting this culture of cruelty to the growing influence of neoliberal policies across all sectors, I suggest that this disturbing new enjoyment of the humiliation of others—far from representing an individualized pathology—now infects US society as a whole in a way that portends the demise of the social state, if not any vestige of a real and substantive democracy. Recognizing the power of dominant culture to shape our thoughts, identities, and desires, we must struggle to uncover "instants of truth" that draw upon our compassion for others and rupture the hardened order of reality constructed by the media and other dominant cultural forces.

The third chapter suggests that even as US popular culture increasingly circulates images of mind-crushing brutality,

American political culture in a similar fashion now functions like a theater of cruelty in which spectacles and public policies display gratuitous and unthinking violence toward the most vulnerable groups in the country, especially children. Despite persistent characterizations of terrorists as "other," the greatest threat to US security lies in homegrown, right-wing extremism of a kind similar to that espoused by Anders Behring Breivik, who in July 2011 bombed government buildings in Oslo, killing eight people, and then went on a murderous shooting rampage in Norway, killing sixty-nine youths attending a Labor Party camp. The eruption of violent speech and racist rhetoric within US political discourse indicates a growing tolerance at the highest levels of government of extremist elements and the authoritarian views and racist hatred they deploy to advance their agenda—which includes dismantling the social state, legitimating a governing apparatus based on fear and punishment, undermining critical thought and education through appeals to conformity and authoritarian populism, and disposing of all populations deemed dangerous and threatening to the dominance of a white conservative nationalism. Bespeaking far more than a disturbing turn in US politics and the broader culture, right-wing policymakers abetted by the dominant media are waging a campaign of domestic terrorism against children, the poor, and other vulnerable groups as part of a larger war against democracy and the democratic formative culture on which it depends for survival.

Continuing an exploration of the neoliberal mode of authoritarianism that has infiltrated US politics, Chapter 4 discusses how anti-immigrant and racist political ideology couched in a discourse of patriotism is being translated into regressive educational policies and an attack on critical education. Reminiscent of the book burnings conducted in Nazi Germany, the Arizona state legislature and school board in Tucson have systematically eliminated ethnic studies from elementary schools and banned books that discuss racism and oppression, including several books by Mexican American authors in a school district where more than 60 percent of the students are from a Mexican American background. Within a neoliberal regime that supports corporate hegemony, social and economic inequality, and antidemocratic forms of governance, racism is either privatized by encouraging individual solutions to socially produced problems or disavowed, appearing instead in the guise of a language of punishment that persecutes anyone who even raises the specter of ongoing racism. The censorship of ethnic studies in Arizona and of forms of pedagogy that give voice to oppression points to how ideas that engage people in a struggle for equality and democracy pose a threat to fundamentalist ideologues and their war against the bodies, histories, and modes of knowledge that could produce the critical consciousness and civic courage necessary for a just society.

Chapter 5 examines the politics of austerity in terms of how it releases corporations and the rich from responsibility for the global economic recession and instead inflicts vast amounts of pain and suffering upon the most vulnerable in society. As an extension of the culture of cruelty, austerity measures encode a fear and contempt for social and economic equality, leading not only to the weakening of social protections and tax breaks for the wealthy but also to the criminalization of social problems. Austerity as a form of "trickle-down cruelty" symbolizes much more than neglect—it suggests a new mode of violence mobilized to address pervasive social ills that will only serve to hasten the emergence of punishing states and networks of global violence. Hope for preventing the escalation of human suffering must be situated in a concerted effort both to raise awareness about the damage wreaked by unchecked casino capitalism and to rethink the very nature of what democracy means and might look like in the United States. A capacity for critical thought, compassion, and informed judgment needs to be nurtured against the forms of bigotry, omission, and social irresponsibility that appear increasingly not only to sanction but also to revel in horror stories of inhumanity and destruction.

Tracing the trajectory of class struggle and inequality in America up to the present day, Chapter 6 argues that a growing concentration of wealth in the hands of the ruling elite means that the political system and mode of governance in the United States are no longer democratic, even as state power is subordinated to the interests of corporate sovereignty. In this chapter, an account of the political, social, and economic injustices confronting the vast majority of Americans—the result of a decades-long unchecked supremacy of corporate power, the reign of corrupt financiers, and a ruthless attack on the social state and social protections—sets the stage for what emerged as the Occupy Wall Street movement in September 2011. While making visible the ongoing significance of class as a political category, the Occupiers did much more than rehash the tired rhetoric of "class warfare" (marshaled by their opponents in an effort to position the ruling elites as victims of class resentment). Quite to the contrary, the Occupiers revealed the potential for a broad collective movement both to expose the material realities of inequality and injustice and to counter prevailing antidemocratic narratives while also fundamentally changing the terms of engagement by producing new images, stories, and memories that challenged the complacency of the public and the impoverished imagination of political and corporate leadership in America.

Chapter 7 concludes the book by reviewing the impact and legacy of the Occupy movement, particularly how it exposed the many ways in which US society has mortgaged the future of youth. The Occupiers have become the new public intellectuals, and they are creating a new pedagogy and politics firmly rooted in democracy, social justice, and human dignity that increasingly occupies the terrain of public discourse and poses a fundamental challenge to the control of the public sphere by corporate elites and their teaching machines. At risk of losing ideological dominance, the authorities retaliated against Occupy protesters by resorting to brutal forms of punishment. This police violence at once made visible the modes of authoritarianism and culture of cruelty that permeate American society—as was seen even at universities and colleges across the United States, institutions charged with contributing to the intellectual, social, and moral growth of society's youth.

As I complete the writing of this introduction, the Occupy struggle for social and economic justice continues on American university campuses—where the influence of austerity measures is increasingly being felt, although the working conditions for faculty and the quality of education for students began to deteriorate under the neoliberal ascendancy decades ago. The issues impacting higher education are undoubtedly symptomatic of the accelerated pace with which the withering away of the public realm is happening. The book finishes, however, by suggesting that the Occupy movement is far from over—despite the shrinking of physical space in which it can protest.

As it expands and spreads across the globe, the movement is producing a new public realm of ideas and making important connections between the deteriorating state of education, antidemocratic forces, and the savage inequalities produced by a market society. The response of young people as the new generation of public intellectuals offers us both critique and hope. It is a call to work collectively to foster new modes of thought and action—one that should be actively supported by higher education and other remaining public spheres in the United States, if American democracy is to have a future at all.

◆

CHAPTER 1

Countermemory and the Politics of Loss after 9/11

Violence, the War on Youth, and the Limits of the Social

The crisis consists precisely in the fact that the old is dying
and the new cannot be born.
                                                  —*Antonio Gramsci*

The barely audible whisper protesting the extreme measures
taken by military and state authorities against peaceful demonstrators in 2011 and 2012 becomes more intelligible, though no
less disturbing, when considered in tandem with the decades-
long global campaign to legitimate violence, retaliation, and force
as "just measures" in the wake of the 9/11 terrorist attacks
against the United States. The national security policies of the
Bush/Cheney administration in conjunction with the dominant
media's role in desensitizing the American public toward forms
of mass cruelty worked together to accelerate the militarizing
processes that were already in place before 9/11. The response
to the despicable actions of terrorists against the United States
was manipulated to sanction unthinkable human and civil
rights violations, terrorism, surveillance, and acts of torture
that any properly democratic state would have denounced. As if
handing to terrorists the evidence they required to justify their
heinous acts, the United States-turned-warfare state exposed

1

to the world its true face as a potential instrument of global oppression capable of unrelenting violence. Yet, there was a moment when other choices could have been made that would have taken the United States down a very different path. Now, with economic devastation expanding the dark shadows that continue to enshroud the United States, it becomes an important and purposeful act to remember the light that shone out in the days following 9/11—the resilience, social consciousness, and collective hope of the American people—as a sign that things could and still can be otherwise.

In the hours and days that bled out from the tragic events of September 11, 2001, the unfolding sense of collective vulnerability and loss drew many Americans and others together in a fragile blend of grief, sacrifice, compassion, and a newfound respect for the power of common purpose and commitment. The translation of such traumatic events into acts of public memory and memorializing is crucial, though deeply unsettling. In spite of the militarized moment in which we now live, we must remind ourselves that traumatic events not only bring about states of emergency and the suspension of civil norms and order. They also can, and did, give birth to enormous political, ethical, and social possibilities. Yet, such enlightened moments for the American public proved fleeting. A society has to move with deliberate speed from the act of witnessing its collective pain to the practice of responsible memorializing—in other words, to make self-reflection an integral part of the effort to rethink what politics, ethics, and civic engagement should mean after such a senseless horror as 9/11. Ten years after that tragic day, the struggle to remember and reclaim those moments in good faith is being constantly challenged, and in ways that few of us would have dared to imagine a decade earlier.

We have learned, and continue to learn, about the high cost of living in a society with an overabundance of violence and inequality and an impoverished supply of long-term commitments and permanent bonds. We live in a hyper-market-driven, fast-paced society of consumers committed only to throwing caution to the wind, whose merits are measured in profit margins and gross domestic product. As *New York Times* writer Stephen Holden stated, "the modern corporation [has become] a sterile Darwinian shark tank in which the only thing that matters is the bottom line."[1] As the United States increasingly produces social forms that too quickly exceed their use-by date, uncertainty and precariousness shape every aspect of daily life. Millions no longer have the satisfaction of a decent job or the security that comes with decent health care, pensions, and vacations. For many Americans, especially young people, alienation and cultural dissatisfaction include but go far beyond "joblessness and falling economic prospects."[2] Despair often turns into cynicism, which undercuts the development of any viable opposition. Under such circumstances, memory is often stripped of its responsibility to justice and becomes flat and self-serving, if not expendable when inconvenient. As the gravity of loss is divorced from both the past and the present, memory relinquishes its claim upon social institutions, politics, democracy, and the future. Daily experience in the age of instant pleasure, living for the moment, and the compulsive pursuit of materialism is no longer mediated by our vulnerability or responsibility as a function of memory. Instead, memory is rendered irrelevant by either the pressing demands of consumerism for the privileged few or the cruel reality of lost jobs, smashed hopes, and hard lives for the majority.[3]

In a society that increasingly punishes civic engagement and disavows the greater good, the web of human bonds is weakened through an emphasis on the socially adrift, free-roaming individual. One consequence is a growing disdain for community and a vanishing sense of any moral and political obligation to care for the fate and well-being of the other. How else to explain Republican congressman Ron Paul's comment during a Republican Party presidential debate in 2011 when he stated that letting the uninsured die rather than providing them with government health insurance is "what freedom is all about"?[4] In this instance, a culture of cruelty not only appears as a legitimate form of political discourse but does so with no apologies and a great deal of enthusiasm. In the words of Zygmunt Bauman, we are witnessing "a weakening of democratic pressures, a growing inability to act politically, [and] a massive exit from politics and from responsible citizenship."[5] Politics is emptied of its democratic vitality as more and more Americans make an obsession out of creating wealth, dismiss the welfare state as a pathology, define government as the problem, and reduce popular culture to traffic in pain, humiliation, and spectacular violence. In this instance, "loss tends to be an experience we are advised to 'get past.'"[6]

In the decade after 9/11, it has become clear that loss, memory, and remembrance share a wary embrace. Remembrance can become dysfunctional, erasing the most important elements of history and trivializing what survives of the event through either crude appeals to an untroubled patriotism or a crass commercialization that reduces 9/11 as an object of remembrance to just another commodity. But remembrance can also recover what has been sacrificed to this historical amnesia. It can produce difficult thoughts, bringing forth not only painful memories of personal loss and collective vulnerability but also new understandings of how specific events infuse the present and become a force for how one imagines the future, including, to quote Roger Simon, how "one imagines oneself, one's responsibility to others, and one's civic duty to a larger democratic polity and range of diverse communities."[7] Memory can be an instigator of both despair and hope, often in ways in which the division between desperation and optimism becomes blurred. The spectacularized shock and violence of 9/11 ruptured an arrogant and insular period in American history that had proclaimed the unrivaled triumph of national progress and the end of ideology, history, and conflict—all the while imposing an unbearable experience of loss, grief, sorrow, and pain on large segments of the world's population.

A decade later, the attacks on the Twin Towers and the Pentagon require of us not only the noble burden of remembering the victims of the barbarous violence of 9/11 but also the questioning of what survives from that moment of intense pain and fear when the very possibility of community, solidarity, and compassion returned, however briefly, from the exile imposed by decades of neoliberal governance. What does it mean to transform the experience of loss after 9/11 in order to suggest that what we witnessed for a short time in the days following the terrorist attack was a revitalization of both civic responsibility and democratic public life?[8] I think it is fair to say that in the period immediately following 9/11, the American public was provided with a glimpse of what Etienne Balibar has called "the insurrectional element of democracy" in which "the very possibility of a community among humans" was put into high relief while at the same time the essence of democratic politics and the formative culture that makes it possible appeared to hang in the balance.[9]

Mourning was fused with a renewed sense of idealism immediately following that shocking moment in history. One can hear it in the words of a young man named Jedediah Purdy, who wrote that it had been "amazing to see how in these past few days we—who have been so used to living with our selves front and center—are suddenly all aware that a common condition comes first. We have not been flip, self-involved, needlessly sarcastic or focused on small divisions. We have all been looking for ways to help. All of us. That is new to us."[10] From the smoldering ruins of 9/11 emerged a deep embrace of civic values and a newfound sense of global solidarity. Shared vulnerability elicited compassion rather than contempt for those of us too long marooned on Survivor Island. The galloping materialistic obsessions, rampant greed, antigovernment rhetoric, and Gilded Age cruelty of the 1980s and 1990s gave way to notions of shared sacrifice and collective hope. For a fleeting moment, the social as a democratic and communal register came alive in both a public and an existential sense. The general abandonment of community, public values, and public goods that had advanced in force and intensity since the Reagan era appeared to be in retreat next to a newly rediscovered sense of solidarity and the common good. Public values took precedence over private interests. Communal concerns were given priority over the materialistic fixations of the market and a fatuous celebrity culture. Public servants, especially the 9/11 firefighters and police officers, were praised for their unflagging courage and unwavering commitment to saving lives. And the Bush regime was forced to expand its mandate, providing security not only for the corporate sector but also for the general public in terms of both physical protection and crucial public services. The United States had become the object of near universal goodwill; its democratic ideals and spirit of leadership resonated with the deepest and most profound elements of an embattled global democracy. The French newspaper *Le Monde* proclaimed in banner headlines, "WE ARE ALL AMERICANS."[11]

Echoes of this lost idealism are evident in the accounts of those public servants in whose memories the horrors and the heroism of 9/11 will be forever etched. One such story recounts, ten years later, how a sense of common purpose and shared sacrifice made its appearance, however briefly. It is a story told by former New York City firefighter Ray Pfeifer. Right after the Twin Towers fell, Pfeifer worked at the World Trade Center site for seven months amid "a choking dust cloud—a brew of pulverized cement and known carcinogens such as asbestos, benzene, pcbs, and dioxin"—what he would later call a "toxic soup." Nine years later, he was diagnosed with stage four kidney cancer that eventually spread to his bones and required the removal of his leg and hip and a kidney. Pfeifer believed his cancer was related to the exposure from his work at ground zero. When asked by a CBS news correspondent if he regretted his rescue efforts after 9/11, he replied, "I'd do it again because I was searching for my buddies." He added, "I had a good friend of mine's son ask me, 'Ray are we ever going to find my dad.' ... This is what this kid said to me. And I think we gave a lot of closure to a lot of families."[12]

What seems exceptional in Pfeifer's statement is not only his deep sense of social responsibility but the dignity and compassion he expressed over the suffering of a child in search of his lost father. I say "exceptional" because that period of unselfish being-for-others, that moment of hope and possibility following 9/11, quickly came to an end as the Bush/Cheney regime pushed the United States into an abyss of militarism, fear, insecurity, and what Alex Honneth has termed "a failed sociality."[13] David Simpson has persuasively argued that 9/11 became "a pretext for political opportunism and military adventurism [in which] in less than two years we went from the fall of the Twin Towers and the attack on the Pentagon to the invasion of Iraq, a process marked by propagandist compression and manufactured consent so audacious as to seem unbelievable, except that it happened."[14]

Our collective fall from grace is now well known. Instead of being a threshold to a different future and a restored democratic faith, the decade following 9/11 became an era of buried memories and the monumentalization of what Joan Didion contemptuously called "fixed ideas."[15] Rather than initiating a period of questioning and learning, the war on terror morphed into a war without end, inspiring torture and abuses at home and abroad, all eventually revealed in an elaborate fabric of legal illegality in which practices that violated human rights were legitimated through the rewriting of the law itself. America's status as a symbol of freedom that had once elicited worldwide respect gave way to a culture of fear, mass hysteria, and state secrecy. As the Bush administration waged war overseas, it unleashed equally destructive market forces at home—all camouflaged by a poisonous propaganda machine in which pressing public issues morphed into a catalog of individual failings and an excuse to disparage an overreliance on the state as a pathological culture of dependency. Finance capital replaced human capital, and the mechanisms of governance were now controlled by the apostles of market orthodoxy. Less than 1 percent controlled almost half of all wealth while "45 percent of U.S. residents live in households that struggle to make ends meet. That breaks down to 39 percent of all adults and 55 percent of all children."[16] Economics was detached from ethics and managed to ignore any vestige of social costs. Youth, by definition vulnerable and dependent, became a deficient and dangerous population. The formative culture necessary to produce the next generation of critical citizens collapsed into a rampaging commercialism as citizens were defined exclusively as consumers, or excluded altogether. At the same time, the notion of the social was increasingly seen as a liability rather than a strength.

Shared sacrifice, compassion for others, and acting in concert as a basic condition of American life quickly expired under the Bush/Cheney administration. As Frank Rich reminds us, "the president scuttled the notion on the first weekend after the attack, telling Americans that it was his 'hope' that 'they make no sacrifice whatsoever' beyond, perhaps, tolerating enhanced airline security. Few leaders in either party contradicted him. Bush would soon implore us to 'get down to Disney World in Florida' and would even lend his image to a travel-industry ad promoting tourism."[17] In the face of unimaginable loss, fear, and insecurity, Bush urged the American public to get a grip and go shopping. That wasn't the worst of it. What has emerged in the last decade is an intensification of many antidemocratic forces that were only briefly interrupted by the outpouring of compassion and solidarity following 9/11. In many ways, as one *New York Times* reporter put it, "the New Normal [following 9/11] was very much like the Old Normal."[18]

In fact, the forces that have undermined democracy since the 1980s received new life under the Bush administration.

These included the growing power of corporations in American politics; an intensified attack on unions; the ascendency of the military-security state; a persistent and growing racism, especially targeting immigrants and Muslims; the suppression of civil rights under the Military Commissions Act and the Patriot Act; the consolidation of the punishing state and the mass incarceration of people of color; the rise of a culture of precariousness and fear; the attack on the social state, especially provisions for young people; the increasing privatization of public life; growing support for a cutthroat form of economic Darwinism and its celebration of cruelty; and the reformulation under the Bush/Cheney regime of politics as an extension of war, both abroad and on the domestic front.

In a startling editorial published in 2007, the *New York Times* declared that in the years since 9/11, "lawless behavior has become standard practice," most evident in the attempt on the part of high-ranking government leaders "to cover up the torture of prisoners by Central Intelligence Agency interrogators."[19] The editorial went further, arguing that "the White House used the fear of terrorism and the sense of national unity to ram laws through Congress that ... swept aside international institutions and treaties, sullied America's global image and trampled on the constitutional pillars that have supported our democracy through the most terrifying and challenging of times."[20] The editorial ended with the chilling statement that "there are too many moments these days when we cannot recognize our country."[21] As the Bush/Cheney government repudiated its public purpose, it catered to the power of finance capital, on the one hand, and assumed the role of a punishing state on the other. While pushing the social state to the brink of collapse and leaving destitute an increasing number of people, the punishing state stepped in to take over from the welfare state. More and more public problems were now viewed and addressed less as social issues than as matters to be handled through what has been called the "governing through crime" complex.[22]

In the aftermath of the damage produced by the Bush/Cheney administration, it has become a widespread belief that social problems are caused by individual failings and should be treated as disciplinary problems, further legitimating the massive extension of the "governing through crime" complex throughout our social foundations and cultural landscape.[23]

The vocabulary and architecture of the punishing state now spread, as Michelle Brown puts it, "across families, communities, schools, religion, the military, politics, the economy, and beyond, normalizing punishment and 'governance through crime and fear.'"[24] Loic Wacquant explains the consequences as the new punishing state "offers relief not to the poor but from the poor, by forcibly 'disappearing' the most disruptive of them, from the shrinking welfare rolls on the one hand, and into the swelling dungeons of the carceral castle on the other."[25] Thus, we see the measures taken to alleviate our insecurities become more frightening than fear itself as they permeate the very foundations of our social, judicial, and political structures.

Where is the public outrage in reaction to right-wing extremists in Congress who, as Noam Chomsky points out, use the debt crisis "to undermine what remains of social programs, public education, unions, and, in general, remaining barriers to corporate tyranny"?[26] What has happened to democracy in the United States when a representative of a corrupt mega–financial service industry, JPMorgan Chase, is allowed to evict a 103-year-old woman and her 83-year-old daughter who are facing foreclosure on their home? The sheer cruelty of this act was so obvious that the movers and sheriff's deputies in Atlanta, Georgia, sent to remove the women refused to evict them.[27] That a major exponent of predatory finance such as JPMorgan Chase can be allowed to impose such suffering and hardship on thousands of individuals and families not only speaks volumes regarding the massive power big banks and hedge funds exercise over the larger social order but also highlights the degree to which they operate in a Wild West zone of Gilded Age politics that refuses to hold them accountable.

Such political and moral lawlessness is even more astounding given that JPMorgan Chase is at the heart of the criminal culture of risk-taking and speculation that was partly responsible for the 2008 economic crisis. As Richard R. J. Eskow points out, "Chase has paid out billions to settle charges that include perjury and forgery (in its systemic foreclosure fraud and abuse), investor fraud, and sale of unregistered securities" and more recently has admitted having incurred "at least $2 billion in losses from risky, unsecured, derivatives-types trading."[28] JP-Morgan Chase, Bear Stearns, Bank of America, Goldman Sachs, Barclay, and Merrill Lynch among other financial service institutions have become models of fraud, corruption, and massive financial incompetence protected by morally bankrupt Washington politicians, federal regulators, and an army of antipublic pundits and academics who benefit from such corruption while reproducing a culture of cruelty and a social order marked by vast inequities in wealth, power, and income.

Evidently, remembrance of the profound sacrifice, civic courage, and unity displayed in the aftermath of 9/11 has given way to a hardening of the culture. Growing indifference to those who struggle to survive combined with unresponsiveness to others' suffering does not augur well for either future generations or democracy itself. One symptom of this hardness is the lack of political and moral outrage over a misdirected war in Iraq based on falsehoods—a war in which the human cost was almost unimaginable: more than 4,000 American troops died, and over 10,000 were wounded.[29] We must consider as well that more than one million Iraqis died, and that the war produced 1.8 million refugees and 1.7 million internally displaced people.[30] In this instance, George W. Bush did more than lie and behave badly—he inaugurated an era of endless war, elevated militarism to the status of a national religion, and mortgaged the future of an entire generation of young people. To paraphrase Paul Krugman, Bush poisoned the memory of 9/11, allowing it to "become an occasion for shame."[31]

The expanding symptomology of this decade-long crisis of idealism is also revealed in the refusal of the American public to confront its own vulnerability, its growing inequality in income and wealth, and its own ongoing acts of violent self-sabotage.[32] One dire consequence of this refusal is a present and future in which populations who are in need of social protections and state interventions are viewed as problems threatening society. Poverty is labeled a "'pathological condition' rather than a reflection of structural injustice—a 'pathological dysfunction' of those who are poor, rather than the structural dysfunction of an economic system that generates and reproduces inequality."[33] The plight of the homeless is now defined less as a political and economic issue in need of social reform than as a matter of law and order. At-risk youths have become the risk, such that state budgets for prison construction now eclipse budgets for higher education. The reach of the carceral state is especially evident in the ways in which many public schools now adopt punishment as the main tool for control of the nation's children.[34] In the devalued landscape of public schooling, punishing young people seems to be far more important than educating them.[35] Similarly, as advocates of a market-driven rationality raise an entire generation on the alleged virtues of "unrestricted individual responsibility," the disdain toward the common good finds its counterpart in increasing acts of "collective and political irresponsibility."[36]

The spirit of idealism, solidarity, and compassion associated with the promise of democracy appears to be almost at the vanishing point in America today. We have two mainstream conservative parties: one that seems wedded to corporate interests and a culture of cruelty and another that has remade itself into a centrist-right party that extends and legitimates many of the policies of George W. Bush. Both parties endorse indefinite military detention without due process, including for American citizens; the ruthless deportation of immigrants; the use of gratuitous violence against peaceful protesters; the arming of local police forces with military-grade weapons; the secret killing by drones of "enemies of the state"; and the criminalization of whistle-blowers.[37] Both parties occupy the same side of the class divide, and the conditions of young people are considerably worse as a result of the policies of both parties. The security state is as dangerous as ever; civil liberties are still under attack; and instead of subjecting alleged terrorists to the judgment of the legal system, they are in some cases simply assassinated. President Barack Obama supports the state-secrets privilege and has made war a permanent condition of American society.

The Koch brothers and their rich cronies are rewriting the meaning of American politics, pushing the United States further and further into a mode of soft authoritarianism.[38] It no longer suffices to say the United States is on the brink of authoritarianism—rather, it is on the brink of making sure that the authoritarian state is not challenged. In the past year, people all over the world put their lives at risk in fighting for democracy while in the United States the two main political parties and a business-friendly Supreme Court colluded with the rich and corporate elite to do everything possible to destroy it. How might we proceed to reclaim the spirit of idealism and national unity that emerged after 9/11 in order to reverse the institutions, values, and power relations that have created the current theater and culture of cruelty and pushed the notion of the democratic social to the margins of political discourse? One place to begin, especially for educators, is with the current state of young people in the United States. It is, after all, in their name, in the name of our collective future, that all memory work proceeds.

The Crisis of Youth

Youth has always represented an ambiguous category, but young people are under assault today in ways that are entirely new because they face a world that is far more dangerous than at any other time in recent history. I speak here not just of wars abroad and the war on terror. I have argued for the past decade that the criminalization of social problems has become a mode of governance in the United States, and it coincides with an intensifying assault on young people that can be understood through the related concepts of a "soft war" and a "hard war."[39]

The soft war refers to the changing conditions of youth within the relentless expansion of a global consumer society that devalues and exploits all youths by treating them as markets or as commodities themselves. This low-intensity war is waged by a variety of corporate institutions through the educational force of a culture that both commercializes every aspect of kids' lives and uses the Internet, cell phones, and various social networks along with other new media technologies to address young people as consumers in ways that are more direct and expansive than anything we have seen in the past. The answer to the increasing global economic instability since 9/11 has been aggressive growth—in which youths play both foot soldier and target.

The reach of the new screen and electronic culture among young people is disturbing. For instance, a recent study by the Kaiser Family Foundation found that young people ages eight to eighteen are spending more than seven and a half hours a day with smart phones, computers, television, and other electronic devices, compared with less than six and a half hours five years before.[40] When you add the time youths spend simultaneously texting, talking on their cell phones, or "watching TV while updating Facebook—the number rises to 11 hours of total media content each day."[41] There is more at stake here than what some call a new form of attention deficit disorder. Youth are given few opportunities for thoughtful analysis and engaged modes of reading—and indeed are receiving the message that investing in or taking the time for such tasks is unnecessary.

At the same time, these media are fashioning a new generation of consuming subjects. Advertisers now spend $17 billion a year engaging in what Susan Linn has called a hostile takeover of childhood.[42] General Mills and other food companies use the Internet in order to pitch junk foods to kids without consideration of how such foods contribute "to poor diets, which are implicated in childhood obesity."[43] Further collapsing the distinction between entertainment and advertising, food marketers have also developed online games in order to bypass parents and directly address young children. Profits take precedence over ethical and health considerations, given current estimates that "children influence more than $100 billion in food and beverage purchases each year, and well over half of all cold cereal purchases."[44] Corporations have hit gold with the new media and can inundate young people directly with market-driven values, desires, and identities, all of which are removed from the mediation of parents and other adults. Increasingly, children can recognize themselves only in terms taught by the market.

The hard war is more serious and dangerous for young people and refers to the harsh values and dictates of a growing youth-crime complex that increasingly governs poor minority youths through a logic of punishment, surveillance, and control. The imprint of the youth-crime complex is evident in the increasingly popular practice of organizing schools through disciplinary practices that subject students to constant surveillance by high-tech security technologies while imposing upon them harsh and often thoughtless zero-tolerance policies that closely resemble the culture of prisons. As the corporate state dives deeper into financial turmoil, the punishing state gathers strength, and certain segments of the youth population become the object of a new mode of governance based on the crudest forms of disciplinary control.

We catch a glimpse of how young people have become a generation of suspects in the endless reports of minor school infractions treated as a problem of law and order. For example, when two police officers were called to a day care center in central Indiana to handle an unruly ten-year-old, they Tasered the child and slapped him in the face. This followed another widely reported incident in which a police officer in Arkansas used a stun gun to subdue an allegedly out-of-control ten-year-old girl. One public response to this incident came from Steve Tuttle, a spokesman for Taser International, Inc., who insisted that a "stun gun can be safely used on children."[45] In another widely distributed news story accompanied by a disturbing video, a school-based police officer brutally beat a fifteen-year-old special needs student because his shirt was not tucked into his pants.[46] Sadly, this is but a small sampling of the ways in which children are being punished instead of educated in American schools. Such examples have become all too common and point to how our society responds to vulnerability and dependency. Surely, the growing number of institutions willing to employ a discipline-and-punish mentality not only constitutes a crisis of politics but suggests an emerging symptomology of a society no longer able to question itself or even reproduce itself, given its inability to care for and protect future generations.

As the culture of fear, repression, and militarization that defined post-9/11 foreign relations turned inward, the culture of schooling was reconfigured through the allocation of resources used primarily to hire more police, increase security staff, and purchase more technologies of control and surveillance. In some cases, schools such as those in the Palm Beach County system have established their own police departments. Consequently, schools begin to take on the obscene and violent contours one associates with the "all [too] familiar procedures of efficient prison management,"[47] including unannounced locker searches, armed police patrolling the corridors, mandatory drug testing, and the ever-present phalanx of lockdown security devices such as metal detectors, X-ray machines, and surveillance cameras. Under such circumstances, education and social services have given way to modes of confinement whose purpose is to ensure "custody and control."[48]

Within this regime of harsh disciplinary control, there is no political or moral vocabulary for recognizing the systemic economic, social, and educational problems that young people face or for addressing what it would mean for American society to invest seriously in their future. The combination of school punishments and criminal penalties has proven a lethal mix for many poor minority youths and has transformed too many schools from spaces of youth advocacy, protection, hope, and equity into military fortresses, well positioned to mete out injustice and humiliation. Instead of being viewed as disadvantaged, poor minority youths are seen as lazy and shiftless; instead of being understood in terms of how badly they are served by failing schools, many youths are labeled uneducable and pushed out of schools. They have not just been excluded from "the American dream" but have become its nightmare—and as such are treated as redundant and disposable, waste products of a society that no longer considers them of value. Relegated to zones of social abandonment, they now inhabit "a post-credit-collapse and post-certainty world" that offers them little in the way of decent jobs, social protections, and hope for the future.[49]

Many youths—now subject to a form of racial and class dumping—experience a kind of social death as they are denied job-training opportunities, required to endure rigorous modes of surveillance and criminal sanctions, and viewed less as chronically disadvantaged than as failed consumers and civic felons. According to a 2007 report published by the Children's Defense Fund, a "Black boy born in 2001 has a 1 in 3 chance of going to prison in his lifetime [while] a Latino boy born in 2001 has a 1 in 6 chance of going to prison in his lifetime.... Minority youth make up 39 percent of the juvenile population but are 60 percent of committed juveniles."[50] Against the idealistic rhetoric of a nation that claims it venerates young people lies the reality of a society that views youths through the optic of security and punishment and has become willing to treat them as hardened criminals and make them "disappear" into the furthest reaches of the carceral state. Schools have become pathways to incarceration and dead-end, powerless lives rather than pipelines for intellectual growth and economically productive lives. Shockingly, in the land of the free and the home of the brave, a "jail or detention cell ... is the only universally guaranteed child policy in America."[51]

The late novelist Claude Brown understood something about this war on youth. Offering testimony of another social catastrophe fifty years prior to 9/11, *Manchild in the Promised Land* (1965) explores the consequences of racist exploitation and exclusion in Harlem in the 1960s. Take the following passage:

If Reno was in a bad mood—if he didn't have any money and he wasn't high—he'd say, "Man, Sonny, they ain't got no kids in Harlem. I ain't never seen any. I've seen some real small people actin' like kids, but they don't have any kids in Harlem, because nobody has time for a childhood. Man, do you ever remember bein' a kid? Not me. Shit, kids are happy, kids laugh, kids are secure. They ain't scared a nothin'. You ever been a kid, Sonny? Damn, you lucky. I ain't never been a kid, man. I don't ever remember bein' happy and not scared. I don't know what happened, man, but I think I missed out on that childhood thing, because I don't ever recall bein' a kid."[52]

In *Manchild in the Promised Land*, Claude Brown wrote about the doomed lives of his friends, families, and neighborhood acquaintances. The book is mostly remembered as a brilliant but devastating portrait of Harlem under siege—a community ravaged by drugs, poverty, unemployment, crime, and police brutality. But what Brown made visible was the fact that the raw violence and dead-end existence that plagued so many young people in Harlem had stolen not only their future but their childhood as well. In the midst of the social collapse and psychological trauma wrought by the systemic fusion of racism and class exploitation, children in Harlem were held hostage by forces that robbed them of the innocence that comes with childhood and that pushed them to assume the risks and burdens of daily survival from which older generations were unable to shield them.

At the heart of Brown's narrative, written in the midst of the civil rights struggle of the 1960s, is the "manchild"—a metaphor that indicts a society that was waging war on poor black children who had been forced to grow up too quickly. The hybridized concept of the manchild marked a liminal space of witness in which innocence was imperceptibly lost and childhood stolen. Harlem was a well-contained, internal colony, and its street life provided the conditions and the very necessity for insurrection. But the many forms of rebellion young people expressed in response—from the public and progressive to the interiorized and self-destructive—came with a price, which Brown reveals near the end of the book. He writes, "It seemed as though most of the cats that we'd come up with just hadn't made it. Almost everybody was dead or in jail."[53]

Brown's story of stolen childhood did not exhort the marginalized and downtrodden to help themselves out of trouble—

that shortsighted and mendacious appeal to self-help would instead define the reactionary reform efforts of the 1980s and 1990s, from Reagan's hatred of government to Clinton's attack on welfare reform. Rather, Brown's story was a clarion call for condemning a social order that denied children a viable and life-enhancing future—a social order characterized by massive inequalities and a rigid racial divide. He created the image of a society without children in order to raise questions about the future of a country that had turned its back on its most vulnerable population. After Jacques Derrida, we might call this evidence of one of America's first autoimmune disorders, in which containment and control in the name of security made society more dangerous, more unsafe.

Nearly fifty years later, Brown's metaphor of the manchild is just as relevant and "the Promised Land" is more mythic than ever as his account of the plight of poor minority children resonates powerfully in light of the 2008 economic meltdown and the dashed hopes of an entire generation now viewed as one without prospects for a decent future. The suffering and hardships many poor minority and immigrant children face in the United States have been greatly amplified by the current economic crisis and the ongoing social disinvestment and devaluation of young people. Many young people today live in a state of perpetual emergency, and through no fault of their own (or of their parents, for that matter) lack food, health care, adequate shelter, clothing, and even spaces to play. They inhabit a rough world where childhood is nonexistent, crushed under the heavy material and existential burdens they are forced to bear.

Current statistics paint a bleak picture for the nation's young people. According to the Bureau of Labor Statistics, 18.6 million youths ages sixteen to twenty-four were unemployed in July 2011.[54] These figures become even more alarming when analyzed through the harsh realities of economic deprivation and persistent racial disadvantage. In a country where white families now possess twenty times the wealth of black families and communities—the largest racial wealth gap recorded by the US Census Bureau in over twenty-five years—poor minority youths are left to navigate an expanding landscape of deprivation, poverty, and despair largely on their own.[55] Joblessness among black youths is almost 50 percent, and the jobless rate for African American school dropouts aged sixteen to twenty-four is a staggering 69 percent.[56] According to US census data, 16.4 million—or 22 percent of all children—live in families with incomes below the poverty level, which is equal to $22,050 a year for a family of four.[57] In what amounts to a national disgrace, children in 2011 made up more than one-third of all people living in poverty. These figures become even more ominous in light of the fact that "recent reports suggest that almost 50% of Americans are in poverty or at a 'low income' level."[58] And the long-term effects of poverty on children are extensive. As the National Center for Children in Poverty makes clear,

> Poverty can impede children's ability to learn and contribute to social, emotional, and behavioral problems. Poverty also can contribute to poor health and mental health. Risks are greatest for children who experience poverty when they are young and/ or experience deep and persistent poverty. Research is clear that poverty is the single greatest threat to children's well-being. But effective public policies—to make work pay for low-income parents and to provide high-quality early care and learning experiences for their children—can make a difference. Investments in the most vulnerable children are also critical.[59]

Adding to this disturbing picture, Mark Rank, a sociologist at Washington University in St. Louis, reports that nearly half of all US children and 90 percent of black youngsters will be on food stamps at some point during childhood, and the fallout from the current recession could push those numbers even higher.[60] The National Association for the Education of Homeless Children and Youth recently reported that there are over a million homeless students in the United States.[61] It gets worse. According to the National Center on Family Homelessness, "one in 45 children in the USA—1.6 million children—were living on the street, in homeless shelters or motels, or doubled up with other families" in 2010. This figure is up 38 percent since 2007.[62]

What is unique about these kids is not just the severity of deprivations they experience daily but how they have been forced to view the world and redefine the nature of their own childhood within its borders of hopelessness and despair. Unlike in Brown's narrative, there is no lingering sense of a hopeful future lying just beyond highly policed, ghettoized spaces as well as the ever-expanding spaces of detention and deportation.

The reality is that an entire generation will not have access to decent jobs, material comforts, or the security made available to previous generations. These youths are a new generation of manchildren who have to think, act, and talk like adults; worry about their families, which may be headed by a single parent or two out of work and searching for jobs; and wonder how they are going to get the money to buy food and what it will take to pay for a doctor in the case of illness. These children are no longer confined to so-called ghettoes. As the burgeoning landscape of poverty and despair increasingly finds expression in our cities, suburbs, and rural areas, these children make their presence felt—they are too many to ignore or hide away in the usually contained and invisible spaces of disposability. They constitute a new and more unsettling scene of suffering, one that not only reveals the vast and destabilizing inequalities in our economic landscape but also portends a future that has no purchase on the hope that should characterize a vibrant democracy.

Defending Youth and Democracy in the Twenty-First Century

The conditions of young people today are considerably worse as a result of the shortsighted policies of three successive US governments. Obama's education policies are largely an extension of the discredited Bush approach to schooling—or, as Diane Ravitch puts it, Obama has given Bush's educational policies a third term.[63] Arne Duncan, Obama's appointed secretary of education, appears unusually obtuse when it comes to devising a democratic vision for education, especially in light of his all-too-apparent love for market measures, military schools, and high-stakes testing schemes and his evident dislike for any mode of knowledge and classroom pedagogy that cannot be quantified.[64] In the last decade, under both the Bush and the Obama administrations, young people have been increasingly removed from the inventory of social concerns and the list of cherished public assets, and in the larger culture they have been either disparaged as a symbol of danger or simply rendered invisible. What does it say about a society when the elected government invests close to $4 trillion of taxpayer dollars in two wars, offers generous tax cuts for the rich, and bails out corrupt banks and insurance industries but does not provide a decent education and job-training opportunities for its most disadvantaged youths? What happens to the fate of democracy in a society in which "states spend on average two and a half times more per prisoner than per school pupil"?[65] The ideals that emerged initially after 9/11 are now barely visible in a society that spends $6 billion a year training Afghan military and police but fires thousands of firefighters, teachers, and other public servants. Advocates of finance capital, right-wing politicians, and neoliberal pundits do their best to develop corporate-friendly and military policies that increase the deficit; eliminate food-stamp programs; refuse to provide health care for millions of children; and, under the current leadership held in a stranglehold by the Republican Party, attempt to balance the budget on the backs of young people, working people, the poor, and the elderly. Since 9/11, the war on terror has come home, and war has become a form of governance, a primary organizing principle of society, and the foundation of politics itself. As Stephen Graham argues, war as a form of governance has become part of a new military doctrine "that engenders a notion of war as a permanent boundless exercise, pitting high-tech militaries and security operations—along with private-sector outsources and military corporations—against a wide array of non-state adversaries. All of this occurs within an environment marked by intense mediatizing, a high degree of mobility and the rapid exploitation of new military technologies."[66]

The shameful condition of America's youths exposes not only their unbearable victimization but also those larger social and political forces that speak to the hardening of a society that actively produces the suffering and death of its children. The nihilism of a market society, the move from a welfare to a warfare state, the persistent racism of the alleged "raceless" society, the collapse of education into training and test-taking—all work together to numb us to the suffering of others, especially children. It is now more necessary than ever to register youth as a central theoretical, moral, and political concern. Doing so reminds adults of their ethical and political responsibility to future generations, and it legitimates investing in youths both for their own sake and as a symbol for nurturing civic imagination and collective resistance in response to the suffering of others. Youth also provides a powerful referent for a critical discussion about the long-term consequences of economic and social policies while gesturing toward the need for putting into place those conditions that make a democratic future possible.

One way of addressing our collapsing intellectual and moral visions regarding young people is to reclaim and reimagine those moments of compassion, social relations, and democratic ideals that surfaced for a short time after 9/11 but now seem lost in a society more intent on forgetting than remembering its civic and social responsibilities. Such a task speaks to the need for a form of countermemory in which we rethink the notion of loss, if not of memory itself, in terms of the possibility of opening up democratic public life. Countermemory of this kind refashions social protections, rights, and relations as central to any notion of remembrance. In the aftermath of 9/11 we must ask, What elements of democracy are missing in a country dominated by the forces of militarism, casino capitalism, insecurity, fear, and cruelty? The events of 9/11 need to be reclaimed as one of those crucial moments that conveys a society's struggle to come to grips with human catastrophe and signals, at the same time, a most frightening truth about the changing nature of democracy. Belief in the promise of democracy requires the American public to engage in a form of memory work in which loss both evokes our collective vulnerability and our communal responsibility and reinforces the ethical imperative to provide young people, especially those marginalized by race and class, with the economic, social, and educational conditions that make life livable and the future sustainable.

What is at stake here is not a one-off bailout or temporary fix but real political and social reform. Needless to say, the remembrance practices associated with 9/11 have not gone in this direction. They have neither remembered the collapse of the social amid the wreckage and debris that fell that day nor called for restorative and just social and economic reforms. What is needed urgently today is a form of memory work that insists on putting into place basic supports, including a system of national health insurance that covers everybody along with provisions for affordable housing. A politics true to the ideals of democratization needs policies that prevent poor families from going bankrupt. Young people need a federally funded jobs-creation program and wage subsidies that would provide year-round employment for out-of-school youths and summer jobs for in-school, low-income youths. Public and higher education, increasingly shaped by corporate and instrumental values, must be reclaimed as democratic public spheres committed to teaching young people about how to govern rather than merely how to be governed in an increasingly authoritarian society. Any viable notion of educational reform must include equitable funding schemes for schools and the recognition that the problems facing public schools cannot be solved with corporate takeovers or law enforcement strategies. Incarceration should be the absolute last resort, not the strategy of choice, for dealing with our children. Educators, parents, and young people need to get the police out of public schools; greatly reduce spending for prisons and military purposes; and invest in more teachers, support staff, and community people in order to eliminate what the Children's Defense Fund calls America's cradle-to-prison pipeline.

But, of course, none of this will take place unless the institutions, social relations, and values that legitimate and reproduce current levels of inequality, power, and human suffering are dismantled.[67] The widening gap between the rich and the poor has to be addressed if young people are to have a viable future. As Stanley Aronowitz has argued, progressives need a new multifront movement that addresses egregious levels of economic inequality and a long-term strategy for challenging the "corporate-style top-down nature of work, education, and other key parts of daily life" while addressing the "task of re-shaping American institutions along genuinely democratic lines."[68] This will require large-scale structural reforms that constitute a real shift in both power and politics away from the current market-driven system that views too many children as disposable. Clearly, there is a need for the American public to reimagine what liberty, equality, and freedom might mean as truly democratic values and practices.

Any society that endorses market principles as a template for shaping all aspects of social life and cares more about the accumulation of capital than it does about the fate of young people is in trouble. Next to the needs of the marketplace, life has become cheap, if not irrelevant. Too many of us have lived too long with governments and institutions that make lofty claims to democracy while selectively punishing those considered expendable—in prisons, public schools, foster care institutions, and urban slums. As public life is commercialized, commodified, and policed, the pathology of individual entitlement and narcissism erodes those public spaces in which the conditions for good conscience, decency, self-respect, and collective dignity take root. Those who believe in justice and human rights need to liberate the discourse and spaces of freedom from the plagues of militarism and consumer narcissism and struggle to build those public spaces where democratic ideals, visions, and social relations can be nurtured and developed as part of a genuinely meaningful education and politics.

As Americans remember the events of 9/11, both now and in the future, they have an opportunity to recast the conversation about the value of public life, the social state, our democratic institutions, and the future of young people. They can honor the lives of those killed on 9/11 as well as the heroic actions of the first responders who sought to save the lives of others by celebrating the selflessness, common humanity, and collective hospitality that emerged in the aftermath of those tragic events. This challenge is particularly urgent at such a dark time in our history as a nation. And it is not a fight that can be won through individual struggles or fragmented, single-issue political movements—it demands that the American public reclaim the principles, values, and social relations that constitute the promise of a democracy to come. For a brief moment after 9/11, Americans were given a glimpse of the power and dignity of those ideals that make a substantive democracy possible.

What the collective response to 9/11 signified amid the suffering and despair was a gesture of hope, a recognition that in the behavior of those who sacrificed themselves in helping others was a bittersweet beacon of the repressed spirit of democracy. Such a call to witnessing and countermemory exceeds the despair of that dark moment and speaks to the future; it is a call that is prophetic in its insistence that the economic, political, and social conditions be created for upcoming generations so they can decide their own future and in doing so take back their country from the ethical, economic, and political abyss into which it has fallen. This is a historical juncture at which young people are making clear that the space of the possible is always larger than the one currently on display. This is particularly evident as young people across the globe are protesting the savage cruelty and massive suffering caused by neoliberal capitalism and other forms of economic and political domination. We are witnessing new forces emerging and making a claim on what Balibar has called the utopian elements of a democracy that is prophetic and filled with new possibilities.[69] The Arab Spring has provided youths all over the globe with a renewed spirit of confidence and resistance. Not only have they challenged the rule of experts, the rise of hegemonic neoliberalism, and regimes of inequality but they have also revived "the almost forgotten practice of participatory democracy."[70] While the promise of democracy has yet to be realized in Egypt, the movement's spirit of resistance spawned ongoing struggles among youths across the globe. This is a diverse movement of youths, workers, and others marginalized by class, ethnicity, and race attempting to reclaim and restore those conditions that enable a democratic politics, affirm the very possibility of community, and reject the ongoing transformation of the welfare state into the punishing state.

This may sound a bit utopian given the depth of the current political and economic crises and the authoritarian forces mobilized to crush the resistance of resurgent youths across the United States, but the American public has few choices if it is going to provide young people with a future that does more for them than does the present. Increasing levels of force against young people are making it clear that expressing dissent against the status quo is now viewed by authorities as a criminal act, one that has produced egregious acts of violence against youthful protesters from Oakland to New York City. Outbreaks of democracy, especially among young people and déclassé intellectuals, pose a real danger to state authorities and the corporate elite. Lacking any real ideas or solutions to the myriad crises now faced by the United States, the state resorts to violent acts. The deteriorating economic, political, and social state of American youth may be the most serious and potentially explosive challenge the United States will face in the twenty-first century. This is a crisis that calls for a new understanding of politics and the real practices that make democracy possible. This is a challenge that demands that individual and collective resistance intensify against a form of casino capitalism in which "all values are now determined by economic calculations."[71] Young people are confronting both the power relations bolstered by finance capital and a ruthless intensification of state-sponsored disciplinary practices that extends from the classroom to the streets. The ongoing attacks by the police and private security forces on the constitutional rights of young people to assembly and protest are only one measure of these increased disciplinary practices. The "failed sociality" of an utterly privatized and commodified culture is now subject to a much-needed critique by young people all over the globe. These emerging critiques and protests are changing the conversation about what politics might mean as they reconfigure relations of power and recall ideological projects indebted to those struggles and memories of educated hope. Such memories both lie hidden in the past and are blossoming anew in a politics that not only names problems but actually confronts them.

The redemptive memories that emerged out of the tragedy of 9/11 provided a glimpse of a formative culture in which democracy once again seemed possible—in which the possibilities of a social contract were matched by an embrace of a democratic community grounded in the principles of social responsibility and social justice. Such memories offer one example of the resources needed to confront the challenge of contemporary urgent political and economic struggles that require us to think beyond the given, imagine the unimaginable, and combine the lofty ideals of democracy with a willingness to fight for its realization. The expansive spirit of community, courage, and surge of compassion we witnessed for a short time after 9/11 provide a countermemory that reminds us that the possibility of collective struggle and shared hopes is far from a lost moment in history.

◇

Chapter 2

Disturbing Pleasures

The Depravity of Aesthetics and the "Kill Team" Photos

Lacking the truth, [we] will however find *instants of truth,* and those instants are in fact all we have available to us to give some order to this chaos of horror. These instants arise spontaneously, like oases in the desert. They are anecdotes and they reveal in their brevity what it is all about.... This is what happens when men decide to turn the world upside down.

—*Hannah Arendt*

For a few brief moments following 9/11, we experienced our common humanity as an "instant of truth" that might have led America to a greater self-understanding and compassion for others; instead, a very different course was chosen by the trifecta of political leadership, corporate elite, and military power brokers governing the United States. In the past decade, we have witnessed not only the sheer force of US military power in pursuing "enemy terrorists" but also the emergence of a dominant culture marked by a virulent notion of hardness and aggressive masculinity.[1] This culture of depravity appears to have infiltrated every aspect of US society, seducing young and old alike. John Cory is right in arguing that much of the media in the United States has become an "ugly circus." This is the media that have "embraced celebrity over content and corporate sponsors over substance, and mindless entertainment over education illumination."[2] But that is not all the media do. They also produce a formative culture in which violence becomes the most important element of identity, a crucial bedrock of power, and the most acceptable mediating force in shaping social relations. Such a culture—with its surrender of historical consciousness to the pleasures of the moment—should not be underestimated in terms of how its narratives and images can either open up or close off possibilities for political, social, and cultural awareness. In the absence of critical mediation and robust counternarratives, the corporate media dominating American popular culture work their influence by condensing pain, humiliation, and abuse into digestible spectacles of violence endlessly circulated through TV broadcasts, video games, YouTube postings, and proliferating forms of the new digital media.

This ideology of hardness and the economy of pleasure it justifies are also behind the unscrupulous relations of power that have intensified since the Reagan presidency, when a shift in government policies first took place and set the stage for the emergence of unchecked torture and state violence under the Bush/Cheney regime.[3] Conservative and liberal politicians alike now spend trillions waging wars around the globe, funding the largest military state in the world, and providing huge tax benefits to the ultrarich and major corporations; at the same time, they drain public coffers, increase the scale of human poverty and misery, and eliminate all viable public spheres—whether they be the social state, public schools, public transportation, or any other aspect of a formative culture that addresses the needs of the common good, or for that matter contributes to the building of viable and caring communities.

What C. Wright Mills once termed "the cultural apparatus" matters even more fifty years later.[4] At the dawn of the twenty-first century, this apparatus has grown into a vast web of media monopolies that serves to entertain global audiences, provide information about the world, create consumer desires, and occasionally offer insights about existing social problems. But these monopolies do even more. They also function as teaching machines, producing and legitimating particular modes of identity and providing the framing mechanisms that drive the questions, interests, and values that shape a society. Through the sheer power of their size and ubiquity, the media and their digital extensions influence major institutions, shape the larger culture, and reproduce particular social values. They also set standards; exert influence on politics; and often privilege the trivial over the substantive, the consumer over the citizen, and the narrowest of interests over larger ethical and social considerations. As the old and new media take over the space of the public and the private, they have become a more insistent and aggressive antidemocratic force corrupting politics; demeaning public goods; trading in campaigns of fear; substituting opinions for legitimate argument; and turning news outlets into spectacles of pain and perversion, if not worse. Think of the preponderance of hate-radio and -television shows that feature the likes of Glenn Beck, Michael Savage, Sean Hannity, and Bill O'Reilly. And bear in mind the narcissistic messages endlessly paraded on reality TV shows. Listen to the often cruel and homophobic nonsense vomited up from the mouths of right-wing luminaries such as Michele Bachmann and Sarah Palin and how the mainstream media report such invective as a serious species of argument.

The scandalous example of Rupert Murdoch is a case in point of money and greed combining with a politics of corruption and shock to produce a culture of cruelty that tarnished everything it touched. Not only did News Corporation inundate the world with schlock tabloids, it also invaded the privacy and violated the dignity of the British royal family, various celebrities, and the victims of the 2005 terrorist attack in London by hacking into their voice-mail accounts. By some accounts, News Corporation is likely guilty of the same criminal activities in the United States.[5] But the most offensive hacking News Corporation has done is its hacking into people's minds to fill their everyday lives with gossip, spectacle, the relentless sexualization of women, and incessant cheerleading for a market-driven society in which all that matters is winning and making money. Unfortunately, what is often left out of existing narratives about the rise of big media and their commitment to shock and political conservatism is the role they play as a vehicle for public pedagogy, as an educational force that demeans any viable notion of democratic values, social relations, and critical agency.

What does it mean that exaggerated violence now rules screen culture? What are the social and psychological costs of a culture in which violent injury, needless cruelty, and regressive spectacles of violence saturate society with an intensity unlike anything produced in the past? How can we respond to violence responsibly when narratives of violence, humiliation, and victimhood become the major engines of entertainment and there is no way for "accountability to be understood apart from the claims of vengeance"?[6] The public pedagogy of entertainment is rampant with extreme images of violence, human suffering, and torture splashed across giant movie screens, some in 3-D, offering viewers every imaginable portrayal of violent acts, each more shocking and brutal than the last. The growing taste for sadism can be seen in the media's fascination with Peter Moskos's book *In Defense of Flogging,* in which the author seriously proposes that prisoners be given a choice between a standard sentence and a number of lashes administered in public.[7] In the name of reform, Moskos argues without irony that public flogging is a more honest and surefire way of reducing the prison population. Not only is this book being given massive air time in the mainstream media, but its advocacy of corporal punishment is being treated as if it were a legitimate proposal for reform. Mind-crushing punishment is presented as the only choice for prisoners aside from serving their sentences. Moreover, this medieval type of punishment inflicts pain on the body as part of a public spectacle. Moskos seems to miss how the legacy of slavery informs his proposal, given that flogging was one of the preferred punishments handed out to slaves and that 70 percent of all current prisoners in the United States are people of color. Surely, the next step will be a reality TV franchise in which millions tune in to watch public floggings. This is not merely barbarism parading as reform, it is also a blatant indicator of the degree to which sadism and the infatuation with violence have become normalized in a society that seems to delight in dehumanizing itself.

As the social is devalued along with rationality, ethics, and any vestige of democracy, spectacles of violence and brutality now merge into forms of collective pleasure that constitute what I believe is an important and new symbiosis among visual pleasure, violence, and suffering. Reveling in the suffering of others should no longer be reduced to a matter of individual pathology, as it now registers a larger economy of pleasure across the broader cultural and social landscape. My emphasis here is on the sadistic impulse and how it merges spectacles of violence and brutality with forms of collective pleasure. This is what I call the *depravity of aesthetics*—the emergence of a new aesthetic of amplified voyeurism characteristic of a social order that has narrowed the range of social expression and values, turning instead to the pursuit of pleasure and the receipt of instant gratification as its sole imperatives. Fundamental to this new aesthetic, with its refiguring of the relationship between violence and the economy of pleasure, is a type of mad violence that not only bears down, often savagely, on young people but also provides them with one of the few registers through which to experience themselves and their relationships to others. In this context, neoliberal capitalism has produced not merely a culture of selfishness and greed but one dominated by a mode of militaristic violence in which the suffering and death of others become a source of entertainment—even of joy. Before building on the relationship between aesthetics and violence put on display in the "Kill Team" photos, I will draw upon critical discussions of the aestheticization of human suffering in order to underscore what has shifted in the broader culture since an aesthetics of depravity was first conceptualized, and what is at stake in the emerging depravity of aesthetics.

The Aesthetics of Depravity

Susan Sontag believed that capitalist societies require images in order to infiltrate the culture of everyday life, legitimate official power, and anesthetize their subjects through visual spectacles.[8] Such images also enable the circulation of information along with militaristic modes of surveillance and control. Sontag argued in her later work that war and photography had become inseparable, and as a result of that fusion, representations of violence no longer compelled occasions for self-awareness and social critique. Rather, shocking images increasingly emerged as a mode of entertainment, advancing the machinery of consumption and undermining democratic relations and social formations. She was particularly concerned about an aesthetics that traffics in images of human suffering that are subordinated to the formal properties of beauty, design, and taste—thus serving in the main to "bleach out a moral response to what is shown."[9]

For Sontag and many other critical theorists, the aesthetics of depravity reveals itself when it takes as its "transcendent" object the misery of others—murderous displays of torture, mutilated bodies, and intense suffering—while simultaneously erasing the names, histories, and voices of the victims of such brutal and horrible acts. What is worth noting, especially in the current historical context, is that there seems to be a perverse pleasure to be had in the erasure of the victims' names, voices, and histories. Similarly, Paul Virilio, in a meditation on the extermination of bodies and the environment from Auschwitz to Chernobyl, refers to this depraved form of art as an "aesthetics of disappearance that would come to characterize the whole fin-de-siècle" of the twentieth century.[10] An example of this mode of aesthetics was on full display in the mainstream media's coverage of the photographs depicting the torture of prisoners at Abu Ghraib prison. As Mark Reinhardt points out, the dominant media had no qualms about showing the faces of the victims, thus violating their dignity, but expressed widespread indignation over reproducing the naked bodies of the victims, claiming that it would demonstrate bad taste.[11] In this instance, concerns of beauty, etiquette, and an empty moralism displaced subject matter—and indeed the subjecthood of the victims—while sheltering the viewer from any sense of complicity in such crimes.

Needless to say, the events at Abu Ghraib were not isolated, though they confirmed the escalation of a desire to view voluptuous depravity that had been honed among the American public for decades. For instance, since the early 1990s, Benetton, the famous clothing manufacturer, has proven that trafficking in pain and human suffering is not only good for business but also good for providing a patina of legitimacy to the company as an artsy brand with philanthropic concerns.[12] Benetton's United Colors campaign appropriated shocking and visually arresting representations of violence and pain in order to sell clothes and attract global attention to its brand. In doing so, Benetton did more than conjoin the worlds of beauty and suffering; it also pushed a mode of commercial advertising in which the subjects of often horrendous misfortunes and acts of suffering disappeared into the all-embracing world of logos and brand names. For example, Benetton used the colorized image of David Kirby, a dying AIDS patient, to sell sweaters. Another poignant example of the reconfiguring of the aesthetic in order to exploit images of suffering can be found in an unpublished interview in which Jacqueline Lichtenstein recounts her experience of visiting the museum at Auschwitz. She writes,

> When I visited the Museum at Auschwitz, I stood in front of the display cases. What I saw there were images from contemporary art and I found that absolutely terrifying. Looking at the exhibits of suitcases, prosthetics, children's toys, I didn't feel frightened. I didn't collapse. I wasn't completely overcome the way I had been walking around the camp. No. In the Museum, I suddenly had the impression I was in a museum of contemporary art. I took the train back, telling myself that they had won! They had won since they'd produced forms of perception that are all of a piece with a mode of destruction they made their own.[13]

As we move into the second decade of the twenty-first century, ethical considerations and social costs are further eclipsed by market-driven policies and values. Images of human suffering are increasingly abstracted from social and political contexts and the conditions that make such suffering possible—and thus they become visually alluring. Moreover, as public issues collapse into private considerations, matters of agency, responsibility, and ethics are now framed within the discourse of extreme individualism. According to this neoliberal logic, individuals and the problems they confront are removed from any larger consideration of public values, social responsibility, and compassion. The endurance of the social and the formative culture that makes human bonds possible are now outmatched, though hardly defeated, by the rise of a Darwinian ethic of greed and self-interest in which violence, aggressiveness, and sadism have become the primary metric for living and dying. As the social contract is replaced by the chaotic disintegration of the social order, a culture of cruelty has emerged in American society. This new mode of collective behavior resembles Freud's theory of the death drive, though it is reconfigured less as a desire to return to nothingness, and thus to quiet forever dangerous sensations, than as the apogee of an eternal present of titillation achieved through the serial production, circulation, and consumption of images of death. Increasingly, as representations of violence permeate every aspect of the machinery of cultural production and screen culture, desire seems only to come alive when people are aroused by the spectacle of high-intensity violence and images of death, mutilation, and suffering.

Death and violence have become the mediating link between America's domestic policy—the state's treatment of its own citizens—and US foreign policy, between the tedium of ever-expanding workdays and the thrill of sadistic release. Disposable bodies now waste away in American prisons, schools, and shelters just as they have littered the battlefields of Iraq and Afghanistan. America has become a permanent warfare state, with a deep investment in a cultural politics and the corollary cultural apparatuses that legitimate and sanctify its machinery of death. The American public's fascination with violence and death is obvious not only in the recent popular obsession with vampire and zombie films and books. We also see it in serious Hollywood films such as the 2010 Academy Award–winning *The Hurt Locker,* in which the American bomb-disposal expert William James (Jeremy Renner) repeatedly puts himself at risk in order to defuse bomb threats—thus highlighting the film-maker's concern with a growing "addiction" to war. But, as Mark Featherstone points out, the film represents the appeal of the reckless behavior of immature and hypermasculine soldiers without so much as offering a critique of it. The James character

> takes unnecessary risks and lives for the limit experience.... He feels most alive when he is closest to death, a condition supported by the philosopher Martin Heidegger, who spoke about being-towards-death, and told us that we should live every moment as though it was our last, in order that we might live a full and meaningful life. When James ... throws the bomb suit away and stands before the bomb with no protection, he puts himself at the mercy of the bomb, the embodiment of the death drive. Herein lies James' ethic of deadly risk, his attempt to realize Heidegger's idea, being-towards-death, in what for Freud would be a per-verse form, being-with-bombs.... In Freudian/Kleinian terms, the bomb is also a projection of the self because it consists of a hard shell containing powerful explosive material.[14]

Featherstone coarsens Heidegger's concept of "being-towards-death," but his notion of the "hard shell" echoes Theodor Adorno's reference to an ideology of hardness that Adorno believed was one of the root causes of the Holocaust.[15]

According to Adorno, violence became entrenched in German culture as the rituals of aggression, brutality, and sadism became a bureaucratized and normalized part of everyday life. More specifically, Adorno believed the "inability to identify with others was unquestionably the most important psychological condition for the fact that something like Auschwitz could have occurred in the midst of more or less civilized and innocent people."[16] One of the consequences of this psychological state was the production of a virulent masculinity that augured both a pathological relationship with the body, pain, and violence and a disdain for compassion, human rights, and social justice.

More than a trace of this mode of aggression and moral indifference now dominates contemporary American society, which also displays disturbing signs of having moved away from providing social protections and safeguarding civil liberties toward the establishment of legislative programs intent on promoting shared fears and increasing disciplinary modes of governance that rely on the criminalization of social problems, precarious forms of punishment, and the disposability of certain vulnerable groups of people.[17] Punishment rather than governance becomes the central feature of politics with the resultant withdrawal of moral and ethical considerations from public conscience.

As violence becomes the most important element of power, there is growing disdain for sustaining any vestige of managed social welfare, leaving citizens who are ravaged by a predatory free-market fundamentalism and a growing police state to fend for themselves. The hardening of American culture has been matched by a disdain for those who are poor, regardless of the fact that they may have no control over their fate and misfortune. Even though half of the American population lives in poverty, with many Americans living on the street or in parking lots, tents, and underground drains and tunnels, the poor and homeless are more despised than are the systemic conditions that produce such hardships. Even though social mobility for most Americans has ground to a near halt in the United States, widespread poverty is seen as a personal failing, and those who are poor are increasingly the object of disdain, fear, loathing, and criminalization.[18]

The right-wing authoritarian answer to poverty or any other of a number of social problems extending from joblessness to lack of adequate health insurance and care is that people have only themselves to blame and that their problems, however dire, can be solved only if people help themselves. Commenting on this form of relentless individualization central to casino capitalism, Zygmunt Bauman sums up its legitimating ideology: "It is then one of those cases when institutions 'for overcoming problems' are transformed into institutions for causing problems; you are, on the one hand, made responsible for yourself, but on the other hand are 'dependent on conditions which completely elude your grasp' (and in most cases also your knowledge); under such conditions, how one lives becomes the biographical solution of systemic contradictions."[19] This is not only a cruel and savage attitude, one that justifies a "punitive attitude to the weak and poor," but one that also signals an emotional callousness that is a precondition for a creeping authoritarianism in the United States.[20]

The broader cultural turn toward unchecked individualization, the death drive, and the strange economy of desire it produces are also evident in the American public's apparent willingness to derive pleasure from images that portray gratuitous violence and calamity. Such portrayals give credence to Walter Benjamin's claim that in late modernity the mesmerizing and seductive language of power underlies captivating spectacles that inextricably fuse aesthetics with a fascist politics.[21] Benjamin recognized the affective force of aesthetics and its at times perverse ability to "privilege cultural forms over ethical norms" while mobilizing emotions, desires, and pleasures that delight in human suffering and become parasitic upon the pain of others.[22] Benjamin's notion of the aesthetic and its relation to fascism is important, in spite of appearing deterministic, because it highlights how fascist spectacles use the force of titillating sensations and serve to privilege the emotive and visceral at the expense of thoughtful engagement. In his analysis of Benjamin's notion of the aesthetic, Lutz Koepnick develops this point further by exploring how the fascist aesthetic "mobilizes people's feelings primarily to neutralize their senses, massaging minds and emotions so that the individual succumbs to the charisma of vitalistic power."[23]

Rather than reject the aesthetics of depravity as being exclusively tied to the pleasure of consumption and the spectacle of violence, if not fascism itself, Sontag modified Benjamin's position on the aesthetic, arguing that it can have a more productive pedagogical role. Against a conventional view of aesthetics limited to a depoliticized embrace of formal properties, she championed images that were ugly, destabilizing, and shocking. Such images, argued Sontag, harbor a capacity to show great cruelties precisely in order to arouse compassion and empathy rather than mere titillation. She asserted, "For photographs to accuse, and possibly to alter conduct, they must shock."[24] Shock and rupture become the pedagogical registers of resistance in which the image might talk back to power, unsettling commonsense perceptions while offering "an invitation to pay attention, to reflect, to learn, to examine the rationalizations for mass suffering offered by established powers."[25] Sontag realized that the aesthetic is not always on the side of oppression when presenting images of suffering. Of course, she was just as aware that in a society that makes a spectacle out of violence and human suffering, images that attempt to shock might well reinforce a media-induced habituation to and comfort with "the horror of certain images."[26]

The Depravity of Aesthetics

The aesthetics of depravity addressed by Sontag, Benjamin, Virilio, and others focuses on suffering through the formal qualities of beauty and design, registering the consumption of images of human pain as a matter of personal pleasure and taste rather than as part of a broader engaged social-political discourse. What I call the depravity of aesthetics, by contrast, considers representations of human suffering, humiliation, and death as part of a wider economy of pleasure that is collectively indulged. This notion of aesthetics focuses on the death drive and uses the spectacles of violence that feed it to generate a source of gratification and intense, socially experienced pleasure. As images of degradation and human suffering become more palatable and pleasurable, individual bodies as well as the body politic no longer become the privileged space of agency but instead become "the location of violence, crime, and social pathology."[27] As decadence and despair are normalized in the wider culture—though far from accomplishing the goal to remove all dissent—people are increasingly exploited for their pleasure quotient while any viable notion of the social is subordinated to the violence of a deregulated market economy and its ongoing production of a culture of cruelty.[28]

Representations of human suffering should not be abstracted from a broader neoliberal regime in which the machinery of consumption endlessly trades in the production of spectacular images designed to excite, stimulate, and offer the lure of intense sensations. This is especially true for the spectacles of violence that are now not only stylistically extraordinary and grotesque but also grotesque depictions of the culture that produces them. No longer mere bystanders to "every act of violence and violation," the American public eagerly substitutes a pleasure in images of human suffering for any viable sense of moral accountability.[29] How else to explain the insistent demand by many conservative and liberal pundits and the American public at large that the government release the grisly images of Osama bin Laden's corpse, even though the fact of his assassination was never in doubt? How might we understand the growing support among the American populace for state-sanctioned torture and the rising indifference to images that reveal its horrible injustices? Just as torture is sanctioned by the state and becomes normalized for many Americans, the spectacle of violence spreads through the culture with ever-greater intensity.

A carnival of simulated and real violence now produces the depravity of aesthetics in which the culture of cruelty flourishes, fueled by a desperate energy and an endless menagerie of pain that meld intense excitement with a sense of fulfillment, release, instant arousal, and pleasure. Terry Eagleton comments on the political implications and social costs of this regime of unfettered desires and sensations. He writes, "Sensation in such conditions becomes a matter of commodified shock-value regardless of content: everything can now become pleasure, just as the desensitized morphine addict will grab indiscriminately at any drug. To posit the body and its pleasures as an unquestionably affirmative category is a dangerous illusion, in a social order which reifies and regulates corporeal pleasure for its own ends just as relentlessly as it colonizes the mind."[30] As the pleasure principle is unconstrained by a moral compass based on a respect for others, it is increasingly shaped by the need for intense excitement and a never-ending flood of heightened sensations. What has led to this immunity and insensitivity to cruelty and prurient images of violence? Part of this process is due to the fact that the American public is bombarded by an unprecedented "huge volume of exposure to ... images of human suffering."[31] As Bauman argues, there are social costs that come with this immersion in a culture of staged violence. One consequence is that "the sheer numbers and monotony of images may have a 'wearing off' impact [and] to stave off the 'viewing fatigue,' they must be increasingly gory, shocking, and otherwise 'inventive' to arouse any sentiments at all or indeed draw attention. The level of 'familiar' violence, below which the cruelty of cruel acts escapes attention, is constantly rising."[32] Hyperviolence and spectacular representations of cruelty disrupt and block our ability to respond politically and ethically to the violence as it is actually happening on the ground. In this instance, unfamiliar violence such as extreme images of torture and death becomes banally familiar, whereas familiar violence that occurs daily is barely recognized, becoming if not boring then relegated to the realm of the unnoticed and unnoticeable.

Cruel acts, while contributing to the further depravity of aesthetics, often escape attention for yet another reason. With the rise of new and highly advanced computer-generated digital and screen technologies, the distance between images and the consequences of real violence becomes greater and less meaningful, just as real violence becomes easier to perform. Video games, for instance, do more than indulge young participants in cartoonish orgies of violence, slaughter, and mayhem. They are also viewed as a source of valuable training for twenty-year-olds who are hired by the Department of Defense because of their video-game skills to sit in secluded rooms in California while manipulating drone aircraft designed to target and kill America's enemies in countries such as Iraq, Pakistan, and Afghanistan. Killing in this instance becomes entirely removed from ethical responsibility, and humane actions are reduced to computer errors. Cruelty manifests itself in a depravity that is pleasure-driven and incited by the possibility of a kill, regardless of whether the latter includes innocent victims such as women and children—as has happened in Afghanistan and has been portrayed in the now famous *Collateral Murder* video from Iraq. Released by WikiLeaks, "[the] graphic video from Baghdad shows a July 2007 attack in which U.S. forces, firing from helicopter gunships, wounded two children and killed more than a dozen Iraqis, including two Reuters employees."[33] The video verifies the presence of two photographers and a man who, though severely wounded, was later purposely killed along with the civilians who tried to rescue him. The voices of the computer warriors on the tape are merciless, intense, and clearly excited by the pleasure gained from pursuing the deliberate and reckless killings.

The cruelty displayed within an increasingly militarized popular culture includes examples already mentioned: reality TV shows that trade in ruthless modes of competition and the threat of exclusion and Hollywood films, such as *Fast Five* (2011) and *Acts of Valor* (2012), that drench the screen in lawlessness and provide fast-rising volumes of sledgehammer blood feasts. The producers of *Acts of Valor* boast that the film uses live ammunition and shamelessly tout it as a venue for recruiting Navy SEALs and other soldiers needed for special operations missions in the age of permanent war.[34] But the culture of cruelty also runs the gamut of media sources, saturating the mainstream news, advertising, and much of what circulates online in the United States. Violence follows a desperate search for new markets and finds its way into advertisements that sell toys to children, just as it is used to produce the subject positions and consumer tastes necessary to influence slightly older children. For instance, films such as *Let Me In* (2010), *Hanna* (2011), and *Sucker Punch* (2011) move from celebrating hyperviolent women to fetishizing hyperviolent young girls.[35] Rather than gain stature through a coming-of-age process that unfolds amid representations of innocence and complicated negotiations with the world, young girls are now valorized for their ability to produce high body counts and their dexterity as killing machines in training. Hollywood films such as the *Saw* series, *Inglourious Basterds* (2009), *Zombieland* (2009), *The Killer Inside Me* (2010), and *Scream 4* (2011) transcend the typical slasher fare and also offer viewers endless, supercharged representations of torture, rape, animal cruelty, revenge, genital mutilation, and much more. For another example of such intensely charged images, see the final image of the music video "Bad Romance," with Lady Gaga posing in a sexually suggestive manner with a corpse—presumably the remains of the lover she has set on fire.[36]

Whatever bleeds—now gratuitously and luxuriously—brings in box-office profits, dominates media headlines, and leads the news broadcasts despite being often presented without any viable context for making sense of the imagery or any critical commentary that might undercut or rupture the pleasure viewers are invited to derive from such images. Representations of violence and human tragedy now merge seamlessly with neoliberalism's pedagogy of cruelty in which risk and mayhem reinforce shared fears rather than shared responsibilities and a Hobbesian war-of-all-against-all becomes the organizing principle for structuring a vast array of US institutions and social relations.

As corporate capitalism translates into corporate fascism, prominent politicians such as Sarah Palin, radio hosts such as Rush Limbaugh, and media-monopoly moguls such as those behind Fox News repeatedly deploy the vocabulary of violence to attack the social state, labor unions, immigrants, young people, teachers, and public service employees. At the same time, the depravity of aesthetics gains popular currency in organs of the dominant media that reproduce an endless stream of denigrating images and narratives of people constrained by the forces of poverty, racism, and disability. Their pain and suffering now become a source of delight for late-night comics, radio talk-show hosts, and TV programs that provide ample narratives and images of poor families, individuals, and communities who become fodder for the "poverty porn" industry.[37] Programs such as the reality TV series *Jersey Shore,* the syndicated tabloid TV talk show series *The Jerry Springer Show* (and its endless imitators), and *The Biggest Loser* all exemplify what Gerry Mooney and Lynn Hancock claim is a massive "assault on people experiencing poverty [seizing] on any example of 'dysfunctionality' in poor working class communities ... [exhibiting] expressions of middle-class fears and distrust, [while] also [displaying] a fascination with poverty and the supposedly deviant lifestyles of those affected—where viewers of moral outrage are encouraged to find the worst and weakest moments of people's lives also funny and entertaining."[38]

Spectacles of humiliation provide an important element in shaping a market-driven culture of cruelty that gives new meaning to the merging of an economy of pleasure and images of violence, mutilation, and human suffering. This is not to suggest that the only images available in contemporary America are those saturated with violence and pain—or that such a culture has removed all dissent—but to emphasize that a humane formative culture that produces images that are at odds with, contest, or provide alternatives to such violence seems to be disappearing. Nor am I suggesting that images of violence can only produce an affective economy of sadistic pleasure or be reduced deterministically to one reading and point of view. What I am arguing and will develop in what follows is that American society under a neoliberal regime—far from being a global democratic leader—has devolved into a media-saturated culture that inordinately invests in and legitimates a grim pleasure in the pain of others, especially those considered marginal and disposable. Decentered and disconnected from any moral criteria, the pleasure-in-death principle coupled with the search for ever more intense levels of sensation and excitation becomes the reigning pedagogical and performative force in shaping individual and collective identities. Within this context, the elevation of cruelty to a structuring principle of society is matched by the privatization of pain, and it is precisely through the depravity of aesthetics encouraged by neoliberal capitalism that the pleasure of humiliation and violence is maximized.

Under the regime of neoliberal policies, relations, and values, profit-making in spite of the human cost becomes the only legitimate mode of exchange; private interests replace public concerns; and unbridled individualism infects a society in which the vocabulary of fear, competition, war, and punishment governs all existing relationships. Freedom and agency are reduced to a regressive infantilism and degraded forms of gratification. What Leo Lowenthal called "the atomization of the individual" bespeaks a figure now terrorized by other human beings and reduced to living "in a state of stupor, in a moral coma."[39] This type of depoliticized inward thinking—with its repudiation of the obligations of shared sociality, disengagement from moral responsibility, and outright disdain for those who are disadvantaged by virtue of being poor, young, or elderly—does more than fuel the harsh, militarized, and ultramasculine logic of the news and entertainment sector. This "atomization of the individual" also elevates death over life, selfishness over compassion, and economics over politics. How else to explain the senseless and tragic killing of Trayvon Martin, a seventeen-year-old African American youth, by an overzealous neighborhood watch volunteer in one of Florida's gated communities? Martin's only crime was that he was black and had the temerity to walk through a gated space defined as the preserve of those who increasingly flee to and inhabit privileged spaces of racial and class exclusion.[40]

In other words, precariousness, uncertainty, and misfortune open up a space in which vulnerability offers a pretext for forms of pleasure that reinforce a culture of cruelty.[41] But even more so, bearing witness to such cruelty produces a kind of dysfunctional silence in American society in the face of widespread hardship and suffering—virtually wiping out society's collective memories of moral decency and mutuality, as mentioned in Chapter 1. Neoliberalism's embrace of a "there is no society" ethic is directly related to a diminishing sense of social responsibility. It promotes a kind of individualism that has become pathological in its disdain for community, social values, public life, and the public good. The depravity of aesthetics not only offers the lure of instant personal gratification but also conceals a hidden order of politics that harbors a deep disdain for social responsibility, justice, and democracy. Yet, the marriage of pleasure and depravity should not be seen as the province of individual pathology; rather, it serves the development of a formative culture of social pathology through an economy of affect that traps people in their own narcissistic desires, aestheticizes violence, and promotes an endless spectacle of shocking images.

In a social order marked by the production of atomized, competitive, and militarized subjects, the pleasure principle is now fused with the death drive. Their entwined expression is increasingly circulated and mediated through ever-growing spectacles of violence that feed into a narcissistic and over-the-top consumerist society. As the social state disappears, critical public spheres are commodified, militarized, and hollowed out. One consequence is that democratic institutions, values, and social relations begin to disappear. Under such circumstances, the aesthetics of depravity is reconfigured, transformed into a depravity of aesthetics, thereby relinquishing any power to rupture, transform, enlighten, and critically inform consciousness. Tied to forms of pleasurable consumption and sensations that delight in images of suffering, the depravity of aesthetics functions to anesthetize ethically and politically, prompting passivity or even joy in the "face of trauma and injustice."[42]

In the current historical moment, life reduced to "bare life" elicits imperviousness at best and a new kind of pleasure at worst. Aesthetics as both a normative and a performative practice is now enmeshed in producing a collective disdain for any viable notion of vulnerability, which if left unchecked risks becoming a form of contempt for life itself. The "cultural apparatus," as C. Wright Mills called it, no longer merely traffics between culture and authority. This apparatus and its public pedagogy now seduce Americans, though not simplistically, through both a new register and economy of pleasure and a machinery of affect rooted in the spectacle of hyperviolence. Victims no longer have to be looked in the eye since they often appear as just dots on an electronic screen. Staged violence is now anticipated with bated breath by audiences who all too willingly displace moral criteria with "the aesthetically spaced world, structured by the relevancies of [intense excitement], pleasure-potential, [and] interest arousal."[43] One consequence is that a "thick" world of agents and thus of resistant otherness is dissolved into a depthless world of selfish gratification, a world that is devoid of opposition.

Instants of Truth

Keeping in mind the depravity of aesthetics and culture of cruelty, I want to return to Arendt's notion of "instants of truth." Such instants often come in the form of images, narratives, and stories that shock. They don't accommodate reality as much as they turn it upside down, eviscerating commonsense assumptions a culture has about itself while revealing an intellectual and emotional chasm that runs through established modes of rationality and understanding. Such flash points not only rupture dominant modes of consciousness, they also give rise to heated passions and debates, sometimes leading to massive displays of collective anguish and resistance, even revolutions. Among the notable examples is the horrifying image of the fourteen-year-old African American boy Emmett Till, whose body was mutilated and tortured by white racists after he allegedly whistled at a white woman in Mississippi in 1955. The image of his disfigured body helped launch the civil rights movement in the United States. There are also the four-decades-old iconic photos taken at My Lai that revealed the slaughter of at least five hundred innocent South Vietnamese women, elderly men, and children by American soldiers during the Vietnam War. These photographs served as a tipping point in reinvigorating a more powerful and consolidated antiwar movement. In 2003, the American people were jolted yet again by another set of photographs and videos, this time of detainees at Abu Ghraib prison outside Baghdad being humiliated and tortured by grinning American soldiers—men and women alike. As a result of the Abu Ghraib photographs, the Bush administration lost credibility, but, more crucially, the image of the United States as a defender of democracy was irretrievably tarnished in the eyes of the world because it had used and later defended—with impunity—state-sanctioned torture. Then, in 2011, a number of photographs once again surfaced depicting grotesque acts of violence and murder by a group of American soldiers stationed in Afghanistan. These images were first released by the German weekly *Der Spiegel* and later by *Rolling Stone* in the United States.

The images released by *Rolling Stone* magazine focused on the murderous actions of twelve US soldiers who decided to kill Afghan civilians allegedly for sport. They used the moniker "Kill Team" to refer to themselves, aptly registering both the group's motivation and its monstrous actions. The soldiers' actions exhibited their immersion in the death-driven culture discussed throughout this chapter. Their actions were neither isolated nor individualized but reflected an evident belief that killing for sport was morally acceptable and could take place with impunity. In fact, they proudly bore the title "Kill Team," which one *Time* magazine writer found indicative of "the pure depravity of the alleged crimes."[44] In the five months during which the soldiers went on a murderous rampage in Kandahar province, it was reported that "they engaged in routine substance abuse and brutality toward Afghan locals that led to four premeditated murders of innocent civilians, the ritual mutilation of corpses ... and the snapping of celebratory photographs alongside the deceased as if they were bagged deer."[45] In one particularly disturbing photo celebrating a kill, one of the soldiers, Jeremy Morlock, is shown posing with the body of Gul Mudin, a fifteen-year-old Afghan boy. With a grin on his face and a thumbs-up sign, Morlock is kneeling on the ground next to Mudin's bloody and half-naked corpse, grabbing a handful of hair to lift up his bloodied face.

The platoon's squad leader, Staff Sergeant Calvin Gibbs, was apparently so pleased with the kill that he participated alongside the team in desecrating the young boy's dead body. Mark Boal quotes one soldier's account of the incident: "'It was like another day at the office for him'; Gibbs started 'messing around with the kid, moving his arms and mouth and acting like the kid was talking.'" Boal adds, "Then, using a pair of razor-sharp medic's shears, [Gibbs] reportedly sliced off the dead boy's pinky finger and gave it to [the soldier], as a trophy for killing his first Afghan."[46] The staff sergeant was so intent on killing Afghan civilians that he actually boasted about it, telling one soldier to "come down to the line and we'll find someone to kill."[47] Revealing the depth of his inhumanity, Gibbs reportedly told his soldiers that all Afghans were savages and talked to his squad about inventive ways to kill civilians. In one almost unbelievable scenario, the soldiers considered throwing "candy out of a Stryker vehicle as they drove through a village and shoot[ing] the children who came running to pick up the sweets. According to one soldier, they also talked about a second scenario in which they 'would throw candy out in front and in the rear of the Stryker; the Stryker would then run the children over.'"[48] Gibbs's instinct for barbarism appears so utterly ruthless that it is difficult to find words to describe the sheer horror of his crimes.

What is revealing about the "Kill Team" photos is that they received very little sustained attention in the American media, despite the depravity of the crimes committed by the group of US soldiers. The few attempts by the media to explain the murderous actions of these soldiers fell back on the usual laconic explanations or superficial comparisons to the Abu Ghraib photos, even though these crimes were different in a number of ways from previously reported atrocities. Only a handful of reports even attempted more sophisticated analyses. Seymour Hersh, for one, claimed that "these soldiers had come to accept the killing of civilians—recklessly, as payback, or just at random—as a facet of modern unconventional warfare. In other words, killing itself, whether in a firefight with the Taliban or in sport with innocent bystanders in a strange land with a strange language and strange customs, has become ordinary."[49] According to Hersh, such murderous acts are part of the social costs that come with sending young people to war. David Carr of the *New York Times* extended this sentiment in his claim that photos taken in wartime "carry the full freight of war and its collateral damage."[50] Writing for the *New York Times*, Luke Mogelson argued that "American soldiers have become increasingly more willing to kill."[51] The editors of *Rolling Stone* and staff writer Mark Boal suggested that the killing of innocent civilians is partly due to the failure of leadership in the US Armed Forces as well as the pedagogy of killing that permeates the training the recruits receive before being shipped off to war. A slightly different perspective was reflected in the comments of one older American officer formally in charge of training marines going to war, who pointed less to how young people are trained to kill by the armed services than to the pedagogical mechanisms at work in a wider culture that increasingly nurtures an inability to identify with others and the habitual use of violence to solve problems. This officer stated, "I used to do this job in the '70s during the war in Vietnam. In those years it took six months to train a young person to be prepared to kill a human being. Now I am doing the same job in Iraq, but things have changed. The young men come here already trained. They come here ready to kill."[52] This last comment comes the closest to interpreting the "Kill Team" photos less in terms of the effects of war—however horrifying and unimaginable—and more in terms of the soldiers' willingness to take pleasure in a collective death drive stoked by an unbridled social Darwinism. Generally speaking, the responses addressed neither what was uniquely horrific about the "Kill Team" photographs nor, more importantly, what they revealed about the current state of American society. The pleasure of killing is no longer normalized only in war as the culture and conditions that favor unrelenting violence have become increasingly hardwired into American society.

Unlike the Abu Ghraib prison photos, which were designed to humiliate detainees, the "Kill Team" photos suggest a deeper depravity, an intense pleasure in acts of violence that are planned and executed with no impending costs, culminating in the sadistic collection of body parts of the slain innocents as trophies. The "Kill Team" was after more than humiliation and the objectification of the other; it harbored a deep desire to feel intense excitement through pathological acts of murder and then capture the savagery in photos that served as mementos so the men could revisit and experience once again the delight that came with descending into the sordid pornographic hell that connects violence, pleasure, and death. The smiles on the faces of the young soldiers as they pose among their trophy killings are not the snapshots of privatized violence but images of sadism that are symptoms of a social pathology in which shared pleasure in violence is now commonplace. As my colleague David L. Clark points out, "This isn't Hannibal Lecter, after all, but G.I. Joe. [Yet the smiles in these photos appear as] symptomatic evidence of a certain public enjoyment of violence for the sake of violence, i.e., not the smile of shared pleasures between intimates (one form of the everyday), but a smile that marks a broader acceptance and affirmation of cruelty, killing for sport. Those smiles register a knowing pleasure in that violence, and say that it is okay to kill, and okay to take pleasure in that killing."[53]

This kind of analysis of "Kill Team" photographs is important because the photos do not signify extreme deviance as much as a new register of aesthetics and a deepening of "an abyss of failed sociality."[54] In this instance, the social does not disappear as much as it is overwritten by a sociality of shared violence—a sociality marked not by the injurious violence of the lone sociopath but instead by a growing army of sociopaths. The "Kill Team" photographs offer a glimpse into a larger set of social conditions now constituting a winner-take-all society in which it becomes difficult to imagine pleasure except through the spectacle of violence buttressed by a market-driven culture and survivalist ethic. The blatant display of these photographs illustrates more than what Judith Butler has called a "righteous coldness." It also registers a delight in the suffering of others that points to a "hot" and ever-present pathological economy of aesthetic pleasure.

The question should not be whether the "Kill Team" images are too heinous to undergo aesthetic appraisal but whether the very category of the aesthetic can tell us something about how the attitudes, values, and actions that produced these photos became intelligible in the first place. What is it about these photos that reveals the smear of the pornographic, a titillation grounded in maximizing the pleasure of violence? What are the political, economic, and social forces bearing down on American society that so easily undercut its potential to raise critical questions about war, violence, morality, and human suffering? How is it that the very category of the aesthetic is reconstituted as part of a wider circuit of consumption and spectacles of violence, transformed in the end into a depravity of aesthetics?

This is not to suggest that aesthetic standards and values don't matter but to inquire how they come to function in the broader culture. I am not suggesting that the symbiosis of the pleasure principle, the death drive, and the spectacle suggests once and for all that any consideration of aesthetics simply adds insult to the portrayal of human suffering and thus has no place in an emancipatory notion of politics. Photographers, as Mieke Bal points out, "can deploy art not only as a reflection but also as a form of witnessing that alters the existence of what it witnesses."[55] Bal also insists that art can be used "to reconquer beauty [when] mobilized as a weapon *against* suffering," as represented by Nan Goldin's deeply personal photographs displaying the violence and aggression that marked her relationship with her lover. What is at stake with the rise of the depravity of aesthetics—which offers up representations of human suffering, pain, and death as the ultimate repository of desire and pleasure—is not so much the beginning of a debate on the relevance of the aesthetic as it is a dialogue on the limits of the social and the perversion of a formative culture that renders the democratic social impossible. This latter line of thought raises a different set of questions.

What forms of responsibility and what pedagogical strategies should one invoke in the face of a society that feeds off spectacles of violence and cruelty? What forms of witnessing and education might be called into play in which the feelings of pleasure mobilized by images of human suffering can be used as "a catalyst for critical inquiry and deep thought"?[56] Responding to these questions would mean not only refusing to allow images to dissolve into a neoliberal pleasure machine by interrogating the crimes they portray but also recognizing, resisting, and transforming the pedagogical function of a cultural apparatus that seriously limits and undermines any viable notion of aesthetics that might extend rather than shut down critical thought, agency, and action in the service of a democracy to come. Rather than being reduced to a mechanism for the cathartic release of pleasure, images of a society saturated in violence, aggression, war, and poisonous modes of masculinity must serve as an indictment, a source of memory, and evidence of the need to imagine otherwise.

In pointing to these photos and the emerging culture of cruelty, I don't want to suggest that because neoliberal social formations appear to be winning in the United States, they have won or the struggle is over. I think it is too easy to slide from an analysis of such dominant forces to erasing the important issue that this is an ongoing struggle that operates within a number of different contexts, however uneven. As Larry Grossberg has pointed out, "The fact that one can read, for example, a culture of cruelty off of various articulations does not yet mean that this is how people live their lives. The fact that the cultural discourses are all about markets does not mean that people live their lives with markets as the only definition/locus of value."[57] These new social formations take place within and across diverse contexts, and we need a new language for describing the nature of such forces, the different terrains on which they operate, and the opportunities for resistance. What I am arguing is that recognizing the depravity of aesthetics does not mean that neoliberal domination and social deformation are accomplished and sutured facts; on the contrary, they make more necessary a mindful commitment to truth, justice, and collective struggle. At the heart of such a commitment is the effort to identify and locate ourselves within complex spheres of struggle and to work collectively toward cultural and political renewal.

We must be open to the possibility of change when it arises, when Arendt's "instants of truth" confront us head-on, shock us out of our stupor, and force us into action. The images from Libya, Syria, Egypt, and Iran of the violence and killing of peaceful protesters by state militia thugs were such instants of truth as they were captured on video and circulated the world over. The video of the murder of a twenty-seven-year-old Iranian music student, Neda Agha Soltan, helped to inspire massive waves of protests in Iran that continue to this day. Similarly, terrifying images of the torture and killing of thirteen-year-old Hamza Ali al-Khateeb have spread throughout Syria, indicting the state security forces who murdered him. Such images propel into being a collective mode of critical consciousness that enables people to remember differently and to imagine that which is deemed unimaginable. What is emancipatory about these images, as Georges Didi-Huberman points out in a different context, is that they cannot be processed through what he calls the "disimagination machine"; that is, these are images whose hard reality bears witness to forms of agency, ethical acts, and collective resistance that persist and teach us "in spite of all"—in spite of the continuous attempts at erasure perpetrated by the dominant pedagogy.[58]

Such images have ignited massive collective protests against repressive governments across the Arab world. These images did not feed the basest of collective desires and pleasurable fantasies detached from any real consequences. On the contrary, such images of abuse and suffering inflamed societies willing to struggle to make instants of truth—those glimpses of humanity in the other and in our collective selves—less ephemeral and more permanent in a world crushed by the fist of powerful elites. As the American public witnesses nightly on its television screens the overt violent and illegal practices of the security and surveillance state, the cinematic delight in violence loses its attraction as fantasy entertainment. The American public's obsession with both the reality and images of violence is wearing thin as more and more instants of truth emerge in the United States. Young nonviolent protesters across the United States are being beaten, maced, arrested, and subjected to all manner of surveillance/spying technologies that engage "in facial recognition, Internet data mining, and even drones."[59]

Nightmares are no longer easily transformed into commodified desires or cheap entertainment by mass advertising and the culture industries. On the contrary, with the rise of the Occupy movement in both the United States and across the globe, glamour, spectacle, and entertainment give way to the reality of deeply oppressive authoritarian regimes that have turned on their children. Given the state's unwillingness to address the problems that many young people face, it has turned to the culture of war and violence, abandoning any attempts at ideological legitimation for its soul-numbing mode of governance. Of course, the punishing of protest is not new in the United States, but what is new is the degree to which it is turned against a generation of young people whose only "crime" is that they are protesting the massive structural economic and political injustices that have stolen from them any possibility of a better future. From Quebec and New York City to Paris and

Athens, the punishing of student protests has quickened, just as the collective call for democracy has intensified.[60] Against these acts of violence that undermine any possibility of a democracy or a viable notion of politics, a new formative culture is being developed all across the globe by young people who refuse the violence at the heart of daily life, who are offering a new language, politics, and form of counterpower to once again make democracy a rallying cry for equality, justice, and freedom. When such a formative culture exists on a global scale, it will enable people everywhere to connect emotional investments and desires to a politics in which unthinkable acts of violence are confronted as part of a larger "commitment to political accountability, community, and the importance of positive affect for both belonging and change."[61]

◇

CHAPTER 3

Norway Is Closer Than You Think
Extremism and the Crisis of American Politics

You are operating as a jury, judge, and executioner on behalf of all free Europeans. It is better to kill too many than not enough ... the time for dialogue is over ... the time for armed resistance has come.
—*Anders Behring Breivik, 2083*

Within a week after right-wing Christian extremist Anders Behring Breivik killed seventy-seven people, many of them children, the US Republican Party leadership—in an effort to rally its members in the budget battle with the Obama administration—screened a short clip from the Ben Affleck movie *The Town* (2010).[1] In the clip, an exchange between a young thug, Doug MacRay (Affleck), and one of his fellow ruffians, James Coughlin (Jeremy Renner), proceeds as follows:

MacRay: I need your help. I can't tell you what it is. You can never ask me about it later. And we're going to hurt some people.

Coughlin: Whose car are we going to take?

The two characters then don hockey masks and break into an apartment, bludgeoning two men with sticks and shooting a third in the leg.

Employing such violent imagery as a political strategy is shocking, and for more reason than the fact that it came so closely on the heels of media coverage of the slaughter of scores of innocent young people in Norway by an ideological extremist. Such an open embrace of the relationship between images of violence and hate and the murderous acts that sometimes follow reveals the indifference, if not moral blindness, of the Republican Party leadership to a growing extremism within the party's own ranks and elsewhere. Thomas E. Mann and Norman J. Ornstein, two Washington insiders, reinforced this view in an op-ed in the *Washington Post*, arguing that "the GOP ... is ideologically extreme; scornful of compromise; unmoved by conventional understanding of facts, evidence, and science; and dismissive of the legitimacy of its political opposition."[2] Yet, in the case of using the clip from *The Town*, indifference turned to something more troubling. It appears that Republican leaders used gratuitous images of mind-crushing violence and retribution as a legitimate, even inspiring, framework for motivating support for legislative practices that will have deleterious impacts on vulnerable populations in the United States, especially children. This is not merely barbarism parading as political reform—it is also a blatant indicator of the degree to which sadism and a theater of cruelty have become normalized in the highest reaches of government. Even more, it suggests that the United States has arrived at a moment in its history when politicians take delight in morally indefensible visions and overtly cruel policies of which the vast majority of Americans would be ashamed.

Despite the views propagated by the former Bush administration to justify its "war on terror," extremism is not born and bred only in countries outside the United States, in particular those perceived to be antagonistic to American democracy. In fact, most acts of terrorism in the United States, like the horrific violence in Norway, have been committed by homegrown terrorists, not members of a foreign extremist group.[3] According to researchers working with the National Consortium for the Study of Terrorism and Responses to Terrorism, the "threat of domestic terrorist attacks in the United States ... is significant and growing."[4] The US Department of Homeland Security specifically warns that "right-wing Conservative extremists would be among the groups most likely to commit an act of mass violence in the United States."[5] And yet, forms of terrorism in the United States that are not of a militant Islamist orientation are generally understudied and underemphasized. As the Norwegian sociologist Sindre Bangstad has stated, "available statistics from Europe in recent years have suggested that militant Islamist terror attacks represent only a small fraction of the total number of recorded terrorist attacks on European soil," yet many terrorism experts have argued that the greatest threat comes from radical Islamist movements.[6] There is more at work here than a racist and xenophobic form of social amnesia. Typically unstated in reports about acts of domestic terrorism in the United States is the fact that a disproportionate number of such acts have been waged against children. Recent US history is replete with examples, from routine Ku Klux Klan (KKK) and other racist attacks on black children and their families in the 1950s and 1960s to the shootings at Columbine High School in 1999 and Virginia Tech in 2007.[7]

The tragic slayings in Norway raise anew serious questions about domestic terrorism and its roots in right-wing ideology, fundamentalist movements, and a virulent species of Christian nationalism spreading across the globe. Breivik's manifesto *2083* and his murderous actions remind us of the degree to which right-wing extremism of a reactionary and authoritarian nature is more than a minor threat to American security—a fact we have been too often willing to forget.[8] The foundation of such violence and the insistent threat it poses to every decent principle associated with justice, equality, and the ideals of a substantive democracy are to be found not only in its most excessive and brutal acts but also in the absolutist and racist worldview that produces it.[9] As Mattias Gardell insists, "The terrorist attacks in Oslo were not an outburst of irrational madness, but a calculated act of political violence. The carnage was a manifestation of a certain logic that can and should be explained, if we want to avoid a repetition."[10] Elements of such political logic are on full display in American society and appear to be gaining ground. As indicated earlier, the influence of extremist and fundamentalist ideologies and worldviews—whether embodied in religion, politics, militarism, or the market—can be seen currently in the rhetoric at work at the highest levels of government. How else to explain, just one day after the debt-ceiling settlement in Washington, why the Republican congressman Doug Lamborn of Colorado Springs in an interview with a Denver radio station referred to President Obama as a "tar baby"?[11] It is hard to mistake the racist nature of the term "tar baby," given its long association as a derogatory epithet for African Americans. Soon afterward, Pat Buchanan wrote a column that began with a shockingly overt racist comment: "Mocked by *The Wall Street Journal* and Sen. John McCain as the little people of the Harry Potter books, the Tea Party 'Hobbits' are indeed returning to Middle Earth—to nail the coonskin to the wall."[12] Then there was the Orange County Republican Central Committee member and Tea Party activist Marilyn Davenport, who sent out an e-mail picturing President Barack Obama's face on the body of a baby chimpanzee.[13] What these incidents make clear is that the "coarse language of fundamentalist hatred" is alive and well in American politics; yet it is barely noticed and produces almost no public outrage.[14] They also indicate how this type of racist discourse creates a climate in which hatred and violence become legitimate political and ideological options. And this type of fundamentalism and extremism is about more than just the rise of the Tea Party.

It has become widely acceptable in mainstream US culture to engage in immigrant- and Muslim-bashing, with examples of revolting racism now commonplace on Fox News. The right-wing media also appears comfortably at home in offering up endless racist comments aimed at President Obama. For instance, in June 2011, conservative TV star Eric Bolling referred "to guests of Barack Obama at the White House as 'hoods in the hizzy.'"[15] It gets worse. The *New York Times* reported that on the occasion of a private party celebrating President Obama's fiftieth birthday, *Fox Nation* ran the headline "Obama's Hip-Hop BBQ Didn't Create Jobs." As the *New York Times* pointed out, "Below the headline were photos of Mr. Obama and, separately, three black celebrities who attended the party, the basketball player Charles Barkley, the comedian Chris Rock and the rapper Jay-Z. Not pictured were any attendees of other racial backgrounds, like the actor Tom Hanks or Mayor Rahm Emanuel of Chicago."[16] It increasingly appears that race-baiting among conservative radio and television commentators and Tea Party supporters has become as pervasive and as popular as extreme sports. Both the discourse and the presence of authoritarian populism and extremism have moved from the margins to the center of American life. Rather than represent the obscene underside of American life, racism, violence, and their accompanying sadistic humiliations have become a defining register of American society. They are a growing and ominous force in everyday life, politics, and the media.

As Andrew Bacevich has noted, violence has become the preferred instrument of statecraft in the United States just as war has become the normal condition of foreign and domestic policy.[17] Reckless military adventures are now matched by the perpetuation of militarized culture at home. The Bush and Obama administrations' move toward war "signals both a reversion to the deepest, darkest roots of [our culture] and the new political era to come. It marks the advent of ... a dangerous and unprecedented confluence of our democratic institutions and the military."[18] A rigid, warlike mentality has created an atmosphere in which dialogue is viewed as a weakness and compromise understood as personal failing. As Richard Hofstadter argued over fifty years ago, fundamentalist thinking is predicated on anti-intellectualism and the refusal to engage other points of view.[19] The other is not confronted as someone worthy of respect but as an enemy, a threatening presence that must be utterly vanquished. Michel Foucault elucidated the idea that fundamentalists do not confront the other as "a partner in the search for the truth but an adversary, an enemy who is wrong, who is harmful, and whose very existence constitutes a threat.... There is something even more serious here: in this comedy, one mimics war, battles, annihilations, or unconditional surrenders, putting forward as much of one's killer instinct as possible."[20]

Missing from the fundamentalist toolbox is the necessity for self-reflection: thinking critically about the inevitable limitations of one's arguments and being morally accountable for the social costs of harboring racist ideologies and pushing policies that serve to deepen racist exclusions, mobilize fear, and legitimate a growing government apparatus of punishment and imprisonment.[21] What connects the moral bankruptcy of right-wing Republicans who embrace violent imagery in order to mobilize their followers with the mind-set of extremists such as Breivik is that they share a deep romanticization of violence that is valorized by old and new fundamentalisms—whose ultimate endpoint is a death-dealing blow to the welfare state, young people, immigrants, Muslims, and others deemed dangerous and disposable. War is now waged against society itself, just as "the current mode of production and reproduction has become a mode of *production for elimination,* a reproduction of populations that are not likely to be productively used or exploited but are always already *superfluous,* and therefore can be only eliminated either through 'political' or 'natural' means—what some Latin American sociologists provocatively call *poblacion chatarra,* 'garbage humans,' to be 'thrown' away, out of the global city."[22]

Moreover, growing corporate power and sovereignty, divorced from any regulatory or ethical commitments to sustain human life, traffic in both symbolic and real violence. The dominant media flood the culture with speech, images, and soundtracks that dissolve screen culture into a visceral bloodbath of pathology and hate. As Chapter 2 discussed in detail, the drive for instant pleasure is now an essential part of a popular culture whose ratings are measured by the increasing levels of shock and violence offered up to viewers. Vulgarity, spectacle, and violence intermingle in TV shows such as *Desperate Housewives* and *Maury,* Hollywood films such as *Savages* (2012), and the endless reality TV series in which a survival-of-the-fittest ethic provides a legitimating discourse for the economic Darwinism that governs the larger society. As Bauman points out, "In contemporary dreams . . . the image of 'progress' seems to have moved from the discourse of *shared improvement* to that of individual survival."[23] The poverty of public discourse is matched by a war-of-all-against-all ethic that provides moral justification and a political rationale not only for massive disparities in wealth and income and the production of disposable populations but also for a growing deregulation, privatization, and militarization of everyday life.[24] In a social order dominated by corporations, high finance, and the military, it is not surprising that the United States is mimicking "the wild inequities and social cruelties"[25] that were rampant in the Gilded Age of the late nineteenth century.

Under free-market fundamentalism, the social when named or recognized is pathologized just as responsibility is depoliticized and radically individualized. Everyone now has to negotiate his or her own fate alone, bearing full responsibility for problems that are often not of his or her own making. Violence inhabits what are increasingly known as zones of social abandonment where law and the mechanisms of formal governance give rise to a machinery of vigilantism, states of emergency, and social death. Under such circumstances, the government "rids itself of any obligation whatsoever to provide for the welfare of its citizens except for the ratcheting up of that military and police power that might be needed to quell social unrest."[26] As the welfare state withers, the police state grows. Given the fact that war has become a permanent condition while a culture of cruelty, hyper-masculinity, and violence is hardwired into the social order, the United States has moved effortlessly from the welfare state to a warfare state and a zero-tolerance society. The thinnest of claims on democracy remains, overshadowed by an impoverishment of values, rights, public goods, and public spheres.

Thus, it is not alarming that Breivik's radical anti-Islamic and anti-Marxist views drew repeatedly on the work of American extremists, including Andrew Bostrom, David Horowitz, and Daniel Pipes. Despite the comforting illusions offered by the media, with these individuals we are talking not about the emergence of right-wing lone wolves who explode in a frenzy of hate and violence but about an increasingly pervasive fundamentalist worldview that embraces a circle of certainty, evokes a Manichaean struggle between good and evil, espouses an anti-intellectual populism, calls for the banishing of critical intellectuals from the academy, and rails against critical academic fields such as postcolonial, feminist, peace, and ethnic studies. Although many religious and secular fundamentalists may not argue directly for violence, they spew out a steady stream of hatred that creates the conditions for both symbolic and real violence. Hence it is not surprising either that Breivik is identified as both a Christian and a conservative nationalist or that his manifesto echoes many of the hateful and militant ideals of white Christian nationalists and militant groups in the United States. Echoes of Breivik's claim that Europe was being handed over to Muslims find their counterpart in the United States in the right-wing claim that American society is being invaded by Mexican immigrants.

I am not suggesting that Breivik's actions can be linked in a direct fashion to right-wing extremism in the Congress and broader US society, but it is reasonable to suggest that they share a number of core concerns including a view of immigrants as a threat to national purity, an embrace of anti-Muslim rhetoric, an espousal of militarism and market fundamentalism, and support for a host of retrograde social policies that embrace weakening unions, the rolling back of women's rights, and a deep distrust of equality as the foundation of democracy itself. Chris Hedges outlines the elements of such a fundamentalism when he writes,

> Fundamentalists have no interest in history, culture or social or linguistic differences.... They are provincials.... They peddle a route to assured collective deliverance. And they sanction violence and the physical extermination of other human beings to get there. All fundamentalists worship the same gods—themselves. They worship the future prospect of their own empowerment. They view this empowerment as a necessity for the advancement and protection of civilization or the Christian state. They sanctify the nation. They hold up the ability the industrial state has handed to them as a group and as individuals to shape the world according to their vision as evidence of their own superiority.... The self-absorbed world view of these fundamentalists brings smiles of indulgence from the corporatists who profit, at our expense, from the obliteration of moral and intellectual inquiry.[27]

At work in fundamentalist logic is a moral and political absolutism that dehumanizes young people, immigrants, feminists, Muslims, cultural Marxists, and all others relegated to the outside of the narrow parameters of a public sphere preserved for white, Christian, male citizens. Breivik acted upon his hatred of Muslims, leftists, and immigrants by murdering young people whose activities at a Labor Party camp suggested they might usher in a future at odds with his deeply racist and authoritarian views.[28] As Scott Shane, writing in the *New York Times*, put it (and it bears repeating), Breivik "was deeply influenced by a small group of American bloggers and writers who have warned for years about the threat from Islam."[29] Breivik, like this new generation of American racists, did not endorse a strategy that made a claim for racial superiority on biological grounds; that is, he recognized that it was not wise tactically "to oppose immigration and Islam on racial grounds (an argument that would attract few people)."[30] Instead, he admired and adopted an ideology from those far-right groups that revises old racist beliefs into new anti-Muslim narratives in which immigrants and those deemed other "are not biologically inferior, but [instead] culturally incompatible."[31] In this case, cultural difference rather than biological degeneration is viewed as a threat to democracy.[32]

Breivik named as one of his major influences the right-wing extremist Pamela Geller, "who has called President Obama 'President Jihad' and claimed that Arab language classes are a plot to subvert the United States."[33] More recently, Geller's xenophobic blog *Atlas Shrugs* has repeatedly attempted "to unearth Obama's relationship to Islam [and prove that] Islam is a political ideology [that is] incompatible with democracy."[34] Geller's racist and hate-filled blog implied that Breivik's attack on the Labor Party youth camp may have been somehow justified because, as she put it, the victims might have become "future leaders of the party responsible for flooding Norway with Muslims who refuse to assimilate, who commit major violence against Norwegian natives including violent gang rapes, with impunity, and who live on the dole."[35] As Lee Fang points out, Geller attempts to prove her case by posting a picture taken on the island camp a few hours before Breivik's murderous rampage and writing the following caption, without any sense of remorse: "Note the faces which are more Middle Eastern or mixed than pure Norwegian."[36] While such shocking expressions of racism should not be directly connected to all forms of fundamentalism, there is nothing about those who espouse this worldview that renders them open or willing to exercise the judgment, critical inquiry, and thoughtfulness necessary to counter and resist such perspectives and the violence to which they often lead. Such worldviews operate on the side of certainty, wrap themselves in a logic that is considered unquestionable, refuse compromise and dialogue, and often invoke a militarized vocabulary to define their supporters as soldiers fighting a war for Western civilization. This is a worldview in which ignorance and a flight from thoughtfulness join with violence, sanctified by a fundamentalism that thrives on conformity and authoritarian populism.

While most right-wing politicians, individuals, and groups in the United States denounced the horrendous violence perpetrated by Breivik, they nonetheless produce and contribute to a culture of violence with their own rhetoric of demonization and barely disguised racism that undermines any respect for difference, democratic values, and a capacious notion of personal and social responsibility. As recently stated in a study by the Anti-Defamation League,

> The hateful rhetoric around the immigration debate has gone beyond the rallies, lobbying and media appearances by anti-immigration advocates. A number of media personalities in television and radio, as well as political leaders, have adopted the same language when discussing immigration issues in this country. These extend from [former] national TV correspondent Lou Dobbs to more extreme political commentator Patrick Buchanan to local radio personalities to members of Congress such as Tom Tancredo and Steve King ... the use of anti-immigrant rhetoric has permeated the culture in our country.[37]

There are a few degrees of separation between far-right extremists such as Madeleine Cosman, an alleged medical lawyer, and radio and TV personality Lou Dobbs, and both have argued that Mexican immigrants are criminals and carriers of diseases such as leprosy. This type of xenophobia can also be found in the words and actions of New York Republican representative Peter T. King, who as chairman of the House Homeland Security Committee opened hearings on the radicalization of Muslim Americans, legitimating the absurd notion that only Muslims pose a terrorist threat. This type of racist hysteria (which precludes investigation of other forms of radicalization) turns a blind eye to homegrown hatred and terrorism. Not only does such an investigation ignore a long-standing tradition of racism and Islamophobia in America, particularly since the tragic events of 9/11, but it is aided and abetted by racist diatribes from conservative public figures.

Pat Buchanan, for one, has written columns such as "Goodbye to Los Angeles" filled with apocalyptic visions of the United States being taken over by people of color and calling Muslims in America "a fifth column."[38] The appeal of such rhetoric is widespread in the United States and can be found in the work of the late Harvard scholar Samuel Huntington, anti-Muslim bloggers, Christian fundamentalists, and Fox News commentators as well as in the anti-immigration policies initiated in several states (one of the most pernicious examples was introduced by state legislators in Arizona).[39] Fundamentalism is as homegrown as the KKK, and the views of white militia groups have been given new life within a range of discourses extending from those of the Christian right to those of secular fundamentalists such as Sam Harris.[40] And often in these discourses the line between hate-filled speech and calls to action is difficult to delineate, especially in an emotionally charged and politically volatile atmosphere. This type of rhetoric may be easy politics, but such rhetoric can be transformed into more than words, becoming an incitement to violence.

Bigotry and the life-crushing policies it produces appear to spread like a disease; their targets seem to multiply every day in the United States. Indeed, one could argue that the only successful (though hardly cost-effective) war the United States has waged since the 1980s has been against poor men of color, who now represent 70 percent of all inmates in US prisons.[41] This disturbing notion is buttressed by the fact that, as Michelle Alexander has argued, "today there are more African Americans under correctional control, whether in prison or jail, on probation or on parole, than there were enslaved in 1850. And more African-American men are disenfranchised now because of felon disenfranchisement laws than in 1870."[42]

As the targets of hatred multiply, the intensity and overt hatred embodied in the attacks become more unapologetic and visible. Lesbian, gay, bisexual, and transgendered populations are another target of hate, evident for example in one of Pat Buchanan's recent columns in which he writes, "What is the moral basis of the argument that homosexuality is normal, natural and healthy? In recent years, it has been associated with high levels of AIDS and enteric diseases, and from obits in gay newspapers, early death. Where is the successful society where homosexual marriage was normal?"[43] There is also the war on youth, which is now in high gear with the implosion of social safety nets, decent housing, and health care, and the simultaneous rise of the punishing state—this being the result of the takeover of a number of state legislatures and governorships by radical conservatives and the House of Representatives being controlled by right-wing extremists. Increasingly, Republican extremists at both the state and federal levels of government have also waged a war on the rights of women by instituting harsh antiabortion measures, depriving women of protection against workplace discrimination, curtailing affordable access to birth control, and cutting back on state-supported health care.[44]

Although what is happening in the United States isn't the kind of direct militant violence we saw in Norway, it is a form of warfare just the same. It is less spectacular in the short run but is certain to incur more casualties in the long run. Consider the actions of Jan Brewer, the governor of Arizona, in "spearheading a bill to eliminate KidsCare, the state's Medicaid Program for children ... though twenty three percent of Arizona's children live in poverty."[45] What does one say about Governor Paul LePage of Maine, who "recently signed into law a bill that eases child labor laws, lowering restrictions on the hours and days teenagers can work"?[46] It gets worse. Senator Harry Reid brought attention to the current extremism of the Republican Party by highlighting the introduction of legislation that would cut or eliminate Medicaid and the Children's Health Insurance Program. Over 1.7 million kids would lose health insurance by 2016.[47] The *CommonDreams* news site further reported that "G.O.P. Florida lawmakers have rejected over $50 million in much-needed federal child-abuse prevention money because it was part of Obama's healthcare reform package."[48]

Violence becomes news when its most extreme registers erupt in waves of bloodshed. Yet there is another kind of violence that can rightfully be viewed as a form of domestic terrorism. It can be seen in an array of statistics that point to the current regime of neglect and abuse of children: one in two Americans is low income or poor—adding up to 146 million Americans; one child in five is poor.[49] In addition, "infant mortality, low birth weight, and child deaths under five are ranked among the highest in the U.S. as compared to Western nations and Japan. Among OECD countries, only Mexico, Turkey and the Slovak Republic have higher infant mortality than the U.S."[50] This is the violence legitimated by right-wing conservative policies that contribute to shocking levels of inequality in which the wealth of Hispanics and blacks fell by 66 percent and 55 percent, respectively, between 2005 and 2009. The extent of America's social disintegration is breathtaking. By now it is also well known that the United States has the highest rates of inequality and poverty among the industrialized nations. As Nobel economist Joseph Stiglitz has pointed out, "The upper 1 percent of Americans are now taking in nearly a quarter of the nation's income every year. In terms of wealth rather than income, the top 1 percent control 40 percent.... While the top

1 percent have seen their incomes rise 18 percent over the past decade, those in the middle have actually seen their incomes fall."[51] Social inequalities were made evident by the Occupy Wall Street protests in the wake of a global financial crisis that, as Matt Taibbi pointed out, "saw virtually every major bank and financial company on Wall Street embroiled in obscene criminal scandals that impoverished millions and collectively destroyed hundreds of billions, in fact, trillions of dollars of the world's wealth—and nobody went to jail ... except Bernie Madoff, a flamboyant and pathological celebrity con artist whose victims happened to be other rich and famous people."[52]

Not only has the future of younger Americans been darkened as a result of the corruption and crimes of bankers, Wall Street, and the politicians who have bailed them out, but the Obama administration has retreated into a mind-numbing silence in the face of deregulatory policies that have produced both criminal behavior on the part of the financial elite and massive hardships for millions of Americans. America's political culture is moving in reverse, substituting hate for compassion and legal illegalities for justice as millions of people face the threat of under- and unemployment; are evicted from their homes; and enter a future in which everyone but the financial elite confronts the ever-expanding specter of poverty, homelessness, unemployment, and a future without hope.

Many right-wing pundits and politicians have responded to the discourse about staggering levels of inequality and poverty by claiming that such rhetoric represents a form of class warfare; if this can be believed, then it is a war being waged against the rich, who are positioned as being ruthlessly victimized. When Warren Buffet wrote an op-ed piece in the *New York Times* insisting that the rich be taxed more, *Fox News*'s Sean Hannity and Republican senator Orrin Hatch, among other conservatives, responded by falsely claiming that over 50 percent of American households no longer pay taxes and that the poor should be actually taxed more.[53] In actuality, 47 percent of American households pay no federal income taxes, but they do pay other taxes. According to the Tax Policy Center, these include "federal payroll taxes that fund Social Security and Medicare, and excise taxes on gasoline, aviation, alcohol and cigarettes. Many also pay state or local taxes on sales, income and property."[54] What is ignored here is that 5.3 million people have been affected by the mortgage foreclosure epidemic; 14 million are unemployed, and millions are working in low-skill, underpaid jobs; 20 percent of all children live in poverty; 45 million lack health insurance; and millions more lack any sense of hope. Such statistics point to policies that are not simply mean-spirited but cruel and sadistic and dishonor the government's obligations to young people and to socially and economically marginalized populations. Apparently it is not enough that the fundamentalist wing of the Republican Party promotes policies that further this culture of cruelty. These extremists now want to punish the poor and disadvantaged even more by taking money from them through new taxation laws that would surely drive people even further into destitution. Fundamentalists need a clearly defined enemy, and they have found one in the growing ranks of the poor. *Lord of the Flies* is no longer merely fiction—it is a prophecy unfolding at this very moment as we watch right-wing politicians and pundits in the United States going mad with greed, hatred, bigotry, and power.

Paul Krugman rightly claims that "the G.O.P. budget plan isn't a good-faith effort to put America's fiscal house in order; it's voodoo economics, with an extra dose of fantasy, and a large helping of mean-spiritedness."[55] Krugman goes further and argues that the American government is being held hostage by a group of Republican extremists who purposely want to make government dysfunctional. Far-right zealots such as Michele Bachmann, Newt Gingrich, Ron Paul, Rick Santorum, Texas governor Rick Perry, and their conservative evangelical compatriots embody a mode of fundamentalism that promotes gay-bashing, disdain for social protections, the collapse of distinctions between church and state, and a deep hatred of government—all of which are rooted less in political and economic analyses than in willful ignorance, misrepresentation of biblical strictures, and distorted religious values.[56] Governor Perry opened his failed campaign for the 2012 presidential election by stating, without any hint of irony or for that matter any vestige of self-reflection, that scientists were making up global warming for profit. He dismissed evolution as "a theory that's out there."[57] Congresswoman Bachmann has stated, "If you are involved in the gay and lesbian life style, it's bondage.... It's part of Satan."[58] She has also insisted that if the Obama administration required young people to do mandatory service, they would be forced "to attend re-education camps."[59] Such comments are becoming ever more frequent in American politics and are no longer limited to the lunatic fringe of the political spectrum. For example, Senate minority leader Mitch McConnell (R., Ky.) stated, "After years of discussions and months of negotiations, I have little question that as long as this president is in the Oval Office, a real solution is unattainable."[60]

There is more than covert racism at work here, or the extremist views about Obama that inform much of the Republican Party. There is also a cult of certainty that has given political extremism a disturbing degree of normalcy while at the same time indicating the degree to which such thought now permeates American society. In fact, absolutist thought is now driving official state and federal policy and pushing the allegedly liberal Obama to a far-right position, a move the president cloaks in a cowardly appeal to bipartisanship and a deeply flawed notion of consensus. Not only is the power of market-driven casino capitalism at its zenith, but a culture of fundamentalism has become the driving force in American politics, which now appears only a few degrees away from an outright embrace of a twenty-first-century authoritarianism.

What is interesting, and quite frightening, about Krugman's analysis of the growing fundamentalism and religiosity of American politics is his insightful claim that such a shift is being abetted by a dominant media apparatus that views extremist ideas within what he calls a "cult of balance" in which such views are treated as just one more legitimate opinion. Listen to Brian Williams, the NBC News anchor, on any given night and you get firsthand one of the most egregious proponents of the cult of balance. Krugman is worth citing on this issue. He writes,

News reports portray the parties as equally intransigent; pundits fantasize about some kind of "centrist" uprising, as if the problem was too much partisanship on both sides. Some of us have long complained about the cult of "balance," the insistence on portraying both parties as equally wrong and equally at fault on any issue, never mind the facts. I joked long ago that if one party declared that the earth was flat, the headlines would read "Views Differ on Shape of Planet." But would that cult still rule in a situation as stark as the one we now face, in which one party is clearly engaged in blackmail and the other is dickering over the size of the ransom? The answer, it turns out, is yes. And this is no laughing matter: The cult of balance has played an important role in bringing us to the edge of disaster. For when reporting on political disputes always implies that both sides are to blame, there is no penalty for extremism.[61]

Clearly, as Krugman points out, there is another side to right-wing fundamentalism that needs to be addressed, aside from its xenophobic, homophobic, antigovernment, antifeminist, and youth-hating beliefs, which have become increasingly normalized, legitimated, and defined loosely as just another view in American society. More than the rise of a hate-filled fundamentalism and a populist anti-intellectualism that scorns debate, dialogue, and critical exchange, the cultural shift is also symptomatic of the end of politics and by extension signals the death knell of democracy itself. Politics becomes moribund when dialogue, critical exchange, reasoned arguments, facts, and critical modes of education become objects of derision and contempt. Right-wing extremism is nourished when the formative culture that makes democracy possible is defunded, commercialized, and diminished—when it is increasingly eroded and may one day cease to exist.

Right-wing extremism and the fundamentalist logic it embraces are not merely a security threat; they do not simply produce terrorists. They actively wage a war on the very possibility of judgment, informed argument, and critical agency itself. They open the door for lies and omissions parading as truth, ignorance celebrated as informed reason, and the dismissal of science as just another worthwhile opinion. In the end, violence emerges as a legitimate strategy to weed out those not on the side of an unquestioning moralism. Education is redefined as training; fear is driven by political illiteracy; and authoritarian populism masquerades as the will of the people—all of which speaks to what Hannah Arendt once called "dark times" in reference to that period in history when the forces of totalitarianism and fascism extinguished reason, thoughtful exchange, discerning judgments, justice, and truth.[62] We are once again on the brink of dark times, and the clock is not merely ticking. The alarm is blaring, yet the American public refuses to wake from a nightmare that is about to become a dreadful and punishing reality. Henry Wallace in a 1944 article for the *New York Times* warned that "American fascism will not be really dangerous until there is a purposeful coalition among the cartelists, the deliberate poisoners of public information, and those who stand for the K.K.K. type of demagoguery."[63] The description is not merely prescient but frightening in the way it so eerily describes the current historical moment in American history.

Of course, history is open, not predetermined. We have witnessed in Egypt, Iran, Syria, Greece, Libya, and other countries how men, women, and young people have refused established and emergent forms of authoritarianism, giving rise to collective revolts that display immense courage and hope. And in the United States the Occupy movement has breathed new life into a surging protest movement. Young people are introducing a new political language and reigniting a new political imagination in revealing the immense inequities, inequalities, and suffering that take place under the current regime of casino capitalism. They are making clear that their exclusion from higher education, decent health care, and jobs cannot be separated from an international system of global finance. Although it is not clear where this movement will go or how far it will succeed, there is no doubt that it is time for Americans to look beyond existing forms of leadership, the tired vocabularies of established political parties, the thoughtless stenography dispersed by mainstream media, and the official view of democracy as just another form of consumerism and the empty ritual of voting. It is time to look to those struggles at home and abroad that both embrace democracy and embody a form of civic courage in which thinking and morality inform each other in support of a world where young people can flourish, politics becomes a noble practice, and democracy has a future. It is time for individuals and social movements to take back the promise of a democracy whose institutions, values, and social relations have been hollowed out, reduced to a vehicle for the free market, finance capital, and megacorporations.

◇

CHAPTER 4

Disposable Knowledge and Disposable Bodies
Book Burning in Arizona

They that start by burning books will end by burning men.
—*Heinrich Heine*

Every once in a while events flash before us that might at first seem trivial or commonplace given how in tune they are with the political and ideological temper of the times, but in reality they sometimes contain a hidden order of politics and reveal a flight from social and moral responsibility that convey a frightening truth about the dark, authoritarian forces driving American society. Such forces are often associated with a passion against equality, driven by an appeal to national unity and defended as a fervent act of patriotism. In actuality, the willingness to defend persistent and deeply rooted forms of racial, economic, and social inequality is often impelled by a fear of those deemed other or viewed as threatening, whose presence, voices, and ideas defy the crippling registers of intellectual conformity and forms of knowledge that merely reinforce "common sense," the status quo, and right-wing populism. Resentment of and contempt for equality easily cross over into bigotry as such forces propel conservative politicians and antipublic bureaucrats to punish those marginalized by class, race, and ethnicity. At the same time, conservative and right-wing groups work hard to eliminate those public spheres, critical ideas, bodies of knowledge, and social relations that give voice to the complex histories of difference and the multilayered cultures and cultural memories that allow the designated voiceless to narrate themselves. This is a politics that attempts to make certain groups disappear—a politics that has a long legacy in American history and can be seen currently in attacks on affirmative action, women's reproductive rights, immigrants, Muslims, and increasingly young people. The policies that accompany this politics of resentment, bigotry, and contempt toward those deemed pathological and disposable promote a form of racist-inflected anti-intellectualism and politics whose goal is to regulate those ideas, individuals, and groups that offer a different and often critical reading of history, power, culture, and the social landscape.

Current acts of censorship and state racism are dressed up as a form of ideological purity and moral certainty that attempts to cleanse the broader polity of those modes of remembrance that allegedly sully and contaminate American culture and character. Such acts contain traces of earlier authoritarian ideologies that were fundamental to the shaping of the totalitarian states of Germany and the Soviet Union in the first part of the twentieth century. For instance, in April 1933, the authorities of Nazi Germany ordered a literary purge—a burning of books, papers, and art works considered degenerate because they allegedly undermined what was defined as "pure" German language, culture, and traditional values. Authors whose works were burnt for harboring dangerous ideas and troubling knowledge included Albert Einstein, Sigmund Freud, John Dos Passos, Bertolt Brecht, Walter Benjamin, Ernst Bloch, André Gide, George Grosz, Franz Kafka, André Malraux, and Karl Marx, among others. All of these authors apparently published works that threatened the gatekeepers of ideological purity and political fundamentalism. The identification of such nefarious works led to the passage of a series of laws in which censorship and the burning of books were quickly followed by, as Heinrich Heine notes in the epigraph, the burning of men, women, children, and others deemed a threat to the Nazi politics of ideological and racial purity.

Within a short time after the book burnings, the Nazis passed the Nuremberg Laws institutionalizing the racial theories embraced by the Third Reich. Under these laws, anyone who had three or four Jewish grandparents was defined as a Jew, subject to legal restrictions that revoked their right to citizenship in the Reich, forbade them "to fly the Reich or national flag," and prohibited them from marrying or having sexual relations with persons of "German or related blood."[1] In such instances, laws were introduced to legitimate what might be called legal illegalities—states of exception in which certain individuals and groups, as Giorgio Agamben has noted, could be punished with impunity because the juridical apparatus was now shaped by a notion of governance and sovereignty that had no respect for matters of justice and the democratic rule of law.[2] The state of exception and the laws that produced it eventually became indistinguishable. The power of the courts and the crafting of the law were shaped by a perception of the other as deviant, inferior, and a threat while they simultaneously provided a justification for both subjugating such groups and making them expendable.

These events might seem far removed from a country such as the United States that makes repeated claims to support democratic institutions, humanitarian values, human rights, and equality. Or it might seem reasonable to argue that fascism was the result of a particular historical experience, rooted in, for instance, German national character. But totalitarian forms of domination travel, and rather than being rooted in some historically frozen notion of national character, they are quite at home in societies characterized by what Adorno called "the immense concentration of economical and administrative power [that] leaves the individual no more room to maneuver."[3] Traces of such authoritarianism have become part of the deep structures of American life. For instance, within the United States today increasing numbers of events are signaling not only the emergence of elements of authoritarianism but also the failure of a society to come to grips with the frightening truth that American democracy is under siege and is giving way to forces that are utterly indifferent to the values and ideals of a viable democracy. For instance, within the past decade under President George W. Bush and President Obama we have witnessed an undeniable attack on civil liberties through legislation—extending from the passage of the Patriot Act of 2001 to the National Defense Authorization Act of 2012—that gives the government the right to conduct warrantless surveillance, arrest American citizens for an indefinite period, and use the power of the military to detain suspected terrorists in the United States.[4]

This is not all. The US government now has the legal power to assassinate "any citizen considered a terrorist or an abettor of terrorism,"[5] kidnap citizens and noncitizens and transfer them to other countries to be tortured, suspend due process, expand the prison system, and do all this covertly under the protection of state secrecy laws. It can remain silent with impunity while government officials, including a former president and vice president, sanction state-administered torture. Governance has become a legitimation for war, terror, and the abrogation of civil liberties. As politics has become an extension of war in the United States, particularly in the aftermath of the tragic events of September 2001, national security and the ever-widening nets of surveillance and militarism have trumped any appeal to democratic rights. With the looming edifice of the national security state casting its shadow over the United States, Jim Garrison offers a critique of the National Defense Authorization Act that goes to the heart of the dark clouds of authoritarianism that are gathering over the nation. He writes,

> The question screaming at us through this bill is whether the war on terror is a better model around which to shape our destiny than our constitutional liberties. It compels the question of whether we remain an ongoing experiment in democracy, pioneering new frontiers in the name of liberty and justice for all, or have we become a national security state, having financially corrupted and militarized our democracy to such an extent that we define ourselves, as Sparta did, only through the exigencies of war?[6]

Indeed, it increasingly appears that the United States has given up on its claim to democracy, however tainted its democratic ideals may have been before 9/11.

Authoritarian societies mark their presence in more ways than the suspension of civil liberties and the ongoing militarization of everyday life. They are generally preceded by an antidemocratic formative culture—notable for its hatred of critical thinking; scorn for reasoned arguments and evidence; disdain for the truth; and devaluation of compassion, civic courage, and social responsibility. This is a formative culture whose pedagogical task is to create subjects who are mobilized by fear, self-interest, and political conformity. Evoking a populist discourse, current versions of this authoritarian culture mobilize anti–big government, antipublic rhetoric in order to convince the American people to imagine the government and the public sector either as private industries or as subordinated to corporate interests. At stake here is the creation of subjects, identities, and desires willing to invest emotionally and politically in regimes that cripple the individual's and public's sense of agency. Such regimes immerse people in "a language that erases everything that matters"[7] and can offer them only a space in which they assume the role of detached bystanders, indifferent to the demands of ethical responsibility and justice for all. In a society that elevates a survival-of-the-fittest ethic to a national ideal, there is no room to appeal to human solidarity or call for a moral response to instances of suffering and widespread racial targeting. At the present moment in American society, human solidarity and democratic values are scorned just as a moral response to the plight of the other is viewed with contempt and seen as a sign of weakness.

Witness the culture of cruelty touted by the 2012 run of Republican presidential candidates who barely blinked when asked about how capital punishment embodies the legacy of slavery, unapologetically suggested that child labor laws be suspended so poor youth of color can work as janitors in their schools, or endlessly complained that the poor lack a work ethic and are undeserving of social protections.[8] Mitt Romney, Rick Santorum, and Newt Gingrich believe that the social safety net, rather than being inadequate, is overextended and promotes a nation of dependents, an army of unrepentant moochers, creating what right-wing politicians and antipublic intellectuals call an "entitlement society." Mitt Romney, the Republican Party presidential nominee, who echoes the fiscal policies of Paul Ryan, the chairman of the House Budget Committee, advocates austerity measures that in reality gut social spending while providing huge tax cuts for corporations and the wealthy. Paul Krugman rightly argues that such policies will have little to do with reducing deficits and are basically an excuse for "attacking Medicare, Medicaid, Social Security and food stamps."[9]

In actuality, such policies reveal the ugly and savage face of a form of economic Darwinism at the heart of casino capitalism. As Krugman points out, what "fake deficit hawks" such as Romney and Ryan espouse are policies that are designed "to snatch food from the mouths of babes (literally, via cuts in crucial nutritional aid programs), [and] that's a positive from their point of view—the social safety net, says Mr. Ryan, should not become 'a hammock that lulls able-bodied people to lives of dependency and complacency' [while] maintaining low taxes on profits and capital gains, and indeed cutting those taxes further, are, however, sacrosanct."[10] The supposed cure is to abolish the safety net and let the free market work its delusional magic so that the poor, elderly, sick, unemployed, and homeless can rely on their own resources.

What's missing in the right-wing analysis of the issues facing Americans is not only any sense of compassion or social responsibility but also any understanding of the social and economic costs of such policies. Although the political rhetoric marshaled by politicians such as Gingrich, Santorum, and Romney is as delusional as it is cruel and unjust, the real issue here is the high price to be paid in human suffering for these types of political and economic measures. The contemporary neoliberal mantra to downsize, privatize, outsource, and deregulate continues to promote economic policies characterized by moral and political lawlessness. Not only do such norms and policies create massive inequalities in income and power, they also produce practices that are responsible for massive suffering. Despite the devastation wreaked by the economic crisis of 2008, the high priests of casino capitalism remain undeterred in their drive to accumulate capital for the few while promoting immiseration for everyone else. Witness the recent malfeasance committed by JPMorgan Chase and the mind-numbing criminal behavior and scandal displayed by Barclay, both of which raised barely a peep from the American public.

Under the regime of neoliberal capitalism, social spending and existing US social safety nets are vastly inadequate: 39 percent of all adults and 55 percent of all children live at or below the poverty line; approximately 146 million Americans—one in two—are low income or poor. Worse, as Diane Sweet points out, is the lack of affordable housing: "Approximately 3.5 million people in the U.S. are homeless, many of them veterans. . . . In addition, 1.6 million kids are homeless at some point in a year."[11] In the richest country in the world, over 30 million are unemployed and 48 million are without health care, and 1.4 million filed for bankruptcy in 2009.[12] Under such circumstances, politics works to create heartless and savage zones of disposability, or what Achille Mbembe calls "death worlds"—a form of "death in life."[13] Young people's existence is marked by extreme precariousness due to the emergence of zones of social abandonment in the form of deteriorating schools, punishing detention centers, dehumanizing workplaces, and other places that accelerate the degradation if not spiritual and social death of entire generations. Market values work their magic through an appeal to common sense in order to remove any vestige of social responsibility from any talk about agency. Under such conditions, the isolated automaton does not have to assume a sense of social responsibility or inquire into the symbolic and structural relations of power that fuel casino capitalism. Hollowed out and stripped of its civic functions, politics takes as its first priority creating the conditions for corporations and financial institutions to act without restraint, while modalities of hypermasculinity, unchecked individualism, and armed power become the measure of national greatness. The formative culture that supports such a politics is one in which the celebration of market fundamentalism and war are destined to become the most enduring symbols of the American way of life.

In such a society, justice becomes the first casualty of emerging authoritarian tendencies, which disable our abilities even to conceive of fairness, equality, and justice, let alone defend them. Arundhati Roy offers a prophetic warning:

> Today, it is not merely justice itself, but the idea of justice that is under attack. The assault on vulnerable, fragile sections of society is at once so complete, so cruel and so clever—all encompassing and yet specifically targeted, blatantly brutal and yet unbelievably insidious—that its sheer audacity has eroded our definition of justice. It has forced us to lower our sights, and curtail our expectations.[14]

As Roy rightly argues, the ground in which the formative culture of authoritarianism takes root and is then sustained can be located among those abstract realms of law, policy, and national security. What is often revealed in associated practices, values, and discourses is the fact that an unrelenting desire to pursue the imperatives of justice—which should be fundamental to any viable democracy—is redirected to achieve something like its opposite: the individual's right to the "pursuit of material self-interest" at any social cost; an ardent and uncritical admiration for consumerism and unfettered markets;

a persistent indifference to the rise of "broken highways, bankrupt cities, collapsing bridges, failed schools, the unemployed, the underpaid and the uninsured"; and a disdain for the public sector so venomous that it seeks nothing less than the death of the social.[15] Business-oriented pedagogies now merge with a politics of fear and a revived and unapologetic racism in order to facilitate the rule of an uncivil society that trades in terror, exclusion, racial segregation, "ardent consumerism and Hobbesian anarchy."[16] What we are witnessing in the United States is the rise of a right-wing political and economic class that wants to take the country back to the inequalities and social cruelties that marked the Gilded Age of the late nineteenth century.[17]

It is worth remembering the period in the late nineteenth century when giant corporations and robber barons controlled state and national politics and subjected blacks, women, immigrants, and the poor to the savage rule of free-market capitalism, leaving the disadvantaged on their own and often defenseless to confront the effects of the structural violence and ideologically powered social Darwinism that shaped the forces governing their lives.[18] It was also a period in which dissent was viewed as un-American and those who had the courage to speak out against political corruption were treated with disdain, often subjected to police brutality or simply fired from their jobs. Furthermore, it was a period in which racial and ethnic differences rather than bigotry were seen as the enemy of democracy. Historical memory was whitewashed, regarded as sacred and worthy of unquestioning adoration rather than given a respect based in critical dialogue, thoughtful interrogation, and informed judgment and debate. Cultural memory's claim to historical legitimacy was invalidated because it was invoked only to devalue the truth by erasing from history those narratives, stories, and modes of analysis that challenged the dominant histories written by the elites in order to serve the interest of the privileged few who controlled the commanding economic, political, and cultural apparatuses of the times. These tarnished dominant histories and their legacy of distortion are on the rise again.

As our contemporary social order convulses, the American public stands witness to a symptomatic and troubling rebirth of those dark forces that once shaped the institutional structures and policies of the Gilded Age, now championed by the financial elite with an unabashed arrogance. Yet perhaps no historical precedent aspired to reach the depths of moral emptiness, political corruption, and savage cruelty that characterizes those bankers, hedge fund managers, and financial tycoons who have swindled away the wealth of the working and middle classes in order to make themselves one of the wealthiest and greediest classes on the face of the globe (e.g., witness the 2012 Libor banking scandal). With such egregiously unequal wealth and power comes more than privilege. Worse still, there is also the use of unlimited resources to devalue, marginalize, and punish those individuals and groups who desire to share in the wealth, abundance, and opportunities that nourish what has been called the American dream. Critical thinking, informed judgment, and literacy itself have taken a hit as an obsession with profit margins has eclipsed the value of wisdom, the civic functions of the arts and humanities, and the complex labor of creating a diverse body of informed citizens. The call to competitiveness hides a deep fear, if not hatred, of those considered expendable, foreign, or unreliable consumers. At the current moment in American history, the merging of the punishing state, an increasingly persistent racism, and a growing inequality in wealth and income has produced an America comfortably settling into a moral coma and a politics of fear and resentment.[19]

Two recent events in Arizona provide flagrant examples of what might be called the emergence of a virulent racism in the service of repressive educational policies and cultural practices fueled by antidemocratic and authoritarian interests. The first event involves the banning of ethnic studies as a result of the passage of Arizona House Bill 2281, which prevents public schools as well as charter schools in the state from offering courses that "promote the overthrow of the U.S. government," "promote resentment toward a race or class of people," "are designed primarily for pupils of a particular ethnic group," or "advocate for ethnic solidarity instead of the treatment of pupils as individuals."[20] Crafted at a time when Arizona is at the forefront of a number of states in enacting a right-wing offensive that produces anti-immigrant and anti-Latino opinions, sentiments, and policies, the law was designed not only to provide political cachet for Arizona conservatives seeking political office but also to impose regulations "which [would] dismantle the state's popular Mexican-American/ Raza Studies programs."[21] In one highly popularized incident, the current Tea Party conservative superintendent of public instruction, John Huppenthal—making good on an earlier claim that he would "stop la raza"—notified the Tucson Unified School District (TUSD) that as a result of the new law banning ethnic studies, the popular Mexican American studies program was in violation of the ban, and TUSD would lose $15 million in annual state aid unless the program was terminated. It was eventually eliminated in spite of the fact that it was credited "with reducing dropout rates, discipline problems, poor attendance and failure rates among Latino Students."[22]

The attack on ethnic studies was soon followed with a decision by the TUSD board to ban a number of books associated with this field of study. The list of removed books, in some cases literally taken out of the hands of crying students, included classic texts such as *Rethinking Columbus: The Next 500 Years*, published by Rethinking Schools; *Occupied America: A History of Chicanos*, by Rodolfo Acuna; and the internationally acclaimed *Pedagogy of the Oppressed*, by Paulo Freire. In an attempt to eliminate any texts or class units where "race, ethnicity and oppression are central themes," the TUSD board also banned Shakespeare's play *The Tempest*. What is important to note about the book-banning structure is that it applies to a school district not only founded by a Mexican American but also one in which more than 60 percent of the students are from a Mexican American background. As Jeff Biggers suggests, the racism at work in this form of "book burning" is not hidden because "the administration also removed every textbook dealing with Mexican-American history, including *Chicano!: The History of the Mexican Civil Rights Movement* by Arturo Rosales, which features a biography of long-time Tucson educator Salomon Baldenegro. Other books removed from the school include *500 Years of Chicano History in Pictures* by Elizabeth Martinez and the textbook *Critical Race Theory* by scholars Richard Delgado and Jean Stefancic."[23]

There is more at work in the attack on ethnic studies and the banning of books considered dangerous to children in the Arizona schools than the rise of Tea Party politics and specific acts of censorship. There is also the emergence of deeper structures of a systemic racism and the increasing mobilization of neoliberal ideology to justify the ongoing attacks on people of color, immigrants, and those considered other by virtue of their class and ethnicity. Under neoliberal regimes, race is not—at least in the first instance—ignored. On the contrary, it is either coded as a style or a commodity or devalued as a criminal culture and defined as a threat to a supposedly under-siege white Christian nation. What follows is that race is more and more erased as a political category and reduced to the narrow parameters of individual preference, psychology, or prejudice. Privatizing race preserves the dominant power structures that produce modes of structural racism extending from racial discrimination to racial exclusion and practiced by schools, governments, banks, and mortgage companies, among others. Within this type of privatized discourse, racism survives through the guise of neoliberalism as a kind of repartee that imagines human agency as simply a matter of individualized choices—the only obstacle to effective citizenship and agency being a lack of principled self-help and moral responsibility. Privatizing racism functions as a racial mythology that both encourages individual solutions to socially produced problems and reveals a false sense of conceit used by those who claim that racism is nothing more than "a psychological space free of racial tension."[24] Even worse is when racism is disavowed yet appears in another guise through a language of punishment that persecutes and demonizes anyone who even raises the charge of racism. For instance, as Professor Roberto Rodriquez makes clear,

> students ... protesting the elimination of the [Tucson School] district's Mexican American studies program, have—without a hearing—been directed to perform janitorial duties this Saturday: an amazing message, right out of Newt Gingrich's playbook (he has been campaigning in the GOP presidential nomination race, proposing the idea that students should be hired as janitors to teach them a work ethic). Apparently, TUSD administrators are paying attention.[25]

Meanwhile, many of the institutions that deal with youth—schools, juvenile detention centers, and the criminal justice system—continue to adopt punishment strategies instead of addressing systemic racism. This is evident, for example, in the rise of zero-tolerance policies in schools, which disproportionately punish African American youths, but also in many routine disciplinary practices.

The fear is that ethnic studies can be taught in ways that provide a critical reading of history, power, ideas, and institutional mappings. This is viewed as dangerous by conservatives and white supremacists because classroom learning can be used to expose specific modes of racial exclusion, class inequalities, and the ongoing punishment and silencing of young people. Even though Mexican American students make up the vast majority of public school students in Tucson, a curriculum that addresses their heritage and culture is considered not simply subversive but anti-American. Clearly, right-wing Christian extremists cannot bear the thought of minority students becoming literate in their history, self-reflective about what they are taught, and empowered to act as engaged critical citizens. Racist fear and bigotry prevent the state's politicians and conservative supporters from rewarding and expanding a program in which Mexican American youths graduate at twice the rate of other Latino students.

What many of the newly elected Tea Party ideologues recognize is that critical pedagogy has the power to challenge persistent racial injustice in the United States. More importantly, they fear the role that such a pedagogy can play in empowering minority students to become informed citizens who might exercise their rights by changing the fundamental institutions and power structures that affect their lives. One response is for school districts to suppress or minimize the histories along with other "forms and possibilities of representation of the subaltern with the state apparatus itself."[26] Destroying the existing or potential political, cultural, and social bonds of subaltern groups provides the basis for making such groups disappear from history and the social order they inhabit. How else to explain Arizona attorney general Tom Horne's persistent disparagement of ethnic studies courses for allegedly promoting ethnic resentment, teaching rudeness, and privileging groups over individuals—even when an audit commissioned by Arizona's right-wing superintendent of schools proved these claims false?[27] What is ignored in this updated notion of racist blabber is that racial hierarchies already in existence are rooted in unequal relations of power and at this very moment are making a significant difference in influencing people's lives and shaping contemporary American society. As Charles Gallagher explains, "this approach erases America's racial hierarchy by implying that social, economic and political power and mobility is equally shared among all racial groups. Ignoring the extent or ways in which race shapes life chances validates whites' social location in the existing racial hierarchy while legitimating the political and economic arrangements which perpetuate and reproduce racial inequality and privilege."[28] Not only has Horne invoked racist attacks against Mexican Americans for over a decade, but he also has a long history of corrupt if not criminal behavior, including being banned for life from the Securities and Exchange Commission. As a Tea Party favorite, he has been able to indulge his anti-immigrant racism with impunity, particularly since assuming public office in a state whose tough immigration laws are notorious for targeting and waging a racist attack on immigrants and all Latinos.

The Arizona superintendent of public instruction, John Huppenthal, has become the most prominent public figure defending the banning of ethnic studies and the books associated with it. Jeff Biggers's characterization of Huppenthal as "the Sheriff Arpaio of ethnic studies may be understated."[29] Huppenthal has been a spokesperson at Tea Party gatherings, attended a rally where "participants openly called President Obama a 'Nazi,'" and stated that the Mexican American studies program produced modes of indoctrination similar to what was replicated in the education of the Hitler Youth, that is, the Hitler Nazi Jugend paramilitary organization.[30] Huppenthal has argued for modes of pedagogy "based on the corporate management schemes of the Fortune 500."[31] What is clear is that he lacks any understanding of education unless it is shaped largely by market-driven values and dominant power structures. Hence, it is not surprising that he has dismissed the work of the internationally celebrated educator Paulo Freire because Freire used the word "oppressed" in the title of his most famous book. Huppenthal labels the author of *Pedagogy of the Oppressed* a Marxist and demagogue, revealing that he knows nothing about Freire's philosophical grounding in the work of liberation theology, humanism, linguistics, and a range of other fields. Nor does he know anything about Freire's work on critical literacy, dialogue, empowerment, and social responsibility or the principle that education should be used to prepare children for a more ethically just life.[32] Huppenthal appears both confused and confusing in that he argues without irony that banning books is the best way to teach kids how to think critically.[33]

Buried beneath Arizona's new mode of education, pedagogy, and politics is a return to a frightening antidemocratic ideology and a set of reactionary policies. This turn to censorship, banning ethnic studies and attacking critical thought, suggests a new intensification of the culture wars of the 1980s and represents a new and determined effort on the part of Christian extremists and political fundamentalists to make sure public and higher education do not enfranchise emerging generations of Mexican Americans and others marginalized by race and class.[34] Superintendent Huppenthal, Attorney General Horne, and their government-employed talking heads target critical thinking, literacy, and informed dialogue as the enemies of education. Any historical narrative that challenges the status quo is dismissed as indoctrination because it may be provocative and unsettling—more threatening apparently to Huppenthal's own identity than to the identities of the students who have actually taken the Mexican American studies courses and who repudiate his arguments. His claim that teaching courses in Mexican American studies promotes racial resentment is simply a cover for his own racist disdain for knowledge that troubles a right-wing belief in a conflict-free narrative of American history. If Huppenthal had his way, US classrooms would be permitted to teach only the Donald Trump/Walt Disney view of history, one that celebrates the growth of corporations, the pioneering role of business in promoting progress throughout the world, the centrality of the military in American life, the ethos of the nineteenth-century robber barons, and an uncritical view of American society based on white Christian narratives and principles. This is a chamber of commerce narrative on steroids.

Huppenthal is in love with what Howard Zinn famously critiqued in his *People's History of the United States* as a triumphalist examination of "history written by the victors." Unfortunately, in Huppenthal's worldview, fidelity to this version of history demands more than defending dominant historical narratives. It also means banishing from classrooms any alternative view of history, especially if it promotes the culture, struggles, and stories of those often considered powerless, who through the power of the word contested and resisted the imperial, cultural, and political legacy of dominant ideologies. How else to explain in the initial introduction of Arizona Senate Bill 1202 a passage that forbids teachers to use partisan books, promote partisan doctrine, or conduct any partisan exercise in schools? While the bill was later amended to remove the prohibition of partisan books, the censorship continues through the banning of books considered specifically dangerous, which in this case provide a dialogical encounter with diverse cultural narratives, promote intellectual excitement, and engage history as part of a critical dialogue. Or Senate Bill 1205, which forbids teachers to say words in the classroom that would violate Federal Communications Commission regulations concerning obscenity, profanity, and indecency?[35] Under this rule it would be illegal to teach classics such as *The Canterbury Tales* and *The Catcher in the Rye*—or for that matter to discuss law cases that have profane words in their titles. It comes as no surprise that the same religious fundamentalist lawmakers who want to turn the classroom into an incubator for thoughtless students also want "to create a high school course that teaches about the Bible and its role in Western culture."[36] Gesturing toward authoritarian regimes of the past in which Jews, intellectuals, and those deemed dangerous to the state were made to disappear, the soft-edged fascism of the current historical moment emerging in states such as Arizona engages in a different type of "disappearing" in that it begins the long march toward "dark times" by making ideas, books, films, and other dissident cultural artifacts disappear.

Horne, Huppenthal, and their followers recognize that the continuing significance of race generates contested meanings of history, challenges traditional modes of curricula and knowledge, implies taking seriously the diverse histories and complex voices of students, and raises serious critiques about the discriminatory and disciplinary practices that minorities of class and color are subjected to in America's public schools.[37] Haunted by the specter of antiracist critiques, pedagogies, and social relations, Horne and Huppenthal attempt to eliminate those approaches to critical pedagogy that would make visible the need to interrogate the histories, cultural artifacts, texts, and policies that sustain complex forms of racism and racial exclusion in the schools, government, and other commanding edifices of the larger society. Thus, there is more at work in the Arizona state-sponsored attack on ethnic studies than the racist conceit of an alleged academic neutrality. School policy functions in this case as part of a much larger design by the American right to leave its own distorted history behind while erasing all of those forms of government support, public spheres, languages, pedagogies, and modes of critique that provide the pedagogical conditions for constructing critical agents that make a democracy functional.

Arizona is but one example of how at the current moment what goes into American culture, what is aired in the media, and what is taught in both public and higher education are being intensely policed by right-wing fundamentalists in all sectors of society. What this points to is a war being waged aggressively against immigrants, youths, and those deemed disposable. We are witnessing the rise of new zones of punishment, abandonment, and exclusion—and the growing perception of the other as deviant, inferior, threatening, and expendable becomes a justification for the subjugation of immigrants and poor people of color. This emerging reality needs to be understood as part of a broader war waged against young people, especially those marginalized by class, race, and ethnicity, as well as an attack on the formative cultures that make a democracy possible. Consequently, the pressing question becomes what role do various cultural apparatuses, including schools, play in creating the formative culture and institutional foundation for a growing authoritarianism? What the banning of ethnic studies and its archive of critical literature makes clear is that any pedagogy that challenges dominant notions of history, stands up for the values of freedom and reason, points to a more just world, and embraces public values that promote democracy is not only dangerous to many right-wing ideologues and reactionary politicians but targeted for erasure from the public schools and increasingly the culture at large.

The example of Arizona can show us how cultural pedagogy in the form of school curricula such as Mexican American studies is truly intimidating to racist conservatives because it offers histories that include the voices of the oppressed and marginalized. It presents knowledge that may open the prospect of "encountering the self through the otherness of knowledge ... bring[ing] oneself up against the limits of what one is willing and capable of understanding."[38] The pedagogical notion that things are not what they seem to be and the maxims that justice demands the "translation of responsibility into the language of society" and that a "'just society' is a society which thinks it is not just enough" pose a real threat to the right-wing demagogues, particularly those who now shape American educational policy.[39] Banning courses that might provide a critical voice to the oppressed as well as expand the ethical and political horizons of those not oppressed constructs as the enemy any pedagogy that attempts to empower young people by providing them with the knowledge, skills, and values needed for self-development, critical agency, autonomy, and civic responsibility. What is dangerous to Tea Party types and their ideological cronies is not simply the presence of books and courses that contain critical ideas but the possibility that this kind of learning may persuade young people to contest the modes of education produced in and out of schools and encourage them to engage in antiracist struggles over the distribution of institutional power and its material effects. The ideologues understand—and fear—forms of critical development that translate ideas into social movements engaged in a struggle to democratize resources, power, and access for everyone equally in society.

This chapter began with a comment on book burning by the Nazis. I return to this reference because we are now at a point in US history during which we are incorporating many authoritarian elements of the past into the current social order. Racial exclusion takes many forms and operates through diverse material and ideological institutions and practices—including antidemocratic modes of persuasion and violence. What must be recognized in this instance, in addition to the threat to democracy posed by such practices, is that for democracy to survive at all, it needs to nourish critically informed agents. It requires young people willing to give constant attention to those relations of power, institutions, and public spheres that make a real claim to democracy. To become indifferent to the formative culture that enables informed judgment, critical consciousness, civic courage, and social responsibility is to strip democracy of any meaning, to make it hollow, if not meaningless—and in doing so to prepare the way for an updated twenty-first-century mode of authoritarianism. In other words, what we see happening in Arizona poses a threat both to critical education and to the very nature of democracy itself. Not only does it represent the growing marginalization of youths of color, but it also speaks to a larger war in which certain bodies, histories, and modes of knowledge become pathologized and viewed as disposable.

This is a war in which bodies disappear, histories are erased, and democracy is left in ruins. The Arizona censorship of ethnic studies, along with the destruction of associated knowledges and the silencing of dissent, is one of those events that flash before us in ways that might at first suggest nothing more than a silly, irrational, or anomalous happening. But that is far from the actual case. Placed within a long view of history, it clearly signals the formation of those antidemocratic forces waiting for an opportune moment to plummet the United States into a deepening abyss of authoritarianism.

The antidemocratic nature of the book-burning policies being promoted in Arizona make clear that the war on youth is partly directed against those institutions capable of teaching young people how to think critically and engage the larger world with a keen sense of social responsibility. In Arizona and other states waging a war on young people, the enemy is not democracy in the abstract but the formative cultures, agents, and institutions that enable young people to exercise critical thought, think imaginatively, learn to hold power accountable, and act in the world with a degree of civic courage. The targets in this case are not only young people but also teachers, classrooms, and schools that take seriously their role as critical educators and vital democratic public spheres, and the result of such attacks is a notion of education that is as pedagogically irresponsible as it is morally bankrupt. This antidemocratic script proceeds at its own peril. And while it works hard to position young people in a world marked by a high degree of illiteracy, historical amnesia, and political passivity, it also creates the conditions for widespread generational dissatisfaction and collective resistance. In light of the growing global youth revolts in Montreal, Paris, Athens, London, and cities all over the United States, Otto Neugebauer, the famed historian of mathematics and astronomy in the ancient world, appears to have provided an important insight in his insistence that "no system of education known to man is capable of ruining everyone."[40]

◇

Chapter 5

Trickle-Down Cruelty and the Politics of Austerity

One of the great liabilities of history is that all too many people fail to remain awake through great periods of social change. Every society has its protectors of the status quo and its fraternities of the indifferent who are notorious for sleeping through revolutions. Today, our very survival depends on our ability to stay awake, to adjust to new ideas, to remain vigilant and to face the challenge of change.
—Martin Luther King Jr.

Disturbing signs that US society is moving toward an authoritarian state largely controlled by corporations and a grotesquely irresponsible financial elite appear to be multiplying, along with the malignant politics and policies that increase the hard currency of human suffering for everyone else.[1] Long-term investments are replaced by short-term gains and profits while compassion is viewed as a weakness and democratic public values are scorned because they subordinate market considerations to the common good. Morality in this instance becomes painless, stripped of any obligations to the other or responsibility for our collective well-being. As the language of privatization, deregulation, and commodification replaces the discourse of the public good, all things public—from public schools and libraries to public services—are either viewed as a drain on the market or rendered as a pathology. In addition,

89

inequality in wealth and income expands, spreading like a toxin through everyday life, poisoning democracy and relegating more and more individuals to a growing army of disposable human waste.[2] The culture of cruelty is echoed and mimicked in market discourses, values, and policy documents. Government policies are now designed to benefit the financial service industries; megacorporations; and the well-off, top 10 percent while at the same time drastically slashing education, health care, and other social services and imposing "particularly brutal forms of regulation" on poor racial minorities.[3]

Right-wing politicians go out of their way to slander the poor, suggesting that their plight is due to their lack of self-reliance and bad character. For instance, during the 2012 Republican primary race, Newt Gingrich unapologetically denounced child labor laws as "truly stupid," suggesting that schools could fire janitors and hire students under the age of sixteen to do their work. In this case, Newt wanted to take away low-income jobs from poor people and hire their children to do the work for yet lower wages. Brilliant! When attacked for this truly Dickensian position, he defended himself by claiming that poor kids lack decent work habits because nobody around them works. This is more than mean-spirited ignorance given the fact that "83 percent of all poor children live in households with at least one adult who works."[4] Newt also seemed to be unaware that the unemployment rate for youths between the ages of sixteen and twenty-four is at an all-time high of 18.1 percent and that over 4.1 million young people cannot find work. Lack of jobs, not the existence of child labor laws, is what prevents young people from working.

The culture of cruelty is also evident in widely popular slogans such as "Government is too big," "Competition and self-interest work best," "Greed is good," "Collective bargaining is a form of socialism," and "People on welfare are pathological moochers." These are more than clichés and caricatures; they are powerful framing mechanisms that denounce health care, quality education, and valuable social services as government hoaxes and an undeserved handout to the poor and less fortunate. And yet those at the top with soaring salaries who create very few jobs and gamble with the country's future while they rake in obscene amounts of money are held up as national heroes. All the while, the policies they promote produce vast amounts of inequality in wealth, income, and opportunity. With great wealth for the few comes massive suffering for the many. Neighborhoods with poverty rates over 40 percent are increasing at a rapid rate and stretching over broader areas of America.[5] The proportion of poor people living "in high poverty neighborhoods jumped from 11.2% in 2000 to 15.1% last year."[6] At the same time poverty in the suburbs has risen by 26 percent over the past decade. Only the top 5 percent have experienced income growth since 1980, whereas 50 percent of Americans are living in poverty or at what is cautiously termed a barely life-sustaining "low income level."[7] Over 10,000 mortgages are foreclosed each day in America, adding precipitously to the eight million homes foreclosed since 2009.[8] In one of the richest countries in the world, 48 million people are on food stamps, an increase of 20 million since 2007. Of course, these figures can only hint at the amount of suffering produced by the gross inequities in power, wealth, and income that are pushing America into a state of utter disrepair economically and politically and into a moral abyss that makes the country's claims on justice and democracy disingenuous, if not delusional. Yet, Mitt Romney, the 2012 Republican presidential nominee, has put forward a budget offer that increases the military budget and "gives a $250K tax cut, on average, to everyone earning over a million dollars a year" while at the same time slashing Medicare, Medicaid, food stamps for the poor, and Pell Grants for students.[9] As America staggers back to the Gilded Age of the late nineteenth century, welfare has become a slush program for the super rich and democracy nothing more than a metaphor for deception and class warfare.

The working and middle classes have been condemned to "a new modernity in which there can be only one kind of value, market value; one kind of success, profit; one kind of existence, commodities; and one kind of social relationship, markets."[10] The global recession has only intensified the war against the American public as professionals and politicians who make up a global business class now displace democracy with the call for austerity and, in doing so, produce a hidden order of politics in which the "demand for the people's austerity hides processes of the uneven distribution of risk and vulnerability."[11] Indeed, austerity measures that would affect the rich are almost nonexistent. Richard D. Wolff provides the details in looking at what he calls "some alternative 'reasonable' kinds of austerity." He writes,

> Serious efforts to collect income taxes from U.S.-based multi-national corporations, especially those who use internal pricing mechanisms to escape U.S. taxation, would generate vast new federal revenues. The same applies to wealthy individuals. The U.S. has no federal property tax on holdings of stocks, bonds, and cash accounts (states and localities levy no such property taxes either). If the federal government levied a 1 per cent tax on assets between $100,000 to 499,000, and 1.5 per cent on assets above $500,000, that would raise much new federal revenue (everyone's first $100,000 could be exempted just as the existing U.S. income tax exempts the first few thousands of dollars of individual incomes). Exiting the Iraq and Afghanistan disasters would do likewise. Ending tax exemptions for super-rich private educational institutions (Harvard, Yale, etc.) and for religious institutions (church-goers would then need to pay the costs of their churches) would be among the many other such alternative "reasonable" austerity measures. Comparable alternatives apply—and are being struggled over—in other countries.[12]

These suggestions make better sense than heaping the burden of debt and a growing employment crisis onto the shoulders of the already disadvantaged, but nowhere is it evident that the call for austerity is driven by common sense. One side effect of the irrational, if not corrupt, mode of austerity now being imposed is what I call the politics of trickle-down cruelty.

Under the guise of austerity, politically motivated attacks are now being waged on young people, low-skilled workers, the poor, labor unions, African Americans, and the elderly. Severe and senseless cruelty is evident in policies in which austerity-based cuts are used to reward corporations and bil-lionaires with tax breaks while simultaneously exploiting the budget crisis in order to eliminate protections provided by the welfare state. The resulting reductions in state spending have drastically cut basic social services so as to endanger the lives of many young people and others at the margins of a society structured by massive financial inequality. For example, in Philadelphia, "fire departments have been closed on a daily rotating basis," delaying response time. One unfortunate and possibly preventable consequence occurred "when two children were pulled from a burning row home too little too late.... Mike

Kane of the Philadelphia Firefighters Union Local 22 said there was no way to tell whether the children would have lived had the fire station been open, but if not for the brownouts, 'maybe those kids would have had a shot.'"[13] In Arizona, Governor Jan Brewer signed a bill that effectively denied health care to over 47,000 low-income children.[14] More recently, a fifty-nine-year-old man in Gastonia, North Carolina, robbed a bank for $1 so he could get access to health care. He handed the bank teller a note asking for only a dollar and medical attention. He sat in a chair in the bank waiting for the police to arrive. As he pointed out to the press, he had lost his job of seventeen years as a Coca-Cola deliveryman and ended up taking a part-time position in a convenience store. But the work was backbreaking, and his suffering was compounded by the fact that he had arthritis, carpal tunnel syndrome, and a painful lump on his chest. With no health insurance, he decided that the best option in America would be to rob a bank and get health care in prison.[15]

We also hear about the return of debtors' prisons, supposedly abolished in the United States in the nineteenth century. The *Minneapolis Star Tribune* reports that "people are routinely being thrown in jail for failing to pay debts," and in some cases "people stay in jail until they raise minimum payment. In January [2010] a judge sentenced a Kenney, Ill., man to 'indefinite incarceration' until he came up with $300 toward a lumber yard debt."[16] Joy Uhlmeyer, a fifty-seven-year-old patient care advocate, spent sixteen hours in jail because she missed a court hearing over a credit-card debt.[17] It is hard to miss the irony of putting someone in jail for not paying a small debt while, as Matt Taibbi has pointed out, law enforcement under the Obama regime has not convicted a "single executive who ran the companies that cooked up and cashed in on the phony financial boom—an industry wide scam that involved the mass sale of mismarked, fraudulent mortgage-backed securities."[18] These financial crooks hid billions from investors and ripped off the American people, causing untold suffering and hardship. And yet law enforcement does not consider them liable for the crimes they committed, and the Obama administration rewards them with weak regulatory laws and an open season on obscene bonuses.

The culture of cruelty operates off the assumption that lack of money correlates with a lack of morals. The message resonates powerfully in a society that stigmatizes poor people as disposable and punishes them disproportionately for behaviors that have little to do with what might loosely be called an act of lawlessness. How else to explain a police officers' union in California selling T-shirts with the message "U raise 'em, we cage 'em"?[19] It is one thing to harass poor youths but another to slander their parents with a form of mockery that is not merely inane but poisonous in its implications. In this instance, the police do more than reinforce an egregious form of racial profiling; they actually target youths from poor families as unavoidable criminals while placing the blame for such behavior on the child-rearing practices of the parents. State-sponsored racism is so unapologetic that it now dresses up its racist practices in a disturbing type of street humor.

When aimed at people marginalized by race and class, the criminal justice system increasingly abandons all notions of fairness. For example, what does it say about a society when it sends a homeless mother, Tanya McDowell, to jail for twelve years because she improperly enrolled her son in a kindergarten class in a highly regarded Connecticut school? As Jen Roesch points out, "her 'crime' was to try to send her son to a school where he might have a better chance of getting a good education."[20] The Bridgeport school system where McDowell's son should have been sent spends about $8,000 per pupil each year and has a 25 percent dropout rate, whereas the Norwalk schools spend $15,686 in educational services for each pupil and have a much lower dropout rate. The school board president, Jack Chiamonte, claims that the case is about stealing services. However, the real crime is the reproduction of an iniquitous system of school financing that discriminates against the children of the poor and works in tandem with the criminal justice system to implement class- and race-specific modes of segregation. Clearly, there is more at work here than a school system marked by rampant inequality and deep-seated modes of segregation. There is also the emergence of a public school system that has become fully integrated into a punishing state in which there is "a tight connection between racism, poverty, segregation and a criminal justice system that punishes the poor and people of color disproportionately."[21] The most serious crime committed in this instance is that American society has given up on schooling as a public good for which all should pay and to which all should have access. Instead, it has transformed a public good into a private right, thus limiting access and opportunity to those who are wealthy and privileged.[22] What is lost in this privatizing vision is the crucial notion that educated societies are more healthy, equitable, and democratic. This public vision of education is premised on the idea that, as Erika Shaker observes, we all benefit from having an informed citizenry and that we are not paying for simply the education of others but "for the right to live in an educated society. With all the vast benefits that brings."[23]

Such stories serve as flash points for a society in crisis. And, as Bauman points out, even though they may tell us little about deeper causal connections, they "prod the imagination. And sound an alert. They appeal to the conscience as well as to survival instincts.... [They also show] that the ideal that one can 'do it alone' is a fatal mistake which defies the purpose of self-concern and self-care."[24] These examples point to the collateral damage of a casino capitalism that now takes austerity as its clarion call to gut social protections and weaken the rights of labor and unions. Moreover, austerity is designed to reward the wealthy while imposing poverty, suffering, and severe hardship on those marginalized by race, disability, age, and class. For many, the examples I have noted suggest that the writing is on the wall regarding their future, and the message is dark indeed.

Complaints by right-wing politicians and conservative pundits about the growing federal deficit and their call for a harsh politics of austerity are both hypocritical and disingenuous—hypocritical, given their support for massive tax breaks for the rich, and disingenuous, given their blatant goal of implementing a market-based agenda that places the burden of decreased government services and benefits on the backs of the poor, young people, the unemployed, the working class, and middle-class individuals and families. As Wolff suggested in the quotation earlier in this chapter, it is increasingly apparent that austerity measures apply to the poor but not to the rich, who continue to thrive under policies that support government bailouts, deficit-producing wars, tax breaks for the wealthy, and deregulation that benefits only powerful corporations. The conservative and right-wing politicians calling for shared sacrifices in the name of balancing budgets have no interest in promoting the public good. Their policies maximize self-interest, support a culture of organized irresponsibility, and expand the pathologies driving poverty, massive inequality, and military spending. Austerity porn functions within the current political climate to promote deficits for the express purpose of returning the United States to the Gilded Age policies of the 1920s.[25]

There is a certain irony in the fact that the austerity hawks have emerged from what can only be called "the party of debt." They belong to the same Republican Party that gave us two wars, an increase in military spending, and a whopping loss of tax revenues due to tax breaks for megarich corporations and wealthy Americans. This is the party that transformed the Clinton surplus into a massive deficit. Nobel Prize–winning economist Paul Krugman raises the question of what happened to the federal government budget surplus in 2000 and provides the following answer: "Three main things. First, there were the Bush tax cuts, which added roughly $2 trillion to the national debt over the last decade. Second, there were the wars in Iraq and Afghanistan, which added an additional $1.1 trillion or so. And third was the Great Recession, which led both to a collapse in revenue and to a sharp rise in spending on unemployment insurance and other safety-net programs."[26] All told, President George W. Bush added $4 trillion to the national debt—and there was no debate at that time about raising the debt ceiling, which received the support of Congress seven times during the Bush presidency.[27]

What is often missed is that running a deficit is a strategy used by hard right-wing Republicans and some equally conservative Democrats as an excuse for cutting social benefits and generating massive amounts of inequality that benefit the rich.[28] Michael Tomasky further explains, "The Republican Party cares nothing about the public debt. In fact, it wants more.... It is the party of debt. It is the party of deficits. It is the party of recession. It is the party of unemployment. It is the party of inequality. And it is the party of middle-class stagnation and slippage.... They scream about crisis because what they desire is to use the crisis as an excuse to do things to this country that the hard right has wanted to do for 30 years."[29] What Tomasky leaves out is that the current crop of right-wing Republicans controlling the shots in Washington and various states also appears to revel in "a deep urge to inflict pain."[30] How else to explain the 2011 debt negotiations between leaders of both political parties, when the Republican leaders walked out as soon as the Democrats suggested the need to talk about not only cutting programs that benefit the poor but also limiting tax breaks for corporate jets, hedge fund managers, the obscenely wealthy, and corporations?

According to the apostles of Ayn Rand, Milton Friedman, and Ronald Reagan, individual interests and market-driven needs always trump social needs; brilliant individuals are those who have apprenticed within institutions committed to making money and are the most qualified to run government; freedom is best defined as freedom from regulation; and any government that passes policies to provide social protections, regulate corporations, or lessen inequality is either grossly authoritarian or unwise. In this scenario, especially under the administration of Ronald Reagan, government is declared the enemy and the market is given free rein to administer society. Through the 1980s, a series of policies was inaugurated in which there was a sustained assault on the working and middle classes through "the busting of unions, the export of millions of decent-paying jobs, and the transfer of enormous wealth to the already rich. The tax rates for the wealthiest were slashed about in half. Greed was incentivized."[31]

The ideologues of casino capitalism believed, despite all evidence to the contrary, that if the rich and corporations paid less tax and inequality was left unchecked, society as a whole would benefit—wealth would trickle down. Of course, what actually happened and was propelled even further by the unchecked Wild West–type casino capitalism under Bush was that wages for workers stagnated; the top 1 percent of the population became fabulously wealthy; health care deteriorated for the vast majority of the population; schools were turned into test centers; the nation's infrastructure was allowed to rot; and millions of people lost their jobs, homes, and hope. And this situation continues to worsen while two-thirds of US corporations currently pay no taxes. For example, Bank of America did not pay any taxes for 2010 or 2011.[32] Given these conditions, it is perhaps no surprise that social inequality in the United States dwarfs income gaps across the rest of the world, and continued increases in executive pay eviscerate any claim the nation might have to democracy.

The implications of this conservative assault waged in the name of austerity go beyond a cozy support of unaccountable corporate rule and the enactment of reactionary government policies. Behind the politics of deception and domination lies the proliferation of a culture of cruelty whose victims are subjected to harsh and brutalizing tactics of regulation and control, especially young people, people of color, the unemployed, the elderly, the poor, immigrants, and a number of other individuals and groups now bearing the burden of the worst economic recession since the 1920s. Cruelty in this instance is not meant simply to refer to the character flaws of the rich or to appeal to a form of leftist moralism but to register the effects of the merging of the institutions of capital, wealth, and power that has resulted, especially since the 1980s, in vast levels of inequality and the infliction of immense amounts of pain and suffering upon the most vulnerable in society.[33] But it does more. Jonathan Schell points out,

> There have been many signs recently that the United States has been traveling down a steepening path of cruelty. It's hard to say why such a thing is occurring, but it seems to have to do with a steadily growing faith in force as the solution to almost any problem, whether at home or abroad. Enthusiasm for killing is an unmistakable symptom of cruelty. It also appeared after the killing of Osama bin Laden, which touched off raucous celebrations around the country. It is one thing to believe in the unfortunate necessity of killing someone, another to revel in it. This is especially disturbing when it is not only government officials but ordinary people who engage in the effusions.[34]

The growing culture of cruelty in the United States registers the emergence of not only a corrupt and morally broken form of casino capitalism but also a hypermasculine ideology in which the most basic elements of the social state and government are "regarded as feminine, weak, and unmanned, and the anti-social aspects of government and social policy [elitist, militarized, individualist] as masculine and strong."[35] Essentially, we are left with a "Macho individualism [that] undermines ideas of collectivity."[36] This warlike notion of masculinity becomes the ideological dressing for a militarized punishing state in which policy matters concerning austerity, foreign affairs, and the politics of governance make a hasty withdrawal from any notion of social costs or ethical considerations. What should be clear is that the politics of austerity is not about rethinking priorities to benefit the public good. Instead, it has become part of a discourse of shaming the individual, one that emulates the economic policies of casino capitalism and the practices of a politics of cruelty, both of which have little to do with using indignation to imagine a better world. On the contrary, shame is now used to wage a war on the poor rather than on poverty, on young people rather than on those economic and political forces that undermine their future, and on those considered "other" rather than on the underlying structures and ideologies of systemic and state racism. Shame is also used to humiliate teachers by making their individual performance assessments public, as if humiliating teachers in the public press will either motivate them or help to reform any aspect of a broken educational system.[37] We live at a time in which reason is divorced from rationality, and the pain of others, particularly those considered disposable or unworthy, has become the subject not of compassion but of ridicule and amusement in America. The discourse of austerity reveals the hidden politics of a neofeudal social order, paralyzed by its own corruption and unable anymore to make legitimate claims to democracy. Michael Thomas captures this dark shift in American society in the following comments:

> I have lived what now, at 75, is starting to feel like a long life. If anyone asks me what has been the great American story of my lifetime, I have a ready answer. It is the corruption, money-based, that has settled like some all-enveloping excremental mist on the landscape of our hopes, that has permeated every nook of any institution or being that has real influence on the way we live now. Sixty years ago, if you had asked me, on the basis of all that I had been taught, whether I thought this condition of general rot was possible in this country, I would have told you that you were nuts. And I would have been very wrong.[38]

As the welfare state is dismantled, it is being replaced by the harsh realities of the punishing state. Consequently, social problems are criminalized and social protections are either eliminated or fatally weakened. The harsh values of this new social order can be seen in the increasing incarceration of young people; the modeling of public schools after prisons; reactionary anti-immigration laws; and state policies that bail out investment bankers but leave the middle and working classes in a state of poverty, despair, and insecurity. For poor youths and people of color, the prison-industrial complex is particularly lethal. Michelle Alexander has pointed out that there are more African American men under the control of the criminal justice system than were enslaved in 1850, and the aggressive prosecution of drug offenses means that four out of five black youths in some communities can expect to be either in prison or "caught up in the criminal justice system at some point in their lives."[39] In states such as Georgia, Alabama, and South Carolina, new immigration laws

> make it impossible for people without papers to live without fear. They give new powers to local police untrained in immigration law. They force businesses to purge work forces and schools to check students' immigration status. And they greatly increase the danger of unreasonable searches, false arrests, racial profiling and other abuses, not just against immigrants, but anyone who may look like some officer's idea of an illegal immigrant.... The laws also make it illegal to give a ride to the undocumented, so a son could land in jail for driving his mother to the supermarket, or a church volunteer for ferrying families to a soup kitchen.[40]

The Obama administration fares no better on punishing immigrants and "has used its criminal justice system and law enforcement apparatus to deport 393,000 people, at a cost of $5 billion."[41] The administration's stance on immigration suggests something about its own misplaced priorities, as does its refusal to prosecute either Wall Street crooks or the CIA thugs who tortured men, women, and children in Iraq. White-collar crooks produce global financial havoc because of their fraudulent deals and go scot-free while illegal immigrants looking for work that most Americans will not perform are put in jail.

The growing culture of cruelty, illegal legalities, and political illiteracy can also be seen in the practice of socialism for the rich that rejects taxes as a means of wealth redistribution, arguing instead that the market system rewards merit and hard work while intentionally forgetting that every person is simply not granted the same opportunities in life—all the more so for those born into an alleged free-market society. This is a mentality in which government supports for the poor, unemployed, sick, and elderly are derided because they either contribute to an increase in the growing deficit or undermine the market-driven notion of individual responsibility. The trickle-down cruelty of the antitax, antipublic, and antigovernment extremists is on full display in Minnesota, where Republicans have refused Governor Mark Dayton's call for a tax on "the 7,700 Minnesotans who make more than $1 million a year" in order to raise revenue to address the state's budget deficit. Rather than tax the rich, Republican legislators have called for slashing "billions from ... education, health care, and safety programs" and have literally shut down state government to get their way.[42] The result is that 22,000 workers have been laid off, child care subsidies have dried up, and essential services for the poor have been suspended—all so that taxes on the rich will not be raised. The governor of New Jersey, Chris Christie, has followed the same playbook and has used his veto to eliminate $1.3 billion in spending, most of it for schools, Medicaid, and aid to cities. But he also cut smaller items favored by Democrats, such as programs to help abused children and provide legal aid to the poor. It gets worse. As funds for state budgets dry up because of corporate welfare policies, some cities have slashed salaries of public servants. In Scranton, Pennsylvania, the salaries of police, firefighters, and others have been reduced to minimum wage.

It's easy to see that the same critics who attack "big government" defend without irony government support for the ultrawealthy, the bankers, the permanent war economy, and subsidies for corporations deemed to be essential to the nation. Clearly, this is an argument that only benefits the rich and powerful and legitimizes the deregulated Wild West of casino capitalism. As public services are eliminated, health insurance is cut for over a million kids, and teachers and public workers are laid off. The average worker in the United States made $39,000 in 2010 and got a 0.5 percent pay increase in 2011, raising their wages to about $40,100. Meanwhile, corporate profits soared, and Wall Street executives had a bonus year. According to the *New York Times*, "the median pay for top executives at 200 big companies [in 2010] was $10.8 million. That works out to a 23 percent gain from 2009."[43] The moral obscenity that characterizes such salaries becomes clear at a time when 14 million people are looking for work, millions have lost their homes, and thousands are trying to survive on food stamps. How can any society that calls itself democratic and egalitarian justify salaries that are so grotesquely high that it is difficult to imagine how such wealth can be spent? For example, how can anyone justify paying CEOs such as Philippe P. Dauman, the head of Viacom, $85 million in 2010? Or, for that matter, the $32.9 million paid to Michael White of DirecTV?[44]

The hidden order of politics and culture of cruelty become even more apparent when it is revealed that Mark G. Parker, the CEO of Nike, got $13.1 million in 2010 and cut 1,750 jobs, while Peter L. Lynch, the CEO of Winn-Dixie, got $5.3 million and cut 2,000 jobs. One of the worst offenders was Michael Duke, the CEO of Walmart, who got $18.7 million in 2010 while eliminating 13,000 jobs.[45] Even more alarming is that some of the bonuses paid to risk-taking bankers were paid for, in part, with taxpayers' money. For example, Benjamin M. Friedman, writing in the *New York Review of Books*, claims that this is precisely what happened in the case of the bonuses paid to Citigroup's executives:

> Despite the destruction of so much of the stockholders' value, and notwithstanding the enormous taxpayer assistance, Citi's management announced in the spring of 2009 that it was paying out 5.3 billion in bonuses for 2008, including payments of more than $5 million apiece to forty-four employees of the bank. Because of the $45 billion investment of AARP and TIP money, by 2009 the U.S. government was Citigroup's largest shareowner. Hence the issue these lavish bonuses raised was not merely a private firm's right to set its employees' compensation. What Citi's management was giving away was, in significant part, the taxpayers' money. Yet the Obama administration voiced no objection, at least not publicly.[46]

Also disgusting about inflated CEO compensation—even beyond being partly subsidized by taxpayer money—is that executive pay raises serve to deepen inequality in the United States, concentrating enormous amounts of political, economic, and social power in the hands of a few individuals and corporations while entailing enormous human costs in the hardships arising from joblessness when workers are laid off in order to fill the pockets of rich CEOs. In the end, such practices contribute to massive amounts of suffering on the part of millions of Americans, they corrupt politics, and they undermine the promise of a viable democracy. Frank Rich expands this critique in arguing that "as good times roar back for corporate America, it's bad enough that CEOs are collectively sitting on some $1.9 trillion.... What's most galling is how many of these executives are sore winners, crying all the way to Palm Beach while raking in record profits and paying some of the lowest tax rates over the past 50 years."[47] What must one do to one's moral conscience—short of lobotomy—to decry any proposed regulation of financial and corporate institutions as an "intolerable burden" while demanding that the poor and jobless carry the fallout of a debt crisis in which they had no hand in creating?

The rise of austerity measures and the form of economic Darwinism they require could not be enforced through the actions of government alone, albeit a government in the hands of right-wing corporate extremists. Such measures also receive support from a conservative US Supreme Court and rely upon the police and other repressive apparatuses. Perhaps even more importantly, austerity garners public support (or indifference) through being endlessly reproduced by the cultural apparatuses of the new and old media and by institutions in the public sector, even colleges and universities, as well as through the thousands of messages and narratives people are exposed to daily in multiple commercial spheres. In this discourse, the economic order either is sanctioned by God or exists simply as an extension of nature. In other words, the tyranny and suffering that are produced through the neoliberal theater of cruelty are coded as unquestionable, as unmovable as an urban skyscraper.

A society driven solely by market interests is neither a relative nor a friend to democracy. The decadent privileges of the rich and the unchecked power of corporations do more to crush democracy than to uplift society as a whole. Any society that allows the market to constitute the axis and framing mechanisms for all social interactions has not just lost its sense of morality and responsibility; it has also given up its claim on any possibility of a democratic future. Market fundamentalism, along with its structure of extreme inequality and machinery of cruelty, has unilaterally proclaimed a death sentence for democracy.

The good news is that young people protesting all over the United States have made the attack on economic inequality and big-money politics one of the major rallying cries of their movement. Inequality in wealth and income is viewed as symptomatic of a corrupt economic system, a type of casino capitalism that rewards the rich and tramples on everyone else. Most importantly, they have recognized that inequality is a powerful indicator of a neoliberal agenda that has produced the current economic crisis and threatens any viable notion of democracy. Under a market-driven society, inequality performs a legitimating function. Serving as a neutral descriptor for market fundamentalism's love affair with a narrow and insidious notion of self-development, hard work, and individual responsibility, inequality disavows structural relations of power, systemic pressures, or institutional forces. The Occupy movement rejects this coded form of politics, with its flight from social costs and social and political responsibility.

Targeting the 1 percent, protesters have said no to Wall Street, the big corporations, rich hedge funds, oversized banks, and corporate executives making millions of dollars annually. Young people are not only asking big questions about class, power, social relations, and social values; they are also giving new meaning to democratic values and modes of collective resistance. Moreover, they have demonstrated through their persistence and dedication that they believe that they have the power to change the corrupt system that has robbed them of any type of viable and joyous future. Following the spirit of protest that has engulfed an entire generation of young people, the time has come when Americans must ask what can be done to demystify the authoritarianism inherent in casino capitalism and the institutions that mimic its policies, practices, and values. Such a task demands that both the youthful protesters and other individuals and social movements join together to address not only the economic issues such as income distribution plaguing Americans but also what Stanley Aronowitz calls the broader dimensions of "social and cultural alienation that mark this revolt."[48] The time has come not only to join young people in their fight against economic inequality but also to rethink what other interconnected registers of freedom and social justice have to be addressed in order to recognize what a real democracy might look like in the United States and what it will take to actually make it happen.

◇

CHAPTER 6

Got Class Warfare?
Occupy Wall Street's Challenge to Casino Capitalism

We're young, we're poor, we're not going to take it anymore.
—*Occupy Wall Street chant*

Class warfare has once again entered the vocabulary of mainstream national politics, this time, however, with a strange twist. Right-wing politicians such as Paul Ryan and various high-profile conservative media pundits and corporate-funded think-tank spokespeople have made visible what ruling classes have long tried to bury beneath the discourse of meritocracy and the myth of the classless society—that is, the harsh consequences of class power, hierarchical rule, and savage inequality. According to the ruling elite, the real class war is being waged against the belief in free and unfettered markets, the reign of unchecked capital, a culture of individualism, religious freedom, and happiness itself—in spite of the fact that it is precisely these beliefs that serve the interests of Wall Street financiers and hedge fund managers who brought the world economy to the brink of ruin in 2008.

Arthur C. Brooks, the president of the ultraright American Enterprise Institute, says it all in defending the legitimating and empty ideology of the elites: "Free enterprise brings happiness; redistribution does not. The reason is that only free enterprise brings earned success."[1] According to this insipid comment,

105

taking a stance against social and economic inequality amounts to railing against hard-earned success. Brooks's position would carry weight only if every person were born into the same circumstances and offered similar opportunities in life—the only hope for which lies in genuine egalitarianism, not the monopolies of wealth and power encouraged by an unrestricted market system. The secret order of politics that haunts Brooks's statement is a fear of democracy matched only by a hysteria that fuels belief in the virtues of a plutocracy and disdain for democratic ideals. The appeal to "earned success" and individual entrepreneurship rings hollow given the extravagant bonuses paid to failed CEOs and hedge fund managers and an economic recovery that has benefited only banks. With CEOs taking in millions in salaries and bonuses while major corporations are laying off thousands of workers each month, the assertion that only an unfettered market can ensure that one's hard work pays off appears disingenuous and desperate. The concept of earned success rings hollow in an economy in which the financial elite do not produce any viable or tangible goods. On the contrary, they earn their wealth producing junk bonds, derivatives, and fraudulent loans and engaging in other corrupt schemes in which profits are gained through accelerated risks, high-stakes gambling, and high-speed trading, largely with other people's money. What Brooks willfully omits is that any society in which morality disintegrates into bald self-interest, and a cruel disregard for others is celebrated as a central element of the social order, has nothing to do with either freedom or democracy. This is obvious in the endless examples of corporate fraud on display extending from the Enron scandal to the more recent debacles of GlaxoSmithKline, M.F. Global, JPMorgan Chase, and Barclay.

When thousands of youths marched against corporate power and the symbols of Wall Street greed across the United States beginning in September 2011, the political and economic elites responded by revitalizing the tired rhetoric of class warfare while clinging to the celebration of a sharklike culture of casino capitalism, revealing all too clearly their own criminal behavior and its threat to American democracy. Labeling the actions of the Occupiers as arising from an infantilizing class resentment was, of course, not a new tactic rolled out by conservatives. Ruling elites have in the past attempted to discredit or neutralize the concept of class warfare, and for a good reason. It made visible the vast differences in power and other inequalities between the wealthy and everyone else, especially the working classes and poor. It also functioned to focus attention on the violence and social costs of concentrating wealth in the hands of corporations and the rich while others suffered and struggled with the dire material consequences. After all, the historical concept of class struggle conjures up images of American workers fighting collectively and valiantly to secure fair wages, safe working conditions, decent housing, and control over their own labor. And the costs were often high. The struggle for decent working conditions and basic economic and labor rights was often met with the brutal acts of violence on the part of employers, rogue detective agencies, and the National Guard.[2] As Stanley Aronowitz has pointed out in his brilliant book, *How Class Works: Power and Social Movements,* class relations are woven into the fabric of American life, and yet such relations are all but written out of American history; erased from dominant media accounts; and absorbed into the language of meritocracy, morality, and character.[3]

At the current moment, the nature of class struggle has taken a slightly different turn. With the triumph of finance capital and the emergence of a second Gilded Age, conscripted thugs, the police, and the National Guard do not constitute the vanguard or first line of class repression. Physical force, though hardly absent from scenes of protests, takes second place to the war being waged every day at the level of policy, culture, and politics. Within a globalized economy, labor is increasingly viewed as a disposable population—pensions are decimated, increased health insurance costs are passed on to employees, unemployment benefits are slashed, and jobs are outsourced so that capital can relocate "to wherever labor is most exploitable."[4] With the advance of corporate and financial power, violence now comes in the form of corrupt legislation and a political ideology that strips government of its universal social protections; removes government oversight; builds on fear; decimates the power of unions; defunds public institutions; and expands the culture of cruelty, fraud, and avarice through policies that perpetuate a crushing inequality.[5] Of course, this same movement to shrink the role of government expresses no opposition to "big government" when it promotes militarism, gives tax breaks to the rich, enacts laws that de-regulate corporations, and defunds valuable social programs.

Meanwhile, a supine and hypertrophied mass media feed the general populace with a toxic mix of propagandistic hate, racism, immigrant baiting, and labor bashing. The power of the rich and their disdain for vulnerability are strengthened by these emotive discourses, along with the support of a gun culture and unthinking consumption of hyperviolence saturating various screen cultures. Scorn for public servants feeds an authoritarian populism and hijacks democratic language, ideals, and social relations. The dominant media are no longer the mouthpiece of the moral majority and the gatekeeper of the status quo—they are now firmly on the side of the radical conservatism espoused by the ultrawealthy and megacorporations. How else to explain the media's contempt for reason and critical inquiry as they turn news into entertainment and the call for balance into a form of anti-intellectual drivel? At best, the dominant media have attempted to neutralize the issue of class inequality, making it largely invisible. At worst, they served as active accomplices in promoting a hidden agenda of class warfare through their embrace of neoliberal values and refusal to engage with any serious issues that might reveal the terrible human and social costs of a growing social and economic inequality that serves only the rich.

In the United States, we inhabit a moment in history when ruling-class hysteria has reached an all-time high in its aggressive attempts to prevent the federal government from exercising any form of regulation that might make it accountable to the American people. At the same time, Republican class warriors and their corporate backers seek to hollow out the social state by labeling a government that provides social protections and works in the interest of the public good as evil, repressive, and expendable. Robert Kuttner, the coeditor of *The American Prospect*, gets it right when he argues, "One of our major parties has turned nihilist.... Government itself is the devil.... Whether the target is the Environmental Protection Agency, the Dodd-Frank Law or the Affordable Care Act, Republicans are out to destroy government's ability to govern.... The right's reckless assault on our public institutions is not just an attack on government. It is a war on America."[6] The most visible face of this war appeared with the economic crisis of 2008 in which Wall Street bankers and traders packaged mortgage debts they knew would fail, perpetrated widespread fraud on the American public through the promotion of liars' loans, and created a business culture that William Black has called "a criminogenic environment"—an environment that spreads fraud through the lack of regulation and the promotion of a compensation system that creates incentives through which cheaters prosper, "markets become perverse," and honesty is treated as a liability.[7] Behind this environment is the scourge of a "casino capitalism that nearly destroyed the economy and overwhelmed our democracy."[8]

And while the historical circumstances producing modes of class struggle have changed, the basic contours of the struggle have been consistent and highlight an ongoing and unjust division between a bloated class of capitalists and financiers, on the one hand, and the rest of the society on the other. As the refrain of the Occupy Wall Street movement made clear, the 99 percent are now largely subject to the reckless policies of the rich and excluded from the vast wealth, resources, and benefits enjoyed by the top 1 percent of American society. Even a child's reading of history reveals the ironic absurdity of the right's attempt to reissue the term "class warfare" in order to position the rich as victims and discredit the legitimate claims of the Occupiers as petty, adolescent smears. Historically, the ruling elites were hardly above the use of fraud, violence, and force to control the instruments and sites of power, extending from the workplace and financial institutions to local, state, and national governments. Anything could be justified in order to secure their wealth, profits, and privileges, even if such practices reproduced vast economic, political, and cultural inequalities and deadly social costs. One historical example is the Ludlow Massacre, during which the Colorado National Guard used a machine gun to fire randomly into the tent city erected by the striking coal miners. Nineteen people were killed.[9] The same script, involving state and corporate violence against workers and their families, also played out in two incidents in spring 1920 in West Virginia known as the Matewan Massacre and the Battle of Blair Mountain. Hoover-type thuggery also resulted in a government attack on what was known as the Bonus Army in the early 1930s, during which the army shot and wounded fifty-five veterans. These are just a few of the more well-known conflicts waged against working people to protect class privilege over the course of the twentieth century.

Historically, it is clear that class warfare often meant that ruling classes, elites, government officials, and corporations did not hesitate to use violence to legitimate capitalism while also maintaining the status quo and repressing any vestige of worker resistance—however just the demands of workers and other groups might have been. This use of force as an instrument of power coincided with the use of culture, educational institutions, political institutions, and a range of other apparatuses to secure the ongoing privileges and benefits of the rich while keeping the dispossessed and disadvantaged firmly in their place. But the injuries of class, as Richard Sennett and Jonathan Cobb have pointed out,[10] often remained hidden, buried beneath the loss of dignity and hopelessness produced by policies that led to massive poverty, deadly levels of unemployment, inadequate health care, failing schools, political corruption, and a range of other social and economic injustices.

Today, largely due to the Occupy movement's public outreach and engagement of various forms of media, the empirical registers of class oppression have become increasingly evident. The richest 1 percent in the 1970s took in only about "8–9 percent of American total annual income," whereas today they take in 23.5 percent.[11] Furthermore, as University of California–Berkeley professor Emmanuel Saez states in his study of inequality, 10 percent of Americans as of 2007 were receiving 49.7 percent of all wages, "higher than any other year since 1917."[12] In another statistic cited in an editorial in the *Huffington Post,* seventy-four of the richest people in the United States make "$10 million in weekly pay ... [and] made as much as the 19 million lowest-paid people in America, who constitute one in every eight workers."[13] Consider, too, the fact that the net worth of the wealthiest Americans is $1.5 trillion, more than the combined net worth of the poorest 50 percent of the population, or some 155 million people combined.[14] David DeGraw points out that "the economic top one percent of the population now owns over 70% of all financial assets, an all-time record."[15] As Joseph E. Stiglitz makes clear, "In terms of wealth rather than income, the top 1 percent control 40 percent. Their lot in life has improved considerably. Twenty-five years ago, the corresponding figures were 12 percent and 33 percent."[16] According to Robert Reich, one stark measure of the inequality that marks American society today is evident in the fact that "the 5 percent of Americans with the highest incomes now account for 37 percent of all consumer purchases."[17]

Needless to say, the gap between the rich and the poor is widening at a time when economic growth has stalled, unemployment has soared, incarceration is booming, and crucial infrastructures have fallen into grave disrepair. The upward redistribution of wealth comes with heavy social and economic costs. Though I have mentioned these figures in other chapters, they are worth repeating: 1 in 2 Americans is low income or poor—that adds up to 146.4 million Americans—and 1.6 million kids are homeless at any given time in a year, which amounts to 1 in 45 kids. This figure is up 38 percent since 2007. Moreover, as Diane Sweet points out, "since 2007, banks have foreclosed around eight million homes. It is estimated that another eight to ten million homes will be foreclosed before the financial crisis is over. This approach to resolving one part of the financial crisis means many, many families are living without adequate and secure housing [while] there are 18.5 million vacant homes in the country."[18]

Given these ever-worsening circumstances, Warren Buffet is certainly right in claiming that his billionaire friends "have been coddled long enough by a billionaire-friendly Congress."[19] What Buffet missed in spite of the best of intentions is that his billionaire friends and their allies actually now control Congress and are not merely the recipients of its largess. There is no longer any distinction between political and corporate sovereignty. The United States is now a corporate-controlled state, not a democratic entity. The rich and corporate elite control the system and mode of governance and leave a poisonous imprint upon national political culture, perhaps most notably a vociferous disdain for the common good. This political culture, along with financial corruption, breeds civic indifference and a death-dealing cynicism. As more and more citizens are deprived of basic rights, jobs, opportunities, and social protections, human resources are squandered. Social investments in education, technology, and infrastructure are abandoned in the name of market efficiency, and the state is reconfigured so as to shun its welfare obligations and govern largely through its punishing institutions such as the courts, criminal justice system, and prisons.

As the foundations of social protections and security are eroded through the mechanisms of inequality, social problems are viewed exclusively as the responsibility of individuals, scorned as a matter of failed character, and increasingly treated as a matter of law and order. How else to explain a criminal justice system notable for its racism and reeking of savagery and cruelty—because of which more than 2 million people are incarcerated? What are we to make of the fact that, in a country that makes a claim to democracy, "more African American men are in prison or jail, on probation or parole than were enslaved in 1850, before the Civil War began"?[20] And as Michelle Alexander points out, "in some black inner-city communities, four of five black youth can expect to be caught up in the criminal justice system during their lifetimes. As a consequence, a great many black men are disenfranchised ... prevented because of their felony convictions from voting and from living in public housing, discriminated in hiring, excluded from juries, and denied educational opportunities."[21] In addition, as Erica Goode writes, "by age 23, almost a third of Americans have been arrested for a crime [which] researchers say is a measure of growing exposure to the criminal justice system in everyday life," while growth in the number of incarcerated is indicative of the "justice system becoming more punitive and more aggressive in its reach during the last half-century."[22] What is to be made of prison practices, such as the extensive use of solitary confinement, that, "many believe, amount to torture"?[23] Or, for that matter, the public support and barbarous celebration of the ongoing use of capital punishment, even though evidence has been produced (based on DNA testing) proving the innocence of many death-row inmates and repeated cases have demonstrated the inherent racism of the criminal justice system and the failure of justice itself?

It is a curious indication of the rising culture of fraud and cruelty in American society that when the discourse of class warfare is invoked by the rich and powerful, it almost never mentions the effects that harsh policies produced by the rich have on the children of this nation. The right-wing response to being charged with class warfare is that the term is divisive, as if the great crime of class inequality is that it makes rich people defensive or makes them feel bad. While the meaning of class warfare is important, it is the effects that in the end really matter, especially in terms of how the social, economic, and political costs of class warfare wreak havoc on young people.

The ideals that inform a substantive democracy are utterly at odds with the current shameful condition of America's youth. The real face and registers of class warfare can be found in statistics that should make every American citizen feel a sense of moral and political outrage. As Marian Wright Edelman points out, "more than one million children fell into poverty between 2009 and 2010; almost a half million fell into extreme poverty."[24] Yet, from the ways in which the dominant media portray the current state of affairs, one would think it is the rich elite and powerful corporations who continue to be the victims of class warfare, not the children who are defenseless against a savage economic system that benefits a privileged few at the very top of the economic ladder. Of course, the rich will say that any criticism of their wealth and policies undervalues their hard work and invaluable contributions to economic progress. But, as Elizabeth Warren has reminded us, nobody gets rich simply by his or her own initiative. Individual success cannot happen without the existence of a viable social contract that puts in place the conditions that enable personal initiative to occur, never mind succeed. She writes,

> There is nobody in this country who got rich on his own. Nobody! You built a factory out there, good for you! But, I wanna be clear. You moved your goods to market on the roads the rest of us paid for. You hired workers the rest of us paid to educate. You were safe in your factory because of the police forces and fire forces that the rest of us paid for. You didn't have to worry that marauding bands would come and seize everything at your factory and hire someone to protect against this because of the work that the rest of us did. Now look, you built a factory and it turned into something terrific or a great idea, God bless, keep a big hunk of it, but part of the underlying social contract is you take a hunk of that and pay forward for the next kid who comes along.[25]

What is often left out of the insipid and embarrassing claim to entitlement by the ruling elite is that, far from promoting economic progress, they have used their wealth—often made not through hard labor but through financial transactions and trades that border on corruption—to promote economic ruin for vast numbers of people in the United States. Rather than producing jobs, they have bankrupted the economy through financial mismanagement and fraud, imposing a staggering burden on small businesses; people with mortgages; the middle and working classes; and young people who can look forward to a future of unparalleled debt, low-wage jobs, and little hope.

Trickle-down economics—discussed in Chapter 5 as one of the legitimating ideologies of market fundamentalism—is really about trickling down to nothing the residual services for the poor, elderly, working class, and young. In the midst of a crushing economic recession, hedge fund managers, banks, and corporations have produced soaring profits, made partly through government bailouts. Yet, they continue to hoard their money, increasing their capital by further cutting back on jobs rather than creating them. According to the Congressional Budget Office, "a dollar dedicated to the middle class grows the economy three times faster than a dollar devoted to the rich. Yet, Republicans would still give the highest earners another tax cut." All the while, "executive and CEO salaries increased by 23 percent in 2010."[26]

If we accept the view that class warfare is alive and well in the United States, then surely it is to be found in the celebration of narrow self-interest, unchecked greed, and a survival-of-the-fittest mind-set that continues to advance modes of agency and policies that shred the social contract, produce massive suffering on a global level, and reek with the arrogance of power. In a deregulated and privatized regime of casino capitalism, the bonds of solidarity have been eroded, shared responsibilities are replaced by shared fears and increasing levels of violence, and the culture is flooded with the soft porn of consumerism. Private concerns now trump public issues, and all remaining public spaces are increasingly turned into sites of surveillance, detention, containment, incarceration, and disposability.[27] Profits for the rich soar as the swollen military-industrial-carceral state reinforces the "winner-take-all politics" of the ultrawealthy 1 percent along with the society it produces and legitimates.[28] While prevailing political, social, and economic inequalities in the United States emanate from a long history of class warfare by the rich against the middle and lower classes, it appears that class-based oppression in its current incarnation is more ruthless and corrupt than that of previous generations.

At the same time, the battle being waged by the ruling elites has become more difficult to hide, despite efforts by a corrupt media and political culture to distract the electorate away from its most destructive consequences. As the practices of casino capitalism and the corporate state were made increasingly visible, they were met with the first sustained challenge in decades with the emergence of the Occupy Wall Street movement. While recognizing the pernicious effects of class inequality, the Occupy movement was broad and diverse enough to articulate a well-fashioned and collective sense of moral and political outrage over the fact that the war on poverty has been translated into a war on the poor, especially poor minorities of class and color. It channeled the public indignation over the fact that homelessness is now viewed as a violation of civic order and misfortune is regularly defined by conservative politicians as a threat to law and order. It made connections between casino capitalism and a culture of cruelty in which kindness, trust, compassion, and a sense of responsibility for others had given way to a flight from ethical considerations. In its commitment to peaceful protest, it reclaimed an ethics of care and trust that had been all but abandoned by a hardened culture and the widespread view that decency, trust, and civic obligations were liabilities.

Occupy Wall Street showed how barbarism is now the preserve of enclaves of the rich, not the poor. It opened the conversation to discussing the statistics mentioned earlier and all the related policies that produce such grievous social costs—costs that not only stagger the mind but are completely at odds with any viable notion of what a democracy should look like or what it means to take seriously the well-being of all members of a society and the importance of the social contract. And such figures and policies, in truth, do not even come close to capturing adequately the amount of human suffering and the destructive social costs that many adults and young people experience as a result of deepening rigid class divisions. But they do sound an alarm and suggest the need for further analyses that connect economic policies to an ethical consideration of the effects such policies have on those who are caught in an ever-expanding web of human despair and misfortune.

The challenge posed by Occupy Wall Street had little to do with the right-wing charge that the protesters were unfairly heaping abuse on the rich and powerful. On the contrary, the discourse and political concerns raised by the protesters were about reclaiming the mechanisms through which history has been written time and again by the victors. It was about challenging the elite universities and foundations incubating anti-public intellectuals in order to further legitimate a war against democracy, public goods, the commons, and, most of all, young people and other groups now deemed expendable. It was about presenting young people with an alternative to the culture of illiteracy actively produced through an ongoing disinvestment and privatization of public education that make it less possible for young people to recognize what the abuse of power and privilege looks like and how this abuse is bearing down on their lives and future. Occupy Wall Street actively opposed forms of illiteracy that seek to prevent youth from addressing what it might mean to become critical and engaged citizens capable of holding official power accountable. Recognizing how the same culture of illiteracy operates through not only state, economic, and educational institutions but also the dominant media and wider cultural apparatuses, Occupy Wall Street, at least initially, created and occupied various sites with discourses, narratives, and frameworks calling on the rich and powerful corporations to account for the unconscionable damage they do to democratic institutions and those marginalized by race, class, and age.

Until recently, those loud voices speaking with contempt for government and social protections—matched only perhaps by the clamoring of right-wing ideologues in favor of unchecked militarism and an ideological blindness to the basic ideals of a viable democracy—were the only ones being heard, while everyone else appeared muted and those populations who suffered the greatest costs were rendered utterly invisible. What the Occupy Wall Street movement did was wrest away from the right, at least for a time, the critical spaces of public engagement and cultural dialogue. In their manifesto, the Occupy Wall Street protesters marshaled their critical ire against a failing political and economic system that poisons the food supply, takes bailouts from taxpayers with impunity, sells out privacy as a commodity, produces unprecedented disparities in income and wealth, blocks alternate forms of energy, participates in the torture and murder of innocent civilians overseas, and develops economic policies that produce catastrophic financial crises on a global scale. In this instance, the Occupy movement changed the national discourse and developed new framing mechanisms for asking crucial questions about inequality, financial fraud, environmental degradation, militarization, the shredding of civil liberties, and the antidemocratic amassing of corporate and financial power. The dominant media initially claimed that the protest groups were incoherent and unorganized while ignoring the fact that they were pushing against the entire system of corporate greed and making clear what the face of class warfare really looks like as it is being conducted by financial elites and their allies against the American public and the very nature of democracy itself. Rather than limit their protests to a single issue, the protesters came together to condemn mass injustices stemming from an economic system that elevates "profits over people, self-interest over justice, and oppression over equality."[29]

The Occupy Wall Street movement confirmed and continues to show how equality and justice need to be reclaimed as crucial political categories and discursive tools to be used by all of those groups—including workers, young people, people of color, women, and the elderly—for understanding the injustices being waged in such a ruthless fashion against young people and other members of a declining and decaying social order. The inequities reproduced through class warfare in the name of economic progress must be taken seriously by social movements that are struggling to ensure that Americans have a future in which democracy is central rather than marginal to their lives. We caught a glimpse of the potential for resistance in the Occupy Wall Street protests in New York and other cities across the United States because they made visible what has been too often rendered invisible—how material and ideological relations can be structured to promote not only antidemocratic tendencies but a culture of deceit, cruelty, and barbarism.

There is no question that Occupy Wall Street is waging a class struggle precisely because the deeply structured ideologies, modes of governance, and policies that reinforce class differences for the benefit of the rich and privileged have destroyed America's claim to even the weakest notion of democracy. Corporations along with the rich have done more than create the current economic apocalypse with its pervasive joblessness; they have also created economic, political, and social conditions in which the ravages of precariousness, uncertainty, and insecurity are all-consuming and will haunt and disempower existing generations for a lifetime. The class warfare of the second Gilded Age has reduced most social relations to survival status—time spent largely on trying to maintain the minimal conditions to stay alive. The Occupy movement in part has combined civil disobedience with political disobedience as part of a broader effort to create open spaces for dialogue, communities of mutual support, and new modes of solidarity capable of weathering the increasing violence waged by a state that can no longer defend its power or legitimate its ruling ideologies. The claim that the rich are the victims of class warfare echoes the response of an intellectually and morally bankrupt regime.

As the Occupy movement demonstrated, class remains a powerful category for understanding society, politics, history, and justice. Class as a category and mode of politics should matter to everyone because it makes visible power relations that are often hidden from public view and removed from official accounts, particularly those recently rewritten by the Paul Ryans of the world. Any viable notion of politics needs to affirm the reality of class struggle as a means of power and use it as a category for reinvigorating democratic struggles with a renewed sense of urgency. In part, this means making class politics part of a broader struggle committed to the development of wider social movements and substantive political transformations in the interests of human solidarity, equality, and freedom. The Occupy Wall Street protests represented only the beginning of such a movement, one in which the future becomes alive with a new understanding of justice, equality, and freedom and a willingness to fight for the promises of a radical democracy. Alongside the Tahrir Square uprisings; the Arab Spring; and the student revolts taking place in Montreal, Athens, London, Paris, and other cities around the globe, the Occupy movement has hopefully ignited the passion and promise of youth in the United States, encouraging young people to act in the interest of building a far more just and sustainable future than the one presented to them by the market-driven imperatives of casino capitalism. This struggle is in its early stages, and as Dan Bensaid has rightly argued, it must arm itself with a "slow impatience," one that enables it to develop a collaboration of forces into a broad-based social movement that can imagine and experiment with alternative modes of education, political formations, and economic organizations.[30]

The Occupy movement needs to create strategies that address the stark concentration of wealth in the United States and the monopolization of power by the privileged few while it begins to theorize what a truly participatory democracy would look like. This demands more than short-term tactics, street theater, or hit-and-run demonstrations. What is needed are viable democratic enclaves and organizations willing to make the long march through the institutions that have a commanding hold on politics, power, and people's lives. The first step in implementing a radical democracy is recognizing that institutions are open to change; that education is central to producing engaged and critical citizens; and that new alliances must be formed between the generations, labor and youth, intellectuals and artists, parents and educators, and so on. Under such conditions, class struggle is far from a dangerous practice. On the contrary, it becomes a minimal condition for experiencing real freedom, autonomy, and justice.

◇

CHAPTER 7

Against American-Style
Authoritarianism

The Occupy Movement and the Promise of Youth

Not everything that is faced can be changed, but nothing can be changed until it is faced.

—*James Baldwin*

For two electrifying months beginning on September 17, 2011, thousands of people—most of them under thirty years of age—organized peaceful occupations across the United States and worldwide to protest corporate corruption, social and economic inequality, savage cutbacks to social programs, rising student debt, unemployment, and a range of negative impacts linked to the ascendancy of neoliberal capitalism. The Occupy protests in the United States brought together young people and enabled them to delineate for many Americans the contours, values, sensibilities, and hidden politics of a neoliberal mode of authoritarianism that now shapes both the commanding institutions of power in the United States and the everyday relations of the 99 percent, who are increasingly viewed as excess; disposable; and unworthy of living a life of dignity, shared responsibility, and hope.

This task of delineation is never easy: the conditions of domination are layered, complex, and deeply flexible. Yet, it should now be evident to all Americans that young people bear a significant portion of the burden of a multi-trillion-dollar deficit, disappearing social safety nets, stagnant job growth, and decrepit educational institutions at all levels while the current leadership of the United States maintains a collision course headed relentlessly toward the destruction of future generations. It is no longer hyperbolic to suggest that the war effort that once focused on American imperial ambitions abroad has come full circle—and its primary target on the domestic front are youths, especially the most vulnerable.

Challenging an unfettered capitalism that seeks to infiltrate and control all political, economic, and social institutions became the central tenet of the Occupy protesters, who argued that such institutions no longer serve the educational, intellectual, economic, and social interests of a vast majority of Americans. Bearing witness to the human suffering caused by the alliance of the corporate state, corrupt Wall Street financiers, and a political leadership that elevates private interest above the public good, protesting youths changed the rules of the game: they invented a different language and vision of politics than the ones being embraced by corporate elites and those who vie for political leadership in the United States. They are also attempting to create a vast network of communities of mutual support and dialogue that are central to any viable notion of agency, resistance, and collective struggle.

The spirit of action that informs the Occupy movement is not about providing recipes or tossing around facile slogans—it is about using new pedagogical tools, practices, and social relations to educate the rest of the American public about the dangers of casino capitalism as a new form of authoritarianism. The effort represents what the philosopher Bernard E. Harcourt has called a social movement in search of a new form of politics, one that not only rejects the inadequacy of existing laws and institutions but also offers resistance "to the very way in which we are governed: it resists the structure of partisan politics, the demand for policy reforms, the call for party identification, and the very ideologies that dominated the post-war period."[1] Rejecting the limited language of reform, the Occupy protesters have challenged the popular myth that the United States is a representative democracy. In doing so, they have drawn attention not only to the vast inequality in wealth and power that belies any notion of democratic governance but also to the fact that most decisions in the United States are now made by the financial, military, and corporate elite. Similarly, the protesters have drawn the public's attention to the various forms of cruelty imposed by the corporate state and encouraged people to link their everyday suffering to an understanding and critique of broader social and economic forces. They made visible the frontal assault being waged by casino capitalism against women's reproductive rights, workers' protections, students, economic justice, immigrants, unions, economic rights, public servants, democratic public spheres, the notion of the common good, and human dignity itself—an assault that constitutes not only an attack on modes of democratic governance and sovereignty but also an alarming act of barbarism against existing and future generations of young people.

Meanwhile, the absurd response of the politicians who have consistently refused to fund job programs for young people—now facing record unemployment while financial aid for higher education is simultaneously slashed—involved taunting the Occupiers to take showers and find work. But this backlash against democratic expression rang hollow, contrasting with the many ways in which the protesters struggled to establish their claims through sophisticated analyses and meaningful engagement with broad public issues. The protesters articulated and embodied the desire for new forms of collective struggle and modes of solidarity built around social and shared, rather than individualized and competitive, values. Having "occupied" the terrain of public discourse, the peaceful protests elicited a violent reaction from the corporate state that made all the more visible the power of antidemocratic forces backing the current leadership in the United States.

As young people were forcibly moved by authorities out of their makeshift tent cities in Zuccotti Park and other public spaces, the potential for the corporate state—increasingly loosened from any kind of public accountability—to transform itself into a rogue punishing state was writ large on the bodies and spaces of the protesters. The police crackdown that took place in streets, parks, and university campuses bordered on pure thuggery, revealing the willingness of those in power to use measures whose violence extends even beyond what Glenn Greenwald calls "excessive police force."[2] Resorting to physical violence against the Occupiers, though utterly shameful in a country that calls itself a democracy, indicated beyond a shadow of a doubt how the corporate state could no longer fight with ideas because its visions, ideologies, and survival-of-the-fittest ethic had been exposed as bankrupt, fast losing any semblance of legitimacy among the broader public, especially young people.

In an irony that invariably escaped the notice of the dominant media, it was the peaceful protesters who were criminalized and subjected to the ruthless dictates of the punishing state, not the Wall Street executives and bankers who had engaged in various forms of financial fraud, causing savage and ruinous injury to many Americans, and who continue to roam free and unscathed by the criminal justice system. When students organized on the campuses of the University of California at Berkeley and Davis to challenge corporatization and its objectionable impacts on higher education, they directly experienced being arrested, pepper-sprayed at point-blank range, and assaulted by baton-wielding police—or bore witness to their friends and peers undergoing such assaults. These student protesters were beaten on their campuses for simply displaying the courage to protest a system that has robbed them of both a quality education and a viable future. As campus security used violence with impunity, it became clear that even those sites designed for the intellectual growth and well-being of young people—universities and colleges—were now being managed by individuals willing to abdicate the responsibilities and public mission of higher education.

Universities and colleges are places that are identified with young people and should register the larger society's obligation to provide them with a well-rounded education and secure their future. Increasingly, however, such institutions are joining the assault on young people's minds and bodies, one that has been perpetrated for decades by the state against generations of poor minority youths. Such youths have either been subjected to penal forms of schooling that borrow tactics from prisons or been ushered directly into juvenile detention facilities that form part of a growing youth crime-control system in the United States.[3] Misplaced priorities as a result of which the state and federal governments are investing more in building prisons than in supporting education means, as Juan Cole points out, "that students are being hit with massive tuition increases to pay for the penitentiaries and their policing, they are also being treated like unruly inmates by a militarizing police force."[4] Market fundamentalism has little regard for either youths or ethical values, and the overinvestment in militarizing universities is a stark reminder of how the war on youth in the United States has taken a dark turn. One indication of the growing militarization of the university is that "since 2000, universities have seen defense-related research contracts increase 900 percent, from $4.4 billion in 2000 to $46.7 billion in 2006."[5] The simultaneous eclipse of affordable university education and the militarization of all aspects of social life, including publicly funded universities, have created a resurgence of anger and political enthusiasm among youths who are struggling against the increasing merger of economic, corporate, and political power. In solidarity with other youths around the world, the Occupy movement across America represents a promising symbol of hope for change, rejecting both the violent militarization inflicted by authoritarian states and the banal fantasies of consumption offered by corporate capitalism. The way in which the young Occupiers are responding to the neoliberal distortion of public values is informative, particularly as the movement evolves to engage new ideas and spaces of public concern by utilizing diverse modes of pedagogical address.

These youths have become the new public intellectuals of the twenty-first century, using their bodies, social media, digital technologies, and other educational tools to raise new questions, point to new possibilities, and register their criticisms of the antidemocratic elements of casino capitalism and the punishing state. While Americans watched a movement emerge in 2011 as a vibrant collective in the streets, it is now equally imperative that attention be given to how student protesters across the United States continue to organize on college campuses, linking the deteriorating conditions in broader society being addressed by the general Occupy movement to aspects of a bankrupt educational system that once promised them a viable future.

Occupy Higher Education

As protesters occupy colleges and universities, they have used the power of ideas to engage other students, faculty, and anyone else who will listen to them. The call went out from the University of California at Berkeley, Harvard University, Florida

State University, Duke University, Rhode Island College, and over 120 other universities that the time has come to connect not only knowledge to powers of oppression but the power of resistance to knowledge—to the very meaning of what it means to be an engaged intellectual responsive to the possibilities of individual and collective resistance and broad social change. This poses a new challenge for the brave students mobilizing these protests on college campuses, and also for faculty members who too often justify their retreat from public life with the secure and comfortable claim that scholarship should be disinterested, objective, and removed from politics. There is much these students and young people can learn from the conformity of intellectuals within the academy, legitimated by the so-called professionalism of disinterested knowledge and the disinterested intellectual.

Students are starting to recognize that it is crucial to struggle for the university as a democratic public sphere, one of the few left in which it remains possible to educate a generation of new students, faculty, and others about the history of race, racism, politics, identity, power, the state, and the struggle for justice. They are increasingly willing to argue in theoretically insightful and profound ways about what it means to defend the university as a site that opens up and sustains public connections through which people's fragmented, uncertain, incomplete narratives of agency are valued, preserved, and made available for exchange while being related, analytically, to wider contexts of politics and power. The protesters reject the current ubiquitous belief that college either has become irrelevant or largely functions to indoctrinate "the young with left-wing dogmas."[6] Instead, they are moving to reclaim higher education as a site of struggle and the humanities as a sphere that is crucial for grounding ethics, justice, and morality across existing disciplinary terrains. And they are raising both a sense of urgency and a set of relevant questions about what kind of education would be suited to the twenty-first-century university and its global arrangements as part of a larger project of addressing the most urgent issues facing societies in a globalized world.

In the United States and many other countries, neoliberalism is waging a savage battle to eliminate all of those public spheres that might offer a glimmer of critical thought and any viable form of opposition to market-driven policies, institutions, ideology, and values. Public spaces such as libraries are detached from the language of public discourse and viewed increasingly as a waste of taxpayers' money. Almost all commanding cultural apparatuses from the media to schools are now subject to the dictates of a consumer culture, which serves to flatten critical thought and trivialize important ideas. The march to illiteracy is also evident in a highly influential and toxic celebrity culture that spreads its idiocy throughout society, infantilizing everything with which it comes in contact. Similarly, over the past thirty years, neoliberal and neoconservative policies have supported an all-out attack against the social state, gutting the social contract and weakening public resistance through a decades-long public campaign against government regulation, social justice, and collective organization. They have used corporate media culture as a powerful pedagogical tool to cultivate neoliberal subjects who believe in a hyperindividualized form of "common sense" that not only denies people access to the power relations that govern society but also destroys the very concept of the social.

Margaret Thatcher's infamous quip that "there is no such thing as society" has become the new normal among conservative politicians, intellectuals, and right-wing think tanks. The democratic ideal that society is "a set of mutual benefits and duties embodied most visibly in public institutions—public schools, public libraries, public transportation, public hospitals, public parks, public museums, public recreation, public universities, and so on" has become an object of disdain and scorn among the growing army of neoliberal warriors and survival-of-the-fittest advocates of market fundamentalism.[7] Welfare no longer means providing a safety net for the poor but assisting unchecked entitlement as a federal resource for big banks, investment houses, hedge funds, and larger corporations. Anything public such as schools, transit systems, parks, playgrounds, bridges, and hospitals is now viewed as a site to defund and eventually privatize, offering the wealthy new opportunities for making a profit off the public good.

But more than public goods are being privatized. As language and politics become privatized, private troubles are removed from social considerations, and the only unit of analysis through which to gauge the workings of power, ideology, and knowledge is the notion of individual responsibility and character. Stripped of the ability to translate private troubles into public issues, public discourse loses its understanding of the complex interplay of larger social forces and individual agency. Politics in this view is atomized, and society becomes either an object of scorn or an empty concept. Instead of a society, we have a collection of competitive nomads. Instead of the public commons, we have gated communities and the prison-industrial complex. Instead of the demands of citizenship, we have the slavish adoration of consumerism and the stripped-down rationality of an all-embracing, market-driven ethos. Prosperity has been privatized only to be shared by the few, just as misery has been expanded as a defining characteristic of the larger polity and public life in general.

In the midst of this onslaught, whatever public goods exist are generally reserved for the rich, signaling that young people are no longer regarded as an important social investment or as a marker for the state of democracy and the moral life of the nation. Youths have become—along with the educational institutions that purport to serve them—the objects of a direct and damaging assault on a number of political, economic, and cultural fronts. Public and higher education, in particular, are being targeted by right-wing politicians and governments because they embody, at least ideally, spheres in which students learn that democracy entails ruptures; relentless critique; and dialogue about official power, its institutions, and its never-ending attempts to silence dissent.[8]

Higher education in this so-called age of austerity has been one of the most significant spheres to bear the brunt of systematic downsizing and budget reallocations of government-sponsored programs and public institutions. The draconian policies implemented under the call for austerity are designed to shift the burden of and responsibility for the recession from the rich to the most vulnerable elements of society—the elderly, workers, lower-income people, and students. Universities and colleges have responded to cutbacks in state funding by squeezing liberal arts programs and increasing student tuition fees in order to offset the financial burdens they are forced to assume. Simultaneously, banks and loan corporations with their army of lobbyists appear to have declared war on students, killing any legislation that would reduce the cost of schooling and stifling any policy that would make education affordable for all working- and middle-class students. The logic of market models increasingly shapes higher education by articulating its value in terms of private benefits to individuals and the economy rather than viewing it as essential to a formative culture that produces engaged and informed citizens.[9] University campuses are increasingly designed to resemble shopping malls, selling space to corporate advertisers, as students are largely reduced to passive consumers entertained by the spectacles of big sports, mass consumption, and celebrity culture.

Many universities have become complicit with the ideologies and money now used to promote the interests of finance capital and agencies such as the CIA, Department of Defense, Pentagon, private security firms, and other apparatuses of the national security state intent on recruiting students to produce militarized knowledge and create new and ever more sophisticated surveillance systems and weapons of mass destruction.[10] As universities adopt models of corporate governance and solicit military funding, they are aggressively eliminating tenure positions, increasing part-time and full-time positions without the guarantee of tenure, and attacking faculty unions. Not only does the corporatized/militarized academy commodify and militarize knowledge and research, it rarely tolerates dissent and views tenure as an obstacle to controlling the views and power of faculty. Currently, only 27 percent of faculty in the United States are either on a tenure track or in a full-time tenured position. In a number of states such as Ohio and Utah, legislatures have passed bills outlawing tenure, and in Wisconsin the governor has abrogated the bargaining rights of state university faculty.[11]

With the ranks of tenure-track faculty being drastically depleted and replaced by a contingent workforce whose basic rights are also under attack, faculty are removed as stakeholders and voices in institutional governance. They lose their power to influence the conditions of their work; they see their workload increase and the quality of education provided to students deteriorate; they are paid poorly, deprived of office space and supplies, and refused travel money; and, most significantly, they are subjected to policies that allow them to be fired at will.[12] The dismantling of the institutional guarantees that have historically enabled academic freedom is particularly egregious because, when such instability is coupled with an ongoing series of attacks by right-wing ideologues against left-oriented and progressive academics, many faculty members begin to censor themselves in their classes.[13] These measures suggest that the notion of the university as a center of critique and a vital democratic public sphere that cultivates the knowledge, skills, and values necessary for the production of a democratic polity is giving way to a view of the university as a marketing machine beholden to the demand for credentials, meeting the needs of the economy, and providing jobs for students.

Many students view these policies and their evident support of market logic, corporate power, and for-profit industries as not just an assault on the public character of the university but also an attack on civic society and their future. They express deep resentment as they become aware of how conservative politicians defund higher education and cut public spending in order to be able to support tax breaks for corporations and the rich and to allocate funds for sustaining and expanding the warfare state. They recognize that the university has become part of a Ponzi scheme designed to force students to carry an unconscionable amount of debt while subjecting them to the power of commanding financial institutions for years after they graduate. Under this economic model of subservience, there is no future for young people. There is no time to talk about advancing social justice, addressing social problems, promoting critical thinking, cultivating social responsibility, or engaging noncommodified values that might challenge the neoliberal world view. As Zygmunt Bauman points out, in a consumerist society, "the tyranny of the moment makes it difficult to live in the present, never mind understand society within a range of larger totalities."[14] Students can see how the university is losing ground as a place to think in complex ways and develop a culture of questioning, dialogue, and civic enlightenment. In response to this growing instrumentalization of thought and accompanying hostility to critical and oppositional ideas within the university, young people are not only engaging in a great refusal but rethinking what should be the role of the university in a world caught in a nightmarish blend of war, massive economic inequities, and ecological destruction. To paraphrase William Greider, young people in Paris, Athens, Montreal, and New York City have recognized in collective fashion that higher education has increasingly come to resemble "an ecological dead zone" where social relevance and engaged scholarship perish in a polluted, commercialized, market-driven environment.

What is important about the Occupy protesters' criticism of being straddled with onerous debt, viewed as a suspect generation, and subjected to the demands of an audit culture that confuses training with critical education is that such concerns situate the attack on higher education as part of a broader criticism against the withering away of the public realm, public values, and any viable notion of the public good. Many universities have lost touch with bridging the production of knowledge, research, and teaching with the myriad social issues now facing the larger society, including crushing poverty, environmental degradation, racism, the suspension of civil liberties, the colonization of the media by corporations, the rise of the punishing state, religious fanaticism, the corruption of politics by big money, and more. But students are making these connections. Central to their inquiry is examining how higher education has been caught in the grip of larger economic and political forces that undermine the social state, social provisions, and democracy itself. The students have refused either to narrow their focus to the specific interests of the group to which they belong or to justify their arguments in terms of the individual benefits derived from quality education. They have instead demanded the university's full participation in a community of the broadest possible resistance.

Student protesters recognize that higher education, even in its imperfect state, still holds the promise of being able to offer them the complex knowledge and interdisciplinary skills that enable existing and future generations to break the continuity of the status quo. The promise of such an ideal allows them to come to terms with their own power as critical agents, be critical of the authority that speaks to them, translate private considerations into public issues, and assume the responsibility of both being governed and learning how to govern. Inhabiting the role of public intellectuals, students take on the difficult but urgent task of reclaiming the ideals and practices associated with higher education as a site of possibility. When joined to democratic ideals, the students' critiques expand the way democracy is conceived beyond simply a mode of governance toward, as Bill Moyers points out, a means of dignifying people so they can become fully free to claim their moral and political agency. As students and faculty increasingly use the space of the university as a megaphone for a new kind of critical education and politics, they will hopefully reclaim the democratic function of higher education and demonstrate what it means for students, faculty, and others to assume the role of public intellectuals dedicated to creating a formative culture that can provide all people with the knowledge and skills necessary for a radical democracy.

Young People as the New Public Intellectuals

In order to find their way to a more humane future, young people demand a new politics, a new set of values, and a renewed sense of the fragile nature of democracy. A new generation appears poised not only to reclaim democratic public spheres as its collective entitlement but also to frame its own agency as a generation of public intellectuals willing to connect their knowledge, work, research, teaching, and service with broader democratic concerns over equality, justice, and a vision of what society in the future might become. Fighting not merely for a space to survive but also for a society in which matters of dignity and freedom are objects of collective struggle, the Occupy protesters have created a new stage on which young people once again are defining what John Pilger calls the "theater of the possible."[15] Signaling a generational and political crisis that is global in scope, young people have sent a message to the world that they refuse to live any longer under repressive authoritarian regimes sustained by morally bankrupt, market-driven policies. The Occupy movement is about what kind of society we all want to live in, and the current historical moment demands that we all take that question seriously and act as quickly as possible to answer it with passion and conviction.

The Occupy protesters reject the propaganda they have been fed relentlessly by a market-driven culture: the notion that markets should take priority over governments, market values are the best means for ordering society and satisfying human needs, material interests are more important than social needs, and self-interest is the driving force of freedom and the organizing principle of society. They are arguing that although they might support a limited version of a market economy, they do not want to live in a market society—a society in which market values become the template for remedying all social ills. Young people are now challenging the toxic form of casino capitalism penetrating all aspects of social life, and in doing so they are shifting a national conversation that has focused on deficit reduction and taxing the poor toward important issues that range from poverty and joblessness to corporate corruption. Put differently, the Occupy protesters are asking big questions, and they are not simply being moralistic when they do so—in fact, they are creating as well as demanding an alternative vision and set of policies to guide American society.

The Occupy protesters refuse a society that can conceive of agency only in the narrowest of instrumentalist terms, one that views people as commodities bound together in a Darwinian nightmare that celebrates the logic of greed, unchecked individualism, and a disdain for democratic values. They have learned the hard way that beneath this market fundamentalism resides a mode of education and set of values that contain a secret order of politics terribly destructive of democratic social relations, democratic modes of equality, and civic education itself. The old idea of democracy in which the few govern the many through the power of capital and ritualized elections is being replaced with a new understanding of democracy and politics in which power and resources are shared and economic justice and democratic values work in the interest of social responsibility and the common good. This radical notion of democracy is in the making, unfinished and open to connecting people, power, resources, and knowledge.

The figure of the young protester as a public intellectual merges theoretical rigor with civic courage, meaning with the struggle for eliminating injustice wherever it occurs, and hope with a realistic notion of social change. Knowledge is understood to be a crucial instrument of change, while the language of a radical politics does more than articulate hope and outrage: it spurs collective action and demands habitable spaces in order to produce ideas, values, and social relations capable of fighting off those ideological and material forces of casino capitalism that are intent on sabotaging any viable notion of human interaction, community, solidarity, friendship, and justice. Under the present circumstances, once again, it is time to remind ourselves that the university may be one of the few public spheres left that can provide the educational conditions for students, faculty, administrators, and community members to occupy a space of dialogue and unmitigated questioning, imagine different futures, become border-crossers, engage in coalition-building, and develop a language of critique and possibility that makes visible the urgency of a politics necessary to address important social issues and contribute to the quality of public life and the common good.

University educators need to listen to young people in order to try to understand the problems they face and how as academics they might be unknowingly complicit in reproducing such problems. The questions students are raising are important for faculty to rethink those market-based modes of professionalism and social relations that have cut universities off from addressing important social issues and the larger society. Faculty members also need to begin a genuine conversation with students and other academics about how they can become a force for democratic change. Students have more to offer than a serious critique of the university and its complicity with a number of antidemocratic forces now shaping the larger society, for they are also modeling for faculty new modes of participatory democracy and exhibiting forms of pedagogy and education that connect learning with social change and knowledge with more democratic modes of self-development and social empowerment. Clearly, academics have a lot to learn from the ways in which students are changing the conversation about education, important social issues, democracy, and what it might mean to imagine a new understanding of politics and a different future.

The Occupy movements should continue their appropriation of public space within the university. If higher education's public mission is not to be smothered by a reductive corporate logic and technocratic rationality unable to differentiate training from a critical education, we need a chorus of new voices to emphasize how the university should play a central role in keeping critical engagement, civic courage, and a spirit of thoughtfulness alive. There is an urgent need to connect the university with visions that have some hold on the present, defending education as more than an investment opportunity or job credential, students as more than customers, and faculty as more than technicians or a subaltern army of casualized labor. Faculty on a global scale need to join with young people to fight alongside them for a better future, using their knowledge and skills to convince a wider public that quality higher education benefits not only the students but the common good and the entire society.

Together, an emerging global citizenry must challenge the further unraveling of human possibilities, prodding human society to go on questioning itself and prevent that questioning from ever stalling or being declared finished. Corporations and the warfare state should not dictate the needs of public and higher education, or, for that matter, any other democratic public sphere. As the Occupy movement has pointed out, one of the great dangers facing the twenty-first century is not the risk of illusory hopes but those undemocratic forces that destroy imagination and ethical consciousness—powerful forces that promote and protect state terrorism and massive inequality, render some populations utterly disposable, and imagine the future only in terms of immediate financial gains. These forces stock their arsenal with self-serving historical reinventions in which power is measured by the degree to which it evades any sense of actual truth and moral responsibility. Youths today, like their counterparts in the 1960s, are demanding an affordable and high-quality education, a decent job that provides a living wage, and a voice in the shaping of the institutions that bear down heavily on their daily lives. In doing so, they have defied a social order that offers them only a meager life stripped of self-determination and dignity.

What is different about this generation of young people from past generations is that today's youths have been immersed since birth in a relentless, spreading neoliberal pedagogical apparatus with its celebration of an unbridled individualism and its near pathological disdain for community, public values, and the public good. They have been inundated by a market-driven value system that encourages a culture of competitiveness and produces a theater of cruelty resulting in what Bauman calls "a weakening of democratic pressures, a growing inability to act politically, [and] a massive exit from politics and from responsible citizenship."[16] Moreover, they have come alive in a historical conjuncture in which all guarantees about inheriting a secure future have been thrown to the wind. This generation is more than a generation of suspects; it is a generation without a future, a generation for whom educational, economic, social, and political rights have disappeared. Society no longer makes any claims in the name of the social or collective insurance policies for future generations, nor does it produce jobs that provide satisfying work and a decent wage. This generation has inherited "an abyss of failed sociality" in which the suffering and despair of young people arouse little public concern.[17] Bauman has deftly argued that what sets this generation apart from its predecessors is its precariousness. The society young people are struggling to enter no longer offers them safe and reliable jobs. He writes,

> One way or another, members of Generation Y differ from their predecessors by a complete or almost complete absence of job-related illusions, by a lukewarm only (if any) commitment to the jobs currently held and the companies which offer them, and a firm conviction that life is elsewhere and resolution (or at least a desire) to live it elsewhere. This is indeed an attitude seldom to be found among the members of the "boom" and "X" generations.[18]

Debt, joblessness, insecurity, and hopelessness are the defining features of a generation that has been abandoned by its market-obsessed, turn-a-quick-profit elders. As Bauman points out, in a world in which credit has collapsed, visions disappear, and zones of social abandonment proliferate, the new generations of "precarians are defined by having their homes erected (complete with bedrooms and kitchens) on quicksand, and by their own self-confessed ignorance ('no idea what is going to hit me') and impotence ('even if I knew, I wouldn't have the power to divert the blow')."[19] While the despair is widespread, it has not been matched by a cynicism capable of undermining a global sense of outrage and resistance.

Increasingly, as is evident all over the world, young people, students, and other members of the 99 percent are refusing to endure the great injustices they see around them, including the wars in Afghanistan and Iraq, the corruption of American politics by casino capitalism, a permanent war economy, and the growing disinvestment in public and higher education. They have refused to allow a deadening apparatus of force, manufactured ignorance, and ideological domination to shape their lives. Reclaiming the possibilities inherent in the political use of both new digital technologies and social media, American youths have protested in large numbers the ongoing intense attack on higher education and the welfare state, rejecting a social order shaped by the demands of casino capitalism. Similarly, thousands of students are mobilizing in Quebec against a right-wing government that wants to defund higher education while at the same time raising tuition. In this instance, the government response to the Quebec resistance movement has been not only an increase in force used by the police but also the passage of Bill 78, which is a draconian measure designed to impose severe restrictions and fines on protests, forcing those who demonstrate to seek permission and secure permits from the police in order to do so. In other words, it becomes illegal for the students to protest without giving the police eight hours' notice and securing a permit. What is unique about the Quebec resistance movement and offers a promising strategy for Occupy protesters in the United States is that it has expanded into a much wider movement protesting not only Bill 78 but also "Quebec's call for higher fees for health care, the firing of public sector employees, the closure of factories, the corporate exploitation of natural resources, new restrictions on union organizing, and an announced increase in the retirement age."[20]

The Occupy protesters, like their counterparts in London, Montreal, Athens, Paris, and elsewhere, have made clear that casino capitalism not only reproduces political corruption and economic fraud on a massive scale but also perpetuates the destruction of any semblance of critical thinking and agency along with undermining any viable attempt of democracy to deliver on its promises. The collective uproar we have witnessed among young people and others was in part an attempt to expose how violence works when neoliberal capitalism reigns unchecked. It was an attempt to make dominant power accountable, doing so through new forms of solidarity that have been often marginalized, fractured, pathologized, or punished. In fact; within a very short time, the Occupy protesters reclaimed former public spaces and built new public spaces while confronting a brutalizing police apparatus with their bodies and refusing to put up with the right-wing notion that they are part of what is often called a "failed generation."

Although most Occupy sites were within a matter of weeks dismantled by police—the Wall Street protest site having been raided by New York City police on November 15, 2011—the

protesters made clear that physical space is not the only re-
quirement for dissent.[21] Space, in fact, will become indispensable only when its democratic functions and uses are restored,
and to do this we need to develop a new language and invent
a common culture that can sustain an open dialogue within
those spaces. Politics and ideology are the essence of what the
Occupy movement is about, and activism in various forms has
been generated or has acquired new vitality as a result of the
2011 occupations. Truly remarkable about the Occupy movement has been its consistent emphasis on connecting learning
to social change and its willingness to do so through new and
collective modes of education.

The expectations that frame market-driven societies are
losing their grip on young people and others, who refuse to be
seduced or controlled by the tawdry promises and failed re-
turns of corporate-dominated regimes. The Occupy movement
has demonstrated that the social visions embedded in casino
capitalism have lost both their utopian thrust and their ability
to persuade and intimidate through manufactured consent,
threats, coercion, and state violence. Young people have become, at least for the moment, harbingers of democracy fash-
ioned through the desires, dreams, and hopes of a world based
on the principles of equality, justice, and freedom. One of the
most famous slogans of May 1968 was "Be realistic; demand
the impossible." The spirit of that slogan is alive once again.
But what is different this time is that it appears to be more than
a slogan: it now echoes throughout the United States and in
other countries as both a discourse of critique and a vocabulary
of possibility and long-term collective struggle.

The Occupy movement makes clear that it is not—indeed,
cannot be—only a short-term project for reform but is instead
a political and moral movement that needs to intensify, accompanied by the reclaiming of public spaces; the use of digital
technologies; the development of public spheres and new modes
of education; and the safeguarding of places where democratic
expression, new identities, and collective hope can be nurtured
and mobilized. At the same time, there are some crucial short-
term demands that are worth pursuing, such as ending student
debt, initiating funding programs to eradicate the scourge of
poverty affecting 22 percent of American children, developing
much-needed infrastructure, offering mortgage relief for the 50

million living with the "nightmare of foreclosures,"[22] increasing taxes on the wealthy and corporations, and putting into place a public works program for the 25 million unable to find jobs. These calls for change represent only a handful of the policy reforms that will surely continue to be articulated as part of a larger strategy of long-term structural change and social transformation.

It is important to recognize that what young people and many others are now doing is making a claim for a democratically informed politics that embraces the public good, economic justice, and social responsibility. Indeed, it is encouraging that the Occupy movement views its very existence and collective identity as part of a larger struggle for the economic, political, and social conditions that give meaning and substance to what it means to make democracy possible. Central to this struggle is the need to affirm the social in governing while defining freedom not simply through the pursuit of individual needs and the affirmation of self-interest but also as part of a social contract that couples individual and political rights with social rights. Political and individual freedoms are meaningless unless people are free from hunger, poverty, needless suffering, and other material deprivations that undercut any viable possibility of dignity, agency, and justice. In other words, the capacity for individual and political freedom has to take a detour through the social, which provides the economic foundation, public infrastructure, and social supports for making private joys possible and individual dreams realizable. As Bauman points out, political rights lose their viability without social rights:

> Little or no prospect of rescue from individual indolence or impotence can be expected to arrive from a political state that is not, and refuses to be, a *social* state. Without social rights *for all*, a large and in all probability growing number of people will find their political rights of little use and unworthy of their attention. *If political rights are necessary to set social rights in place, social rights are indispensable to make political rights "real" and keep them in operation.* The two rights need each other for their survival; that survival can only be their *joint* achievement.[23]

The Occupy protests—recognizing that social justice and shared responsibilities must be the basis for any real understanding of freedom—have positioned themselves against the forms of social death promoted by a casino capitalism that seeks to replace important elements of a democratic polity with a culture of violence that would turn democracy into a pathology and informed appeals to morality and justice into cruel jokes.

At one point in time, as Fredric Jameson suggested, it may have been easier to imagine the end of the world than the end of capitalism, but this no longer seems true. The cracks in the capitalist edifice of greed and unchecked power have finally split open. While there is no guarantee that new modes of social transformation will manifest, there is a vibrant collective energy on the horizon that at least makes such a possibility imaginable once again. In an age when corporate media often become only a means of mass distraction and entertainment, we are seeing youths reclaim traditional sites of engagement and develop new ones of their own—as physical and virtual spaces where theory and action inform each other and intellectual and creative activities are not divorced from matters of politics, social responsibility, and justice. In response, we must join with these youths in taking up the challenge of developing a politics and a pedagogy that can serve and actualize a democratic notion of the social—that is, we must develop and collectively organize for a politics whose hope lies in defending the shared values, spaces, and public spheres that enable an emergent radical democracy.

It is increasingly imperative for intellectuals, educators, social workers, organized labor, artists, and other cultural workers to collaborate with young people in order to put the question of social and economic rights on the political agenda. In this way, the Occupy movement will connect to the larger world through a conversation that links particular concerns with broader notions of freedom and justice. Against the pedagogical machine and political forces of casino capitalism, an expanding Occupy movement will hopefully energize a collective resistance—determined in its mission to expand the capacities to think otherwise; courageous in its attempts to take risks; brave in its willingness to change the nature of the questions asked; dedicated to its role of holding power accountable; and thoughtful in its efforts to provide the formative culture for young people and everyone else to struggle for those economic, political, social, and cultural conditions that are essential both to their future and to democracy itself.

◇

Notes

Notes for Introduction

1. Clearly, there are many reasons for the various youthful protests across the globe, ranging from the murder of young people and anger against financial corruption to the riots against cuts to social benefits and the rise of educational costs.

2. Christopher McMichael, "The Shock-and-Awe of Mega Sports Events," *OpenDemocracy* (January 30, 2012), online at: http://www.opendemocracy.net/christopher-mcmichael/shock-and-awe-of-mega-sports-events.

3. Zygmunt Bauman, *Wasted Lives* (London: Polity, 2004), p. 76.

4. See Loic Wacquant, *Punishing the Poor: The Neoliberal Government of Social Insecurity* (Durham, NC: Duke University Press, 2009).

5. Amanda Peterson Beadle, "Obama Administration Ends Medicaid Funding for Texas Women's Health Program," *ThinkProgress* (March 16, 2012), online at: http://thinkprogress.org/health/2012/03/16/445894/funding-cut-for-texas-womens-health-program.

6. Maureen Dowd, "Don't Tread on Us," *New York Times* (March 14, 2012), p. A25.

7. See, for example, Daisy Grewal, "How Wealth Reduces Compassion: As Riches Grow, Empathy for Others Seems to Decline," *Scientific American* (Tuesday, April 10, 2012), online at: http://www.scientificamerican.com/article.cfm?id=how-wealth-reduces-compassion&print=true.

8. Azam Ahmed, "The Hunch, the Pounce and the Kill: How Boaz Weinstein and Hedge Funds Outsmarted JPMorgan," *New York Times* (May 27, 2012), p. BU1.

9. Anne-Marie Cusac, *Cruel and Unusual: The Culture of Punishment in America* (New Haven, CT: Yale University Press, 2009), p. 3.

10. David Harvey, *A Brief History of Neoliberalism* (New York: Oxford University Press, 2007), p. 19.

11. Stuart Hall, "The Neo-Liberal Revolution," *Cultural Studies* 25:6 (November 2011): 706.

12. Ibid.

13. Wendy Brown, *Regulating Aversion* (Princeton, NJ: Princeton University Press, 2008), p. 16.

14. Pascale-Anne Brault and Michael Naas, "Translators' Note," in Jean-Luc Nancy, *The Truth of Democracy* (New York: Fordham University Press, 2010), p. ix.

15. Jean-Marie Durand, "For Youth: A Disciplinary Discourse Only," *TruthOut* (November 15, 2009), trans. Leslie Thatcher, online at: http://www.truthout.org/11190911.

16. David Theo Goldberg, *The Threat of Race: Reflections on Racial Neoliberalism* (Malden, MA: Wiley-Blackwell, 2009), p. 347.

17. Zygmunt Bauman, "Has the Future a Left?" *Soundings* 35 (Spring 2007): 5–6.

18. Ibid.

19. Goldberg, *The Threat of Race*, p. 331.

20. Cited in Anson Rabinach, "Unclaimed Heritage: Ernst Bloch's *Heritage of Our Times* and the Theory of Fascism," *New German Critique* (Spring 1997): 8.

21. See *OccupyArrests.com*, http://occupyarrests.moonfruit.com.

22. Durand, "For Youth."

23. Kyle Bella, "Bodies in Alliance: Gender Theorist Judith Butler on the Occupy and SlutWalk Movements," *TruthOut* (December 15, 2011), online at: http://www.truth-out.org/bodies-alliance-gender-theorist-judith-butler-occupy-and-slutwalk-movements/1323880210.

24. Richard Lichtman, "Not a Revolution?" *TruthOut* (December 14, 2011), online at: http://www.truth-out.org/not-revolution/1323801994.

25. Arun Gupta, "Arundhati Roy: 'The People Who Created the Crisis Will Not Be the Ones That Come up with a Solution,'" *Guardian* (November 30, 2011), online at: http://www.guardian.co.uk/world/2011/nov/30/arundhati-roy-interview.

26. Staughton Lynd, "What Is to Be Done Next?" *CounterPunch* (February 29, 2012), online at: http://www.counterpunch.org/2012/02/29/what-is-to-be-done-next.

27. Stanley Aronowitz, "Notes on the Occupy Movement," *Logos* (Fall 2011), online at: http://logosjournal.com/2011/fall_aronowitz.

28. On the rise of the punishing state, see Cusac, *Cruel and Unusual*; Wacquant, *Punishing the Poor*; Angela Y. Davis, *Abolition Democracy: Beyond Empire, Prisons, and Torture* (New York: Seven Stories Press, 2005).

29. Bill Moyers, "Discovering What Democracy Means," *Tom-Paine* (February 12, 2007), online at: http://www.tompaine.com/articles/2007/02/12/discovering_what_democracy_means.php.

30. Daniel Bell, *The End of Ideology: On the Exhaustion of Political Ideas in the Fifties* (New York: Free Press, 1966); and the more recent Francis Fukuyama, *The End of History and the Last Man* (New York: Free Press, 2006).

31. Stuart Hall, "The March of the Neoliberals," *Guardian* (September 12, 2011), online at: http://www.guardian.co.uk/politics/2011/sep/12/march-of-the-neoliberals/.

32. Alex Honneth, *Pathologies of Reason* (New York: Columbia University Press, 2009), p. 188.

33. John Van Houdt, "The Crisis of Negation: An Interview with Alain Badiou," *Continent* 1:4 (2011): 234–238, online at: http://continentcontinent.cc/index.php/continent/article/viewArticle/65.

34. See for instance, Noam Chomsky, *Failed States: The Abuse of Power and the Assault on Democracy* (New York: Holt Paperbacks, 2007).

35. Andrew Bacevich, "After Iraq, War Is US," *Reader Supported News* (December 20, 2011), online at: http://readersupportednews.org/opinion2/424-national-security/9007-after-iraq-war-is-us.

36. C. Wright Mills, *The Power Elite* (New York: Oxford University Press, 2000), p. 222.

37. See Gore Vidal, *Imperial America: Reflections on the United States of Amnesia* (New York: Nation Books, 2004); Gore Vidal, *Perpetual War for Perpetual Peace* (New York: Nation Books, 2002); Chris Hedges, *War Is a Force That Gives Us Meaning* (New York: Anchor Books, 2003); Chalmers Johnson, *The Sorrows of Empire: Militarism, Secrecy, and the End of the Republic* (New York: Metropolitan Books, 2004); Andrew Bacevich, *The New American Militarism* (New York: Oxford University Press, 2005); Chalmers Johnson, *Nemesis: The Last Days of the Republic* (New York: Metropolitan Books); Andrew J. Bacevich, *Washington Rules: America's Path to Permanent War* (New York: Metropolitan Books, 2010); and Nick Turse, *The Complex: How the Military Invades Our Everyday Lives* (New York: Metropolitan Books, 2008).

38. Tony Judt, "The New World Order," *New York Review of Books* 11:2 (July 14, 2005): 17.

39. Cusac, *Cruel and Unusual*, p. 2.

40. Jim Garrison, "Obama's Most Fateful Decision," *Huffington Post* (December 12, 2011), online at: http://www.huffingtonpost.com/jim-garrison/obamas-most-fateful-decis_b_1143005.html.

41. Ibid.

42. Stephen Graham, *Cities under Siege: The New Military Urbanism* (London: Verso, 2010), p. xi.

43. Andrew Becker and G. W. Schulz, "Cops Ready for War," *Reader Supported News* (December 21, 2011), online at: http://readersupportednews.org/news-section2/316-20/9023-focus-cops-ready-for-war.

44. Ibid.

45. Glenn Greenwald, "The Roots of the UC-Davis Pepper-Spraying," *Salon* (November 20, 2011), online at: http://www.salon.com/2011/11/20/the_roots_of_the_uc_davis_pepper_spraying.

46. See, for instance, Steven Rosenfeld, "5 Freedom-Killing Tactics Police Will Use to Crack Down on Protests in 2012," *AlterNet* (March 16, 2012), online at: http://www.alternet.org/story/154577/5_freedom-killing_tactics_police_will_use_to_crack_down_on_protests_in_2012.

47. Erica Goode, "Many in U.S. Are Arrested by Age 23, Study Finds," *New York Times* (December 19, 2011), p. A15.

48. Goldberg, *The Threat of Race*, p. 334.

49. Lauren Kelley, "Occupy Updates: Extreme Police Violence in Berkeley, with Calls for a Strike; Harvard Protesters Shut out of Harvard Yard," *AlterNet* (November 14, 2011), online at: http://www.alternet.org/newsandviews/article/728865/occupy_updates%3A_extreme_police_violence_in_berkeley,_with_calls_for_a_strike%3B_harvard_protesters_shut_out_of_harvard_yard; Conor Friedersdorf, "UC Berkeley Riot Police Use Batons to Clear Students from Sproul Plaza," *Atlantic* (November 10, 2011), online at: http://www.theatlantic.com/national/print/2011/11/uc-berkeley-riot-police-use-batons-to-clear-students-from-sproul-plaza/248228; Al Baker, "When the Police Go Military," *New York Times* (December 3, 2011), p. SR6; and Rania Khalek, "Pepper-Spraying Protesters Is Just the Beginning: Here Are More Hypermilitarized Weapons Your Local Police Force Could Employ," *AlterNet* (November 22, 2011), online at: http://www.alternet.org/story/153147/pepper-spraying_protesters_is_just_the_beginning%3A_here_are_more_hypermilitarized_weapons_your_local_police_force_could_employ.

50. Philip Govrevitch, "Whose Police?" *New Yorker* (November 17, 2011), online at: http://www.newyorker.com/online/blogs/comment/2011/11/occupy-wall-street-police-bloomberg.html.

51. Phil Rockstroh, "The Police State Makes Its Move: Retaining One's Humanity in the Face of Tyranny," *CommonDreams* (November 15, 2011), online at: http://www.commondreams.org/view/2011/11/15.

52. Michael Geyer, "The Militarization of Europe, 1914–1945," in John R. Gillis, ed., *The Militarization of the Western World* (New Brunswick, NJ: Rutgers University Press, 1989), p. 79.

53. Judt, "The New World Order," pp. 14–18.

54. Geoff Martin and Erin Steuter, *Pop Culture Goes to War: Enlist-*

ing and Resisting Militarism in the War on Terror (New York: Lexington Books, 2010).

55. Carl Boggs and Tom Pollard, *The Hollywood War Machine: U.S. Militarism and Popular Culture* (Boulder, CO: Paradigm Publishers, 2006).

56. Kostas Gouliamos and Christos Kassimeris, eds., *The Marketing of War in the Age of Neo-Militarism* (New York: Routledge, 2011).

57. David Cole, "An Executive Power to Kill?" *New York Review of Books* (March 6, 2012), online at: http://www.nybooks.com/blogs/nyrblog/2012/mar/06/targeted-killings-holder-speech.

58. Steve Herbert and Elizabeth Brown, "Conceptions of Space and Crime in the Punitive Neoliberal City," *Antipode* (2006): 757.

59. Davis, *Abolition Democracy*, p. 41.

60. One classic example of this neoliberal screed can be found most recently in an unapologetic defense of social Darwinism by Charles Murray, *Coming Apart: The State of White America, 1960–2010* (New York: Crown Forum, 2012). For a critique of this position, see David Garland, *The Culture of Control: Crime and Social Order in Contemporary Society* (Chicago: University of Chicago Press, 2001); Philip Jenkins, *Decade of Nightmares: The End of the Sixties and the Making of Eighties America* (New York: Oxford University Press, 2006); and Jonathan Simon, *Governing through Crime: How the War on Crime Transformed American Democracy and Created a Culture of Fear* (New York: Oxford University Press, 2007).

61. Chris McGreal, "The US Schools with Their Own Police," *Guardian* (January 9, 2012), online at: http://www.guardian.co.uk/world/2012/jan/09/texas-police-schools.

62. Daniel Tancer, "Student Punished for Refusing to Cite the Pledge," *Psyche, Science, and Society* (February 25, 2010), online at: http://psychoanalystsopposewar.org/blog/2010/02/25/student-punished-for-refusing-to-recite-the-pledge.

63. McGreal, "The US Schools with Their Own Police."

64. Criminal InJustice Kos, "Criminal InJustice Kos: Interrupting the School to Prison Pipeline," *Daily Kos* (March 30, 2011), online at: http://www.dailykos.com/story/2011/03/30/960807/-Criminal-InJustice-Kos:-Interrupting-the-School-to-Prison-Pipeline.

65. "A Failure of Imagination," *Smartypants* (March 3, 2010), online at: http://immasmartypants.blogspot.com/2010/03/failure-of-imagination.html.

66. See Mark P. Fancher, *Reclaiming Michigan's Throwaway Kids: Students Trapped in the School-to-Prison Pipeline* (Michigan: ACLU, 2011), online at: http://www.njjn.org/uploads/digital_library/resource_1287.pdf; and Advancement Project, *Test, Punish, and Push Out: How "Zero Tolerance" and High-Stakes Testing Funnel Youth into*

the School-to-Prison Pipeline (Washington, DC: Advancement Project, March 2010), online at: http://www.advancementproject.org/sites/default/files/publications/rev_fin.pdf.

67. Gilles Deleuze, "Postscript on the Societies of Control," *October* 59 (Winter 1992): 3–7.

68. Alex Honneth, *Pathologies of Reason* (New York: Columbia University Press, 2009), p. 188.

69. Bauman, "Has the Future a Left?" p. 2.

70. Barbara Ehrenreich, "How We Cured 'The Culture of Poverty,' Not Poverty Itself," *Truthout* (March 15, 2012), online at: http://www.truth-out.org/how-we-cured-culture-poverty-not-poverty-itself/1331821823.

71. This theme is taken up in great detail in Jonathan Simon, *Governing through Crime: How the War on Crime Transformed American Democracy and Created a Culture of Fear* (New York: Oxford University Press, 2007).

Notes for Chapter One

1. Stephen Holden, "Perils of the Corporate Ladder: It Hurts When You Fall," *New York Times* (December 10, 2010), p. C9.

2. Stanley Aronowitz, "Notes on the Occupy Movement," *Logos* (Fall 2011), online at: http://logosjournal.com/2011/fall_aronowitz.

3. On the issue of memory and loss, see Roger Simon, *The Touch of the Past: Remembrance, Learning, and Ethics* (New York: Palgrave, 2005). On consumerism, see Zygmunt Bauman, *Consuming Life* (London: Polity Press, 2007) and Zygmunt Bauman, *Does Ethics Have a Chance in a World of Consumers?* (Cambridge, MA: Harvard University Press, 2008).

4. Josh Domer, "Let Him Die?" *The Progress Report* (September 13, 2011), online at: http://thinkprogress.org/progress-report/let-him-die/?post_type=progress-report.

5. Zygmunt Bauman, *The Individualized Society* (London: Polity, 2001), p. 55.

6. Sheldon Wolin takes up this issue in "Political Theory: From Vocation to Invocation," in Jason Frank and John Tambornino, eds., *Vocations of Political Theory* (Minneapolis: University of Minnesota Press, 2000), pp. 3–22.

7. Roger Simon, "A Shock to Thought: Curatorial Judgment and the Public Exhibition of 'Difficult Knowledge,'" *Memory Studies* (February 21, 2011), online at: http://mss.sagepub.com/content/early/2011/02/18/1750698011398170.abstract.

8. Etienne Balibar, *We, the People of Europe? Reflections on*

Transnational Citizenship (Princeton, NJ: Princeton University Press, 2004), p. 116.

9. Ibid., p. 119.

10. Reed Johnson, "Will War on Terrorism Define a Generation?" *Los Angeles Times* (September 23, 2011), online at: http://articles .latimes.com/2001/sep/23/news/cl-48761.

11. Jean-Marie Colombani, "We Are All Americans," *Le Monde* (September 12, 2001), online at: http://www.worldpress.org/1101we_ are_all_americans.htm.

12. "Study Shows Rise of Cancer in 9/11 Firefighters," *CBS Evening News with Scott Pelley* (September 1, 2011), online at: http://www .cbsnews.com/stories/2011/09/01/eveningnews/main20100679 .shtml?tag=contentBody;cbsCarousel.

13. Alex Honneth, *Pathologies of Reason* (New York: Columbia University Press, 2009), p. 188.

14. David Simpson, *9/11: The Culture of Commemoration* (Chicago: University of Chicago Press, 2006), pp. 4–5.

15. Joan Didion quoted in Frank Rich, "Day's End," *New York Magazine* (August 27, 2011), online at: http://nymag.com/news/9-11/10th-anniversary/frank-rich.

16. Reuters, "45% Struggle in US to Make Ends Meet," *MSNBC: Business Stocks and Economy* (November 22, 2011), online at: http://www.msnbc.msn.com/id/45407937/ns/business-stocks _and_economy/#.T3SxhDEgd8E.

17. Rich, "Day's End."

18. Michiko Kakutani, "Outdone by Reality," *New York Times* (September 1, 2011), online at: http://www.nytimes.com/2011/09/01/ us/sept-11-reckoning/culture.html?_r=1&pagewanted=all.

19. Editorial, "Looking at America," *New York Times* (December 31, 2007), p. A20.

20. Ibid.

21. Ibid.

22. Jonathan Simon, *Governing through Crime: How the War on Crime Transformed American Democracy and Created a Culture of Fear* (New York: Oxford University Press, 2007).

23. Ibid.

24. Michelle Brown, *The Culture of Punishment: Prison, Society and Spectacle* (New York: New York University Press, 2009), p. 7.

25. Loïc Wacquant, *Punishing the Poor: The Neoliberal Government of Social Insecurity* (Durham, NC: Duke University Press, 2009), p. 294.

26. Noam Chomsky, "Was There an Alternative? Looking Back on 9/11 a Decade Later," *TomDispatch* (September 6, 2011), online at: http://www.tomdispatch.com/dialogs/print/?id=175436.

27. Mark Davis and Angel K. Brooks, "103-Year-Old Woman Won't Be Evicted from Atlanta Home," *Atlanta Journal-Constitution* (November 30, 2011), online at: http://www.ajc.com/news/atlanta/103-year -old-woman-1245741.html.

28. Richard R. J. Eskow, "Dimon's JPMorgan Chase: Why It's the Scandal of Our Time," *Crooks and Liars* (May 15, 2012), online at: http://crooksandliars.com/richard-rj-eskow/dimons-jpmorgan -chase-why-its-sca.

29. See, for example, Margaret Griffis, ed., "Casualties in Iraq," *Anti-War.com* (July 18, 2011), online at: http://antiwar.com/ casualties.

30. Joseph E. Stiglitz, "The Price of 9/11," *Project Syndicate* (September 11, 2011), online at: http://www.project-syndicate.org/ commentary/stiglitz142/English.

31. Paul Krugman, "The Years of Shame," *New York Times* (September 11, 2011), online at: http://krugman.blogs.nytimes .com/2011/09/11/the-years-of-shame.

32. See Sabrina Tavernise, "Soaring Poverty Cast Spotlight on 'Lost Decade,'" *New York Times* (September 13, 2011), p. A1.

33. Zygmunt Bauman, *Living on Borrowed Time: Conversations with Citlali Rovirosa-Madrazo* (Cambridge, UK: Polity Press, 2010), p. 4.

34. Christopher Robbins, *Expelling Hope: The Assault on Youth and the Militarization of Schooling* (New York: State University of New York Press, 2008); Henry A. Giroux, *Education and the Crisis of Public Values* (New York: Peter Lang, 2012).

35. Erik Eckholm, "School Suspensions Lead to Legal Challenge," *New York Times* (March 18, 2010), p. A14.

36. Wacquant, *Punishing the Poor,* p. 6.

37. See for instance, Glenn Greenwald, "Obama's Illegal Assaults," *In These Times* (August 26, 2011), online at: http://www .inthesetimes.com/article/11787/obamas_illegal_assaults.

38. Jane Mayer, "Covert Operations: The Billionaire Brothers Who Are Waging a War against Obama," *New Yorker* (August 30, 2010), online at: http://www.newyorker.com/reporting/2010/08/30/100830fa _fact_mayer.

39. These concepts are taken up in great detail in Henry A. Giroux, *Youth in a Suspect Society: Democracy or Disposability?* (New York: Palgrave-Macmillan, 2009).

40. Tamar Lewin, "If Your Kids Are Awake, They're Probably Online," *New York Times* (January 20, 2010), p. A1.

41. C. Christine, "Kaiser Study: Kids 8 to 18 Spend More Than Seven Hours a Day with Media," *Spotlight on Digital Media and Learning: MacArthur Foundation* (January 21, 2010), online at: http://

spotlight.macfound.org/blog/entry/kaiser_study_kids_age_8_to_18_spend_more_than_seven_hours_a_day_with_media.

42. Susan Linn, *Consuming Kids: The Hostile Takeover of Childhood* (New York: The New Press, 2004).

43. Matt Richtel, "In Online Games, a Path to Young Consumers," *New York Times* (April 10, 2011), p. A1.

44. Ibid.

45. Carly Everson, "Ind. Officer Uses Stun Gun on Unruly 10-Year-Old," *Guardian* (April 2, 2010), online at: http://www.guardian.co.uk/world/feedarticle/9014651.

46. Henry A. Giroux, "Brutalizing Kids: Painful Lessons in the Pedagogy of School Violence," *Truthout* (October 8, 2009), online at: http://www.truthout.org/10080912.

47. Zygmunt Bauman, *Wasted Lives* (London: Polity Press, 2004), p. 82.

48. Ibid.

49. Zygmunt Bauman, "Youth Unemployment—the Precariat Is Welcoming Generation Y," *Social Europe Journal* (May 22, 2012), online at: http://www.social-europe.eu/2012/05/youth-unemployment-the-precariat-is-welcoming-generation-y.

50. These figures are taken from Children's Defense Fund, *Summary Report: America's Cradle to Prison Pipeline* (2007), pp. 4, 38, online at: http://www.childrensdefense.org/site/DocServer/CPP_report_2007_summary.pdf?docID=6001.

51. Ibid., p. 77.

52. Claude Brown, *Manchild in the Promised Land* (New York: Signet Books, 1965).

53. Ibid., p. 419.

54. Bureau of Labor Statistics, US Department of Labor, "Employment and Unemployment among Youth—Summer 2011," News Release (August 24, 2011), online at: http://www.bls.gov/news.release/pdf/youth.pdf.

55. Joshua Holland, "White Families Have 20 Times the Wealth of Black Families: How Racism's Legacy Created a Crushing Depression in Black America," *AlterNet* (July 27, 2011), online at: http://www.alternet.org/module/printversion/151809.

56. Andrew Sum, Ishwar Khatiwada, and Joe McLaughlin, *The Consequences of Dropping out of High School: Joblessness and Jailing for High School Dropouts and the High Cost for Taxpayers* (Boston: Center for Labor Market Studies, Northeastern University, October 2009), online at: http://iris.lib.neu.edu/cgi/viewcontent.cgi?article=1022&context=clms_pub.

57. Tavernise, "Soaring Poverty Cast Spotlight on 'Lost Decade.'"

58. Paul Buchheit, "Half of America in Poverty?" *CounterPunch* (December 27, 2011), online at: http://www.counterpunch.org/2011/12/27/half-of-america-in-poverty.

59. See National Center for Children in Poverty online at: http://www.nccp.org/topics/childpoverty.html.

60. Lindsey Tanner, "Half of US Kids Will Get Food Stamps, Study Says," *Chicago Tribune* (November 2, 2009), online at: http://www.chicagotribune.com/news/chi-ap-us-med-children-food,0,6055934.story.

61. Erik Eckholm, "Surge in Homeless Pupils Strains Schools," *New York Times* (September 6, 2009), p. A1.

62. Marisol Bello, "Report: Child Homelessness up 33% in 3 Years," *USA Today* (December 13, 2011), online at: http://www.usatoday.com/news/nation/story/2011-12-12/homeless-children-increase/51851146/1.

63. Diane Ravitch, *The Death and Life of a Great American School System: How Testing and Choice Are Undermining Education* (New York: Basic Books, 2010).

64. I take this issue up in more detail in Henry A. Giroux, *Politics after Hope: Obama and the Crisis of Youth, Race, and Democracy* (Boulder: Paradigm Publishers, 2010).

65. Marion Wright Elderman, "Ending the Cradle to Prison Pipeline and Mass Incarceration," *Children's Defense Fund* (July 6, 2012), online at: http://cdf.childrensdefense.org/site/messageviewer?em_id=28962.0&dlv_id=0.

66. Stephen Graham, *Cities under Siege: The New Military Urbanism* (London: Verso, 2010), p. 7.

67. Richard Wilkenson and Kate Pickett, *The Spirit Level: Why Great Equality Makes Societies Stronger* (New York: Bloomsbury Press, 2009). See also Robert Reich, *Aftershock: The Next Economy and America's Future* (New York: Knopf, 2011).

68. Roger Bybee, "Aronowitz: Occupy Movement Needs Both Audacity and Long-March Strategy," *In These Times* (November 17, 2011), online at: http://www.inthesetimes.com/working/entry/12309/aronowitz_movement_needs_both_long_march_strategy_and_audacity.

69. Balibar, *We, the People of Europe*, pp. 119–120.

70. Aronowitz, "Notes on the Occupy Movement."

71. Jeffrey T. Nealon, *Foucault beyond Foucault: Power and Its Intensifications since 1984* (Palo Alto, CA: Stanford University Press, 2008), pp. 70–77.

Notes for Chapter Two

1. Andrew J. Bacevich, *Washington Rules: America's Path to Permanent War* (New York: Metropolitan Books, 2010).

2. John Cory, "The Ugly Circus," *Reader Supported News* (February 19, 2012), online at: http://readersupportednews.org/opinion2/276-74/10044-the-ugly-circus.

3. For the most extensive and exhaustive history of the technology of torture, see Darius Rejali, *Torture and Democracy* (Princeton, NJ: Princeton University Press, 2007). Some of the more instructive books on torture under the George W. Bush administration include Mark Danner, *Torture and Truth: America, Abu Ghraib, and the War on Terror* (New York: New York Review of Books, 2004); Jane Mayer, *The Dark Side: The Inside Story of How the War on Terror Turned into a War on American Ideals* (New York: Doubleday, 2008); and Philippe Sands, *Torture Team: Rumsfeld's Memo and the Betrayal of American Values* (London: Penguin, 2009).

4. C. Wright Mills, "The Cultural Apparatus," *The Politics of Truth: Selected Writings of C. Wright Mills*, selected and introduced by John H. Summers (New York: Oxford University Press, 2008), pp. 203–212.

5. See Russ Baker, "Murdoch US Scandal Brewing?" *WhoWhatWhy.com* (July 21, 2011), online at: http://whowhatwhy.com/2011/07/21/murdoch-us-scandal-brewing.

6. Judith Butler, *Precarious Life: The Powers of Mourning and Violence* (London: Verso Press, 2004), p. 4.

7. Peter Moskos, *In Defense of Flogging* (New York: Basic Books, 2011).

8. Susan Sontag, *On Photography* (New York: Picador, 1973).

9. Susan Sontag, *Regarding the Pain of Others* (New York: Farrar, Straus and Giroux, 2003).

10. Paul Virilio, *Art and Fear* (New York: Continuum, 2004), p. 28.

11. See Mark Reinhardt, "Picturing Violence: Aesthetics and the Anxiety of Critique," in Mark Reinhardt, Holly Edwards, and Erina Duganne, eds., *Beautiful Suffering* (Chicago: University of Chicago Press, 2007), p. 17.

12. I have taken up this issue in great detail in Henry A. Giroux, "Consuming Social Change: The United Colors of Benetton," *Disturbing Pleasures: Learning Popular Culture* (New York: Routledge, 1994), pp. 3–24.

13. Cited in Virilio, *Art and Fear,* p. 28.

14. Mark Featherstone, "The Hurt Locker: What Is the Death Drive?" *Sociology and Criminology at Keele University* (February 25, 2010), online at: http://socandcrimatkeele.blogspot.com/2010/02/hurt-locker-what-is-death-drive.html.

15. Theodor Adorno, "Education after Auschwitz," *Critical Models: Interventions and Catchwords* (New York: Columbia University Press, 1998), pp. 191–204.

16. Ibid., p. 201.

17. See, for instance, Loic Wacquant, *Punishing the Poor: The Neoliberal Government of Social Insecurity* (Durham, NC: Duke University

Press, 2009); Jonathan Simon, *Governing through Crime: How the War on Crime Transformed American Democracy and Created a Culture of Fear* (New York: Oxford University Press, 2007); and Angela Y. Davis, *Abolition Democracy: Beyond Empire, Prisons, and Torture* (New York: Seven Stories Press, 2005).

18. Suzanne Moore, "Instead of Being Disgusted by Poverty, We Are Disgusted by Poor People Themselves," *Guardian* (February 12, 2012), online at: http://www.guardian.co.uk/commentisfree/2012/feb/16/suzanne-moore-disgusted-by-poor.

19. Zygmunt Bauman, *The Individualized Society* (London: Polity Press, 2001), p. 5.

20. Moore, "Instead of Being Disgusted by Poverty."

21. Walter Benjamin, *Illuminations,* trans. Harry Zohn (New York: Schocken Books, 1969). See also Walter Benjamin, "Critique of Violence," *Reflections: Essays, Aphorisms, Autobiographical Writings* (New York: Schocken Books, 1986).

22. Lutz Koepnick, "Aesthetic Politics Today—Walter Benjamin and Post-Fordist Culture," in Peter Uwe Hohendahl and Jaimey Fisher, eds., *Critical Theory—Current State and Future Prospects* (New York: Berghahn Books, 2002), p. 95.

23. Ibid., p. 96. See also Susan Buck-Morss, "Aesthetics and Anaesthetics: Walter Benjamin's Artwork Essay Reconsidered," *October* 62 (Fall 1992): 3–41.

24. Sontag, *Regarding the Pain of Others*, p. 81.

25. Ibid.

26. Ibid.

27. Paul Gilroy, "'After the Love Has Gone': Bio-Politics and Ethepoetics in the Black Public Sphere," *Public Culture* 7:1 (1994): 58.

28. I take up in great detail the notion of a culture of cruelty in Henry A. Giroux, *Zombie Politics and Culture in the Age of Casino Capitalism* (New York: Peter Lang, 2011).

29. Geoffrey Hartman, "Public Memory and Its Discontents," *Raritan* 8:4 (Spring 1994): 25.

30. Terry Eagleton, *The Ideology of the Aesthetic* (Cambridge: Basil Blackwell, 1990), p. 344.

31. Zygmunt Bauman, *Life in Fragments* (Malden: Blackwell, 1995), p. 149.

32. Ibid., pp. 149–150.

33. Sarah Lazare and Ryan Harvey, "WikiLeaks in Baghdad," *Nation* (July 29, 2010), online at: http://www.thenation.com/article/38034/wikileaks-baghdad.

34. For an example of utterly uncritical reporting on this type of over-the-top celebration of violence and the armed forces, see John

Anderson, "On Active Duty for the Movies (Real Ammo)," *New York Times* (February 19, 2012), p. AR16.

35. See, for example, A. O. Scott and Manohla Dargis, "Gosh, Sweetie, That's a Big Gun," *New York Times* (April 27, 2011), p. MT1.

36. The grotesque image closes Lady Gaga's "Bad Romance" video. A still photo can be viewed here: http://www.bjwinslow.com/albums/album90/Lady_Gaga_skeleton.jpg.

37. I have taken the term "poverty porn" from Gerry Mooney and Lynn Hancock, "Poverty Porn and the Broken Society," *Variant* 39/40 (Winter 2010), online at: http://www.variant.org.uk/39_40texts/Variant39_40.html#L4.

38. Ibid.

39. Leo Lowenthal, "Atomization of Man," *False Prophets: Studies in Authoritarianism* (New Brunswick, NJ: Transaction Books, 1987), p. 182.

40. Henry A. Giroux, "Hoodie Politics: Trayvon Martin and Racist Violence in Post-Racial America," *Truthout* (March 2, 2012), online at: http://truth-out.org/news/item/8203-hoodie-politics-and-the-death-of-trayvon-martin.

41. Judith Butler touches on this issue in *Precarious Life: The Powers of Mourning and Violence* (London: Verso Press, 2004).

42. Reinhardt, "Picturing Violence," p. 21.

43. Bauman, *Life in Fragments*, p. 151.

44. Jim Frederick, "Anatomy of a War Crime: Behind the Enabling of the 'Kill Team,'" *Time* (March 29, 2011), online at: http://globalspin.blogs.time.com/2011/03/29/anatomy-of-a-war-crime-behind-the-enabling-of-the-kill-team.

45. Mark Boal, "The Kill Team: How U.S. Soldiers in Afghanistan Murdered Innocent Civilians," *Rolling Stone* (March 27, 2011), online at: http://www.rollingstone.com/politics/news/the-kill-team-20110327.

46. Ibid.

47. Ibid.

48. Ibid.

49. Seymour M. Hersh, "The 'Kill Team' Photographs," *New Yorker* (March 23, 2011), online at: http://www.newyorker.com/online/blogs/newsdesk/2011/03/the-kill-team-photographs.html.

50. David Carr, "War, in Life and Death," *New York Times* (April 24, 2011), p. B1.

51. Luke Mogelson, "A Beast in the Heart of Every Fighting Man," *New York Times Magazine* (April 27, 2011), online at: http://www.nytimes.com/2011/05/01/magazine/mag-01KillTeam-t.html.

52. Cited in Franco Bifo Berardi, *Precarious Rhapsody: Semiocapitalism and the Pathologies of the Post-Alpha Generation* (London: Minor Compositions, 2009), pp. 96–97.

53. David L. Clark, personal correspondence, May 15, 2011.

54. Alex Honneth, *Pathologies of Reason* (New York: Columbia University Press, 2009), p. 188.

55. Mieke Bal, "The Pain of Images," in Mark Reinhardt, Holly Edwards, and Erina Duganne, eds., *Beautiful Suffering* (Chicago: University of Chicago Press, 2007), p. 107.

56. Ibid., p. 111.

57. Lawrence Grossberg, personal correspondence, June 18, 2011.

58. Georges Didi-Huberman, *Images in Spite of All: Four Photographs from Auschwitz*, trans. Shane B. Lillis (Chicago: University of Chicago Press, 2008), pp. 1–2.

59. Erik Hoffner, "Punishing Protest, Policing Dissent: What Is the Justice System For?" *Common Dreams* (February 11, 2012), online at: http://www.commondreams.org/view/2012/02/12-6.

60. Ibid.

61. Clare Hemmings, "Invoking Affect: Cultural Theory and the Ontological Turn," *Cultural Studies* 19:5 (September 2005): 557–558.

Notes for Chapter Three

1. Judd Legum, "House GOP Plays Ben Affleck Movie Clip to Rally Caucus," *ThinkProgress* (July 26, 2011), online at: http://thinkprogress.org/politics/2011/07/26/280239/house-gop-plays-ben-affleck-movie-clip-to-rally-caucus-i-need-your-help-were-going-to-hurt-some-people.

2. Thomas E. Mann and Norman J. Ornstein, "Let's Just Say It: The Republicans Are the Problem," *Washington Post* (April 27, 2012), online at: http://www.washingtonpost.com/opinions/lets-just-say-it-the-republicans-are-the-problem/2012/04/27/gIQAxCVUlT_story.html.

3. As Michael Kazin observes, this type of antigovernment extremism and ideological fundamentalism has been more common on the right than on the left. Most liberals and radicals view the government as one of the few remaining national institutions to provide social protections and social needs not met by businesses and charities. See Michael Kazin, "Paranoia Strikes Deep in America . . . Over and Over," *AlterNet* (September 18, 2009), online at: http://www.alternet.org/story/142690. The best history of right-wing authoritarianism can be found in Sarah Diamond, *Roads to Dominion: Right-Wing Movements and Political Power in the United States* (New York: Guilford Press, 1995); and Sarah Diamond, *Not by Politics Alone: The Enduring Influence of the Christian Right* (New York: Guilford Press, 2000).

4. CNN Wire Staff, "Far Right Domestic Terrorism on Par with Foreign Threat, Experts Say," *CNN.com* (July 25, 2011), online at: http://edition.cnn.com/2011/US/07/25/domestic.extremism/index .html?hpt=hp_bn1. See also Ben Armbruster, "After Right-Wing Pressure, DHS Now Has 'Just One Person' Dealing with Domestic Terrorism," *ThinkProgress* (July 27, 2011), online at: http://thinkprogress .org/security/2011/07/27/280665/dhs-domestic-terrorism-right-wing-pressure.

5. Chauncey DeVega, "A Reminder That Whiteness Is Not Benign: Of Warnings about White, Middle Class Domestic Terrorists in the U.S. and the Norway Massacre," *AlterNet* (July 28, 2011), online at: http://blogs.alternet.org/speakeasy/2011/07/28/a-reminder -that-whiteness-is-not-benign-of-warnings-about-white-middle-class -domestic-terrorists-in-the-u-s-and-the-norway-massacre.

6. Sindre Bangstad, "Norway: Terror and Islamophobia in the Mirror," *OpenDemocracy* (August 22, 2011), online at: http:// www.opendemocracy.net/sindre-bangstad/norway-terror- and-islamophobia-in-mirror?utm_source=feedblitz&utm_medium= FeedBlitzEmail&utm_content=201210&utm_campaign= Nightly_%272011-08-24%2005%3a30%3a00%27.

7. See Douglas Kellner, *Guys and Guns Amok: Domestic Terrorism and School Shootings from the Oklahoma City Bombing to the Virginia Tech Massacre* (Boulder, CO: Paradigm Publishers, 2008).

8. There are some people on the left who defend the term "extremism" as meaning a position that challenges what is defined as the political norm. In this view, the term signifies an act of transgression and does not have a pejorative connotation. I use the term, however, in reference to right-wing populism and to denote a transgression that is both reactionary and authoritarian, one that assaults every decent principle associated with justice, equality, and the ideals of a substantive democracy.

9. See Theodor Adorno's more recently available works on this type of worldview, especially Theodor W. Adorno, *Guilt and Defense: On the Legacies of National Socialism in Postwar Germany*, ed. and trans. Jeffrey K. Olick and Andrew J. Perrin (Cambridge, MA: Harvard University Press, 2010). This followed the classic Theodor W. Adorno, Else Frenkel-Brunswik, and Daniel J. Levinson, *The Authoritarian Personality* (New York: W. W. Norton, 1993 [1950]).

10. Mattias Gardell, "The Roots of Breivik's Ideology: Where Does the Romantic Male Warrior Ideal Come from Today?" *OpenDemocracy* (August 1, 2011), online at: http://www.opendemocracy.net/mattias -gardell/roots-of-breiviks-ideology-where-does-romantic-male -warrior-ideal-come-from-today.

11. Quoted in Aliyah Shahid, "GOP Congressman, Doug Lamborn

of Colorado, Blasted for Likening President Obama to a 'Tar Baby,'" *Daily News* (August 2, 2011), online at: http://www.nydailynews .com/news/politics/2011/08/02/2011-08-02_gop_congressman _doug_lamborn_of_colorado_blasted_for_likening_president_obama _to.html?print=1&page=all.

12. Pat Buchanan, "The Day of the Hobbits," *Town Hall* (August 2, 2011), online at: http://townhall.com/columnists/patbuchanan/ 2011/08/02/the_day_of_the_hobbits.

13. See Luke Roney, "Orange County Republican Censured for Obama-Chimp E-Mail," *Newport Beach News* (May 4, 2011), online at: http://newportbeach.patch.com/articles/orange-county-republican -censured-for-obama-chimp-e-mail.

14. Chris Hedges, "Fundamentalism Kills," *Truthdig* (July 26, 2011), online at: http://www.truthdig.com/report/item/fundamentalism _kills_20110726.

15. Paul Bentley, "Fox Host Forced to Apologise after On-Air Tirade about Obama's 'Hoodlum in the Hizzouse,'" *Daily Mail Online* (June 14, 2011), online at: http://www.dailymail.co.uk/news/ article-2003560/Revoltingly-racist-Fox-host-forced-apologize-air -tirade-Obamas-hoodlum-hizzouse.html.

16. Brian Stelter, "Fox News Site Calls Obama Party a 'Hip-Hop BBQ,'" *New York Times* (August 5, 2011), online at: http://www .msnbc.msn.com/id/44041546/ns/politics-the_new_york_times/ #.TjyTkBzmbqI.

17. See Andrew J. Bacevich, *Washington Rules: America's Path to Permanent War* (New York: Metropolitan Books, 2010).

18. Kevin Baker, "We're in the Army Now: The G.O.P.'s Plan to Militarize Our Culture," *Harper's Magazine* (October 2003), pp. 37–38.

19. Richard Hofstadter, *Anti-Intellectualism in American Life* (New York: Vintage, 1966). See also more recently Susan Jacoby, *The Age of American Unreason* (New York: Pantheon, 2008).

20. Michel Foucault, "Polemics, Politics, and Problematizations: An Interview with Michel Foucault," *Ethics: Subjectivity and Truth: The Essential Works of Michel Foucault 1954–1984*, ed. Paul Rabinow, vol. 1 (New York: The New Press, 1994), pp. 112–113.

21. See Michelle Alexander, *The New Jim Crow: Mass Incarceration in the Age of Colorblindness* (New York: New Press, 2011).

22. Etienne Balibar, *We, The People of Europe? Reflections on Transnational Citizenship* (Princeton, NJ: Princeton University Press, 2004), p. 128.

23. Zygmunt Bauman, *Liquid Times: Living in an Age of Uncertainty* (London: Polity Press, 2007), p. 103.

24. Stephen Graham, *Cities under Siege: The New Military Urbanism* (London: Verso, 2010).

25. Robert Reich, "The Rebirth of Social Darwinism," *Robert Reich* (November 30, 2011), online at: http://robertreich.org/post/13567144944.

26. David Harvey, *A Brief History of Neoliberalism* (New York: Oxford University Press, 2006), pp. 152–153.

27. Hedges, "Fundamentalism Kills."

28. Chip Berlant has long documented in brilliant fashion the rise of the Christian right and other fundamentalist groups in the United States. See his excellent commentary on the relationship between the Breivik manifesto and White Christian nationalism. Berlant also documents Breivik's hatred of cultural Marxism. See Chip Berlant, "Updated: Breivik's Core Thesis Is White Christian Nationalism v. Multiculturalism," *Talk to Action* (August 31, 2011), online at: http://www.talk2action.org/story/2011/7/25/73510/6015.

29. Scott Shane, "Killings in Norway Spotlight Anti-Muslim Thought in U.S.," *New York Times* (July 24, 2011), online at: http://www.nytimes.com/2011/07/25/us/25debate.html?ref=scottshane.

30. Matthew Goodwin, "Norway Attacks: We Can No Longer Ignore the Far-Right Threat," *Guardian* (July 24, 2011), online at: http://www.guardian.co.uk/commentisfree/2011/jul/24/norway-bombing-attack-far-right.

31. Ibid.

32. A brilliant analysis of this type of racism can be found in many of the works of David Theo Goldberg. See, for example, *The Threat of Race: Reflections on Racial Neoliberalism* (Malden, MA: Wiley-Blackwell, 2008).

33. Lee Fang, "Pam Geller Justifies Breivik's Terror: Youth Camp Had More 'Middle Eastern or Mixed' Races Than 'Pure Norwegian,'" *ThinkProgress* (August 1, 2011), online at: http://thinkprogress.org/security/2011/08/01/284011/pam-geller-race-mixing-breivik-right.

34. Ibid.

35. Geller's blog *Atlas Shrugs* can be found at http://atlasshrugs2000.typepad.com/atlas_shrugs.

36. "Under the picture, Geller writes: 'Note the faces which are more Mlddle [sic] Eastern or mixed than pure Norwegian.'" Fang, "Pam Geller Justifies Breivik's Terror."

37. American Anti-Defamation League, *Immigrants Targeted: Extremist Rhetoric Moves into the Mainstream* (July 2007), online at: http://www.adl.org/civil_rights/anti_immigrant/rhetoric.asp.

38. Patrick Buchanan, "Goodbye to Los Angeles," *WorldNetDaily* (June 27, 2011), online at: http://www.wnd.com/index.php?pageId=316201.

39. See, for example, Samuel P. Huntington, *The Clash of*

Civilizations and the Remaking of the World Order (New York: Simon and Schuster, 2011).

40. See Hedges, "Fundamentalism Kills"; also see Kazin, "Paranoia Strikes Deep in America."

41. Alexander, *The New Jim Crow.*

42. Amy Goodman, "On Eve of MLK Day, Michelle Alexander & Randall Robinson on the Mass Incarceration of Black America," *Democracy Now!* (January 13, 2012), online at: http://www.democracynow.org/2012/1/13/on_eve_of_mlk_day_michelle. Also see Alexander, *The New Jim Crow.*

43. The full article and a critical commentary can be found in Murshedz, "MSNBC's Bigotry Problem—Pat Buchanan—Flares Up Again," *Crooks and Liars* (July 2, 2011), online at: http://crooksandliars.com/murshedz/msnbc-s-bigotry-problem-pat-buchanan-flar.

44. CC, "GOP Do NOT Think They're at War with Women & That Speaks Volumes," *Daily Kos* (April 6, 2012), online at: http://www.dailykos.com/story/2012/04/06/1081188/-The-Mere-Fact-GOP-do-NOT-Think-They-re-at-War-with-Women-Speaks-Volumes.

45. Sarah Jaffe, "The 10 Scariest GOP Governors: Bringing a Radical Right-Wing Agenda to a State Near You," *AlterNet* (July 7, 2011), online at: http://www.alternet.org/story/151535/the_10_scariest_gop_governors%3A_bringing_a_radical_right-wing_agenda_to_a_state_near_you?page=entire.

46. Ibid.

47. Harry Reid, "GOP Would Cut Health Insurance for 1.7 Million Kids," *Huffington Post* (May 31, 2011), online at: http://www.huffingtonpost.com/sen-harry-reid.

48. "When Ideology Gets Abusive," *CommonDreams* (July 21, 2011), online at: http://www.commondreams.org/further/2011/07/21-2.

49. Les Leopold, "How Can the World's Richest Country Let Children Go Hungry? 6 Tricks Corporate Elites Use to Hoard All the Wealth," *AlterNet* (December 27, 2011), online at: http://www.alternet.org/module/printversion/153531.

50. Ghali Hassan, "American (Real) Exceptionalism," *Counter Currents* (July 22, 2011), online at: http://www.countercurrents.org/hassan220711.htm.

51. Joseph E. Stiglitz, "Of the 1%, by the 1%, for the 1%," *Vanity Fair* (May 2011), online at: http://www.vanityfair.com/society/features/2011/05/top-one-percent-201105.

52. Matt Taibbi, "Why Isn't Wall Street in Jail?" *Rolling Stone* (February 16, 2011), online at: http://www.rollingstone.com/politics/news/why-isnt-wall-street-in-jail-20110216.

53. Warren Buffett, "Stop Coddling the Super-Rich," *New York Times* (August 15, 2011), p. A21.

54. FiredupinCa, "Sen. Orrin Hatch: The Poor Are Not Taxed Enough," *Daily Kos* (July 7, 2011), online at: http://www.dailykos.com/story/2011/07/07/992277/-Sen-Orrin-Hatch:-The-Poor-Are-Not-Taxed-Enough.

55. Paul Krugman, "Ludicrous and Cruel," *New York Times* (April 7, 2001). For a detailed analysis of how neoliberal ideology and casino capitalism drive these policies, see David Harvey, *A Brief History of Neoliberalism* (New York: Oxford University Press, 2005); also see Jacob S. Hacker and Paul Pierson, *Winner-Take-All Politics* (New York: Simon and Schuster, 2010).

56. See Sarah Posner, "God's Law Is the Only Law: The Genesis of Michele Bachmann," *Religion Dispatches Magazine* (August 1, 2011), online at: http://www.religiondispatches.org/archive/politics/4838/god%E2%80%99s_law_is_the_only_law%3A_the_genesis_of_michele_bachmann. See also Adele M. Stan, "Because the Bible Tells Me So: Why Bachmann and Tea Party Christians Oppose Raising the Debt Ceiling," *AlterNet* (August 1, 2011), online at: http://www.alternet.org/teaparty/151795/because_the_bible_tells_me_so%3A_why_bachmann_and_tea_party_christians_oppose_raising_the_debt_ceiling; Amy Davidson, "Michele Bachmann's Vows," *New Yorker* (July 13, 2011), online at: http://www.newyorker.com/online/blogs/closeread/2011/07/michele-bachmann-debt-ceiling.html; and Ryan Lizza, "Leap of Faith," *New Yorker* (August 15, 2011), online at: http://www.newyorker.com/reporting/2011/08/15/110815fa_fact_lizza.

57. Quoted in Thomas Lane, "Is He Even Trying? Huntsman Seems Determined to Alienate the GOP Base," *TPMMuckracker* (August 19, 2011), online at: http://readersupportednews.org/off-site-opinion-section/72-72/7112-huntsman-seems-determined-to-alienate-the-gop-base.

58. Quoted in Mark Duell, "'Gays Are Part of Satan and Their Life Is Bondage': Bachmann's Thoughts on Homosexuality," *Daily Mail Online* (July 13, 2011), online at: http://www.dailymail.co.uk/news/article-2014289/Michele-Bachmann-says-gays-Satan-homosexual-life-bondage.html#ixzz1UeMCHLZl.

59. Chris Stellar, "Bachmann Fears 'Politically Correct Re-education Camps for Young People,'" *Minnesota Independent* (April 6, 2009), online at: http://minnesotaindependent.com/31237/bachmann-reedcuation-camps.

60. Quoted in Carol E. Lee, Damian Paletta, and Naftali Bendavid, "As Talks Stall, New Debt Plan Offered," *Wall Street Journal* (July 13,

2011), online at: http://online.wsj.com/article/SB10001424052702 30367870457644183301411 6822.html.

61. Paul Krugman, "The Centrist Cop-Out," *New York Times* (July 27, 2011), p. A27.

62. Hannah Arendt, *Men in Dark Times* (Orlando, FL: Harcourt Brace and Company, 1968 [1955]).

63. Henry A. Wallace, "The Dangers of American Fascism," *Truthout* (February 28, 2011), online at: http://www.truth-out.org/ the-dangers-american-fascism68098.

Notes for Chapter Four

1. See "Nuremberg Law for the Protection of German Blood and German Honor, September 15, 1935," online at: http://www.owlnet .rice.edu/~rar4619/blood.html.

2. Giorgio Agamben, *Homo Sacer: Sovereign Power and Bare Life* (Stanford, CA: Stanford University Press, 1998), especially pp. 71–115.

3. Theodor W. Adorno, "Appendix 1: Discussion of Professor Adorno's Lecture 'The Working through the Past,'" *Critical Models: Interviews and Catchwords,* trans. Henry W. Pickford (New York: Columbia University Press, 1998 [1963]), p. 298.

4. See, for example, Glenn Greenwald, *With Liberty and Justice for Some* (New York: Metropolitan Books, 2011).

5. Jonathan Turley, "10 Reasons the U.S. Is No Longer the Land of the Free," *Washington Post* (January 13, 2012), online at: http:// www.washingtonpost.com/opinions/is-the-united-states-still-the -land-of-the-free/2012/01/04/gIQAvcD1wP_story.html.

6. Jim Garrison, "Obama's Most Fateful Decision," *Huffington Post* (December 12, 2011), online at: http://www.huffingtonpost.com/ jim-garrison/obamas-most-fateful-decis_b_1143005.html.

7. Angela Y. Davis, *Abolition Democracy: Beyond Empire, Prisons, and Torture* (New York: Seven Stories Press, 2005), pp. 90–91.

8. See Paul Krugman, "Romney Isn't Concerned," *New York Times* (February 12, 2012), online at: http://www.readersupportednews .org/off-site-opinion-section/72-72/9776-romney-isnt-concerned. See also Paul Thomas, "Gingrich's Strategy: Racism," *Daily Censored* (January 25, 2012), online at: http://dailycensored.com/2012/01/25/ gingrichs-strategy-racism.

9. Paul Krugman, "Big Fiscal Phonies," *New York Times* (May 28, 2012), p. A17.

10. Ibid.

11. Diane Sweet, "3.5 Million Homeless and 18.5 Million Vacant Homes in US," *Occupy America* (December 30, 2011), online at: http://occupyamerica.crooksandliars.com/diane-sweet/35-million-homeless-and-185-million-va.

12. David DeGraw, "The Economic Elite Have Engineered an Extraordinary Coup, Threatening the Very Existence of the Middle Class," *AlterNet* (February 15, 2010), online at: http://www.alternet.org/story/145667.

13. Achille Mbembe, "Necropolitics," trans. Libby Meintjes, *Public Culture* 15:1 (2003): 21.

14. Arundhati Roy, "Peace and the New Corporate Liberation Theory," The 2004 Sydney Peace Prize Lecture, *Sydney Morning Herald* (November 4, 2004), online at: http://www.smh.com.au/news/Opinion/Roys-full-speech/2004/11/04/1099362264349.html.

15. Tony Judt, *Ill Fares the Land* (New York: Penguin, 2010), pp. 2, 12.

16. Jean and John Comaroff, "Criminal Obsessions after Foucault: Postcoloniality, Policing, and the Metaphysic of Disorder," *Critical Inquiry* 30 (Summer 2004): 84.

17. Robert Reich, "The Rebirth of Social Darwinism," *Robert Reich* (November 30, 2011), online at: http://robertreich.org/post/13567144944.

18. I have written about the emergence of the second Gilded Age in great detail in Henry A. Giroux, *Twilight of the Social* (Boulder, CO: Paradigm Publishers, 2012); Henry A. Giroux, *Youth in a Suspect Society* (Boulder, CO: Paradigm Publishers, 2009); Henry A. Giroux, *Public Spaces/Private Lives* (Boulder, CO: Paradigm Publishers, 2003).

19. This theme is taken up brilliantly in Susan Searls Giroux, *Between Race and Reason: Violence, Intellectual Responsibility, and the University to Come* (Stanford, CA: Stanford University Press, 2010).

20. See "Fact Sheet on Arizona House Bill 2281," *Ethnic Studies Week* (October 1–7, 2010), online at: http://ethnicstudiesweekoctober1-7.org/arizona-hb-2281-fact-sheet.html. The legislation can be found at http://www.azleg.gov/legtext/49leg/2r/bills/hb2281s.pdf.

21. Jessica Calefati, "Arizona Bans Ethnic Studies," *Mother Jones* (May 12, 2010), online at: http://motherjones.com/mojo/2010/05/ethnic-studies-banned-arizona.

22. Roxana Rahmani, "Arizona HB 2281 Aims to End Ethnic Studies in Tucson," *Harvard Civil Rights–Civil Liberties Law Review* (April 16, 2011), online at: http://harvardcrcl.org/2011/04/16/arizona-hb-2281-aims-to-end-ethnic-studies-in-tuscon.

23. Jeff Biggers, "Who's Afraid of 'The Tempest'?" *Salon* (January 13, 2012), online at: http://www.salon.com/2012/01/13/

whos_afraid_of_the_tempest. See the important work of Roberto Cintli Rodriquez, who has made a number of important contributions on the attack on indigenous voices, culture, and history. His blog *Dr Cintli* is online at: http://drcintli.blogspot.com/. See also Roberto Cintli Rodriguez, "Arizona's 'Banned' Mexican American Books," *Guardian* (January 18, 2012), online at: http://www.guardian.co.uk/commentisfree/cifamerica/2012/jan/18/arizona-banned-mexican-american-books?newsfeed=true.

24. Charles Gallagher, "Color-Blind Privilege: The Social and Political Functions of Erasing the Color Line in Post Race America," *Race, Gender, and Class* 10:4 (2003), online at: http://aca.lasalle.edu/schools/sas/sscdept/content/faculty/gallagher/Color_Blind_Privilege.pdf. Some of the best work written on critical race theory can be found in a number of books by David Theo Goldberg. See, for example, *The Threat of Race: Reflections on Racial Neoliberalism* (Malden, MA: Wiley-Blackwell, 2008).

25. Cintli Rodriguez, "Arizona's 'Banned' Mexican American Books."

26. Etienne Balibar, "Outline of a Topography of Cruelty: Citizenship and Civility in the Era of Global Violence," *We, the People of Europe? Reflections on Transnational Citizenship* (Princeton, NJ: Princeton University Press, 2004), p. 128.

27. Amy Goodman, "Tucson Orders Closure of Mexican-American School Program as Ethnic Studies Faces Nationwide Threat," *Democracy Now!* (December 29, 2011), online at: http://www.democracynow.org/2011/12/29/tucson_orders_closure_of_mexican_american.

28. Gallagher, "Color-Blind Privilege."

29. Jeff Biggers, "Will Tucson School Board Stand Up and Defend Ethnic Studies?" *Common Dreams* (January 9, 2012), online at: http://www.commondreams.org/view/2012/01/09-9.

30. Jeff Biggers, "AZ School Chief Compares Mexican-American Studies to Hitler Jugend (As He Endorses White Supremacist-Backed Candidate)," *Huffington Post* (January 12, 2012), online at: http://www.huffingtonpost.com/jeff-biggers/az-school-chief-compares-_b_985390.html.

31. Biggers, "Will Tucson School Board Stand Up and Defend Ethnic Studies?"

32. All one has to look at in this case is some of Freire's later work—for instance, *Pedagogy of Hope* (New York: Continuum Press, 1994) and *Pedagogy of Freedom* (Lanham, MD: Rowman and Littlefield Publishers, 1999).

33. Amy Goodman, "Debating Tucson School District's Book Ban after Suspension of Mexican American Studies Program," *Democra-*

cyNow! (January 18, 2012), online at: http://www.democracynow
.org/2012/1/18/debating_tucson_school_districts_book_ban.

34. This theme is taken up brilliantly by Christopher Newfield in
his examination of the culture wars that have plagued higher education in the 1980s. I believe his thesis extends to the attack on public
education as well. Well worth quoting on the issue, he writes, "To
oversimplify somewhat, conservative elites who had been threatened
by the postwar rise of the college-educated economic majority have
put that majority back in its place. Their roundabout weapon has been
the culture wars on higher education in general, and on progressive
cultural trends in the public universities that create and enfranchise
the mass middle class. In *Unmaking the Public University,* I show that
the culture wars have coincided with the majority's economic decline
for the simple reason that these wars propelled the decline by reducing
the public importance and economic claims of the American university
and its graduates. While most commentators have seen the culture
wars as a distraction from economics, I show that the culture wars
were economic wars. They sought to reduce the economic claims of
their target group—the growing college-educated majority—by discred-
iting the cultural framework that had been empowering that group."
Christopher Newfield, *Unmaking the Public University* (Cambridge, MA:
Harvard University Press, 2008), p. 6.

35. For details of Senate Bill 1202, see http://www.azleg.gov/
legtext/49leg/2r/bills/sb1202s.pdf.

36. Paul Davenport, "Arizona House Approves Bill for Bible
Course," *Stamford Advocate* (February 21, 2012), online at: http://
www.stamfordadvocate.com/news/article/Arizona-House-approves
-bill-for-Bible-Course-3347241.php.

37. I have taken up this issue in great detail in Henry A. Giroux,
Youth in a Suspect Society: Democracy or Disposability? (New York:
Palgrave, 2010). See also Christopher Robbins, *Expelling Hope: The
Assault on Youth and the Militarization of Schooling* (New York: State
University of New York Press, 2008).

38. Roger I. Simon, "A Shock to Thought: Curatorial Judgment
and the Public Exhibition of 'Difficult Knowledge,'" *Memory Studies*
(February 25, 2011): 2. See also Deborah Britzman, *Lost Subjects,
Contested Objects: Toward a Psychoanalytic Inquiry of Learning* (Al-
bany: State University of New York, 2003).

39. Zygmunt Bauman and Keith Tester, *Conversations with Zygmunt Bauman* (London: Polity Press, 2001), pp. 65, 63.

40. Cited in Anthony Grafton, "Can the Colleges Be Saved?"
New York Review of Books (May 24, 2012), online at: http://www
.nybooks.com/articles/archives/2012/may/24/can-colleges-be
-saved/?pagination=false.

Notes for Chapter Five

1. There are many books on this issue. Some of the more notable are Sheldon S. Wolin, *Democracy Incorporated: Managed Democracy and the Specter of Inverted Totalitarianism* (Princeton, NJ: Princeton University Press, 2008); Henry A. Giroux, *Against the Terror of Neoliberalism* (Boulder, CO: Paradigm Publishers, 2008); Chris Hedges, *Death of the Liberal Class* (Toronto: Knopf Canada, 2010); and Jacob S. Hacker and Paul Pierson, *Winner-Take-All Politics* (New York: Simon and Schuster, 2010).

2. On the pernicious effects of inequality in US society, see Joseph E. Stiglitz, *The Price of Inequality* (New York: W. W. Norton, 2012); Tony Judt, *Ill Fares the Land* (New York: Penguin Press, 2010). Also see Göran Therborn, "The Killing Fields of Inequality," *Open Democracy* (April 6, 2009), online at: http://www.opendemocracy.net/article/the-killing-fields-of-inequality.

3. Dorothy Roberts, *Fatal Intervention: How Science, Politics, and Big Business Re-Create Race in the Twenty-First Century* (New York: The New Press, 2011), p. xi.

4. Rev. Jesse L. Jackson, "Slandering the Poor," *Counterpunch* (December 14, 2011), online at: http://www.counterpunch.org/2011/12/14/slandering-the-poor.

5. Hope Yen and Laura Wides-Munoz, "US Poorest Poor at Record Highs," *Reader Supported News* (November 4, 2011), online at: http://readersupportednews.org/news-section2/320-80/8235-us-poorest-poor-at-record-highs.

6. Ibid.

7. Paul Buchheit, "Half of America in Poverty?" *CounterPunch* (December 27, 2011), online at: http://www.counterpunch.org/2011/12/27/half-of-america-in-poverty.

8. Diane Sweet, "3.5 Million Homeless and 18.5 Million Vacant Homes in the US," *Occupy America* (December 30, 2011), online at: http://occupyamerica.crooksandliars.com/diane-sweet/35-million-homeless-and-185-million-va.

9. Robert Reich, "Romney's Regressivism," *Robert Reich* (May 25, 2012), online at: http://robertreich.org/post/23708814586.

10. Lawrence Grossberg, *Caught in the Crossfire: Kids, Politics, and America's Future* (Boulder, CO: Paradigm Publishers, 2005), p. 264.

11. Gesa Helms, Marina Vishmidt, and Lauren Berlant, "Affect and the Politics of Austerity: An Interview Exchange with Lauren Berlant," *Variant* 39/40 (Winter 2010), online at: http://www.variant.org.uk/39_40texts/Variant39_40.html#L1.

12. Richard D. Wolff, "Austerity: Why and for Whom?" *In These*

Times (July 15, 2010), online at: http://www.inthesetimes.com/article/6232/austerity_why_and_for_whom.

13. Rania Khalek, "Death by Budget Cut: Why Conservatives and Some Dems Have Blood on Their Hands," *AlterNet* (June 13, 2011), online at: http://www.alternet.org/story/151275/death_by_budget_cut:_why_conservatives_and_some_dems_have_blood_on_their_hands.

14. Khalek, "Death by Budget Cut."

15. Diane Turbyfill, "Bank Robber Planned Crime and Punishment," *Gaston Gazette* (June 16, 2011), online at: http://www.gastongazette.com/articles/bank-58397-richard-hailed.html.

16. Chris Serres and Glenn Howatt, "In Jail for Being in Debt," *Star Tribune* (June 9, 2010), online at: http://www.startribune.com/investigators/95692619.html.

17. Ibid.

18. Matt Taibbi, "Why Isn't Wall Street in Jail?" *Rolling Stone* (February 16, 2011), online at: http://www.rollingstone.com/politics/news/why-isnt-wall-street-in-jail-20110216.

19. Melody Gutierrez, Kim Minugh, and Sam Stanton, "Twin Rivers Police Association Stops Sales of Controversial T-Shirts," *Sacramento Bee* (November 1, 2011), online at: http://www.sacbee.com/2011/11/01/v-mobile/4020655/twin-rivers-police-association.html.

20. Jen Roesch, "How Our War on the Poor Landed One Homeless Mother in Jail," *AlterNet* (March 8, 2012), online at: http://www.alternet.org/story/154458/how_our_war_on_the_poor_landed_one_homeless_mother_in_jail.

21. Ibid.

22. I take this issue up in detail in Henry A. Giroux, *Education and the Crisis of Public Values* (New York: Peter Lang, 2012).

23. Erika Shaker, "Don't Kid Yourself: We Are All Paying for the Defunding of Higher Education," *Common Dreams* (May 12, 2012), online at: http://www.commondreams.org/view/2012/05/12-3.

24. Zygmunt Bauman, *Collateral Damage: Social Inequalities in a Global Age* (Cambridge: Polity Press, 2011), p. 39.

25. James Crotty, "High Deficits Were the Objective of Right Economics," *The Real News* (May 10, 2011), online at: http://therealnews.com/t2/index.php?option=com_content&task=view&id=31&Itemid=74&jumival=6724.

26. Paul Krugman, "The Unwisdom of Elites," *New York Times* (May 8, 2011), p. A23, online at: http://www.nytimes.com/2011/05/09/opinion/09krugman.html.

27. Paul Krugman, "To the Limit," *New York Times* (June 30, 2011), online at: http://www.nytimes.com/2011/07/01/opinion/01krugman.html.

28. Crotty, "High Deficits Were the Objective of Right Economics."

29. Michael Tomasky, "Why The GOP Loves the Debt," *Daily Beast* (July 1, 2011), online at: http://www.thedailybeast.com/articles/2011/07/01/the-gop-party-of-debt-and-deficits.html.

30. Paul Krugman, "The Urge to Purge," *New York Times* (June 27, 2011), online at: http://krugman.blogs.nytimes.com/2011/06/27/the-urge-to-purge.

31. Robert Parry, "If Ayn Rand and the Free Market Fetishists Were Right, We'd Be Living in the Golden Age—Does This Look Like the Golden Age to You?" *AlterNet* (June 28, 2011), online at: http://www.alternet.org/economy/151463/if_ayn_rand_and_the_free_market_fetishists_were_right,_we'd_be_living_in_a_golden_age_—_does_this_look_like_a_golden_age_to_you.

32. Allison Kilkenny, "2/3 of U.S. Corporations Pay Zero Federal Taxes," *AlterNet* (March 27, 2011), online at: http://www.alternet.org/story/150387.

33. This issue is taken up in great detail in Bauman, *Collateral Damage.*

34. Jonathan Schell, "Cruel America," *Nation* (September 28, 2011), online at: http://www.thenation.com/article/163690/cruel-america.

35. Varda Burstyn, *The Rites of Men: Manhood, Politics and the Culture of Sport* (Toronto: University of Toronto Press, 2000), p. 184.

36. Ibid., p. 184.

37. I have taken up this issue in great detail in Henry A. Giroux, *Education and the Crisis of Public Values* (New York: Peter Lang, 2012).

38. Michael Thomas, "'There Will Be Violence, Mark My Words'" *Newsweek* (December 28, 2011), online at: http://www.readersupportednews.org/opinion2/279-82/9142-the-big-lie.

39. Cited in Dick Price, "More Black Men Now in Prison System Than Were Enslaved in 1850," *LA Progressive* (March 31, 2011), online at: http://www.zcommunications.org/more-black-men-now-in-prison-system-than-enslaved-in-1850-by-dick-price. See also Michelle Alexander, *The New Jim Crow: Mass Incarceration in the Age of Colorblindness* (New York: New Press, 2010).

40. "It Gets Even Worse," *New York Times* (July 3, 2011), p. A16.

41. Taibbi, "Why Isn't Wall Street in Jail?"

42. "Antitax Extremism in Minnesota," *New York Times* (July 6, 2011), p. A18.

43. Pradnya Joshi, "We Knew They Got Raises—But This?" *New York Times* (July 2, 2011), p. BU1.

44. Ibid.

45. Josh Harkinson, "10 CEOs Who Got Rich by Squeezing Work-

ers," *Mother Jones* (May 12, 2011), online at: http://motherjones.com/mojo/2011/05/ceo-executive-pay-layoffs.

46. Benjamin M. Friedman, "Cassandra among the Banksters," *New York Review of Books* (June 23, 2011), online at: http://www.nybooks.com/articles/archives/2011/jun/23/cassandra-among-banksters.

47. Frank Rich, "Obama's Original Sin," *New York Magazine* (July 3, 2011), online at: http://nymag.com/news/frank-rich/obama-economy/presidents-failure.

48. Stanley Aronowitz, "Notes on the Occupy Movement," *Logos* (Fall 2011), online at: http://logosjournal.com/2011/fall_aronowitz.

Notes for Chapter Six

1. Arthur C. Brooks, "America's New Culture War: Free Enterprise vs. Government Control," *Washington Post* (May 23, 2010), p. B01.

2. There are numerous histories that chart these struggles. A good place to begin is with Howard Zinn, *A People's History of the United States* (New York: Harper, 2010).

3. Stanley Aronowitz, *How Class Works: Power and Social Movement* (New Haven, CT: Yale University Press, 2003).

4. Philip Green, "Farewell to Democracy?" *Logos* 10:2 (2011), online at: http://logosjournal.com/2011/farewell-to-democracy.

5. Roger Bybee, "Rep. Paul Ryan's Class War," *In These Times* (September 27, 2011), online at: http://inthesetimes.com/working/entry/12010/paul_ryan_and_marie_antoinette_waging_class_war_while_whining_on_taxes. A very different but important critique of economic and social inequality can be found in Richard Wilkenson and Kate Pickett, *The Spirit Level: Why Great Equality Makes Societies Stronger* (New York: Bloomsbury, 2009). See also Robert Reich, *Aftershock: The Next Economy and America's Future* (New York: Knopf, 2011); and Tony Judt, *Ill Fares the Land* (New York: Penguin, 2010).

6. Robert Kuttner, "Land of the Free, Home of the Turncoats," *The American Prospect* 22:8 (2011): 3.

7. Bill Moyers, "Interview with William K. Black," *Bill Moyers Journal* (April 23, 2010), online at: http://www.pbs.org/moyers/journal/04232010/transcript4.html.

8. Robert Reich, "Mitt Romney and the New Gilded Age," *Huffington Post* (July 2, 2012), online at: http://www.huffingtonpost.com/robert-reich/mitt-romney-bain-capital_b_1644856.html.

9. On the Ludlow Massacre, see Howard Zinn, *The Politics of History* (Urbana and Chicago: University of Illinois Press, [1970] 1990), pp. 79–101.

10. Richard Sennett and Jonathan Cobb, *The Hidden Injuries of Class*, rev. ed. (New York: W. W. Norton, 1993).

11. Robert Reich, "Unjust Spoils," *Nation* (July 19, 2010), online at: http://www.thenation.com/article/36893/unjust-spoils.

12. Maxwell Strachan, "15 Facts about U.S. Income Inequality That Everyone Should Know (CHARTS)," *Huffington Post* (September 19, 2011), online at: http://www.huffingtonpost.com/2011/04/05/us-inequality-infographic_n_845042.html.

13. "New Figures Detail Depth of Unemployment Misery, Lower Earnings for All but Super Wealthy (VIDEO)," *Huffington Post* (November 2, 2010), online at: http://www.huffingtonpost.com/2010/10/25/income_inequality_statistics_tax_code_n_773392.html.

14. David DeGraw, "The Richest 1% Have Captured America's Wealth—What's It Going to Take to Get It Back?" *AlterNet* (February 17, 2010), online at: http://www.alternet.org/module/printversion/145705.

15. Ibid.

16. Joseph E. Stiglitz, "Of the 1%, by the 1%, for the 1%," *Vanity Fair* (May 2011), online at: http://www.vanityfair.com/society/features/2011/05/top-one-percent-201105.

17. Robert Reich, "Inequality Has Wrecked the Economy," *Reader Supported News* (September 5, 2011), online at: http://readersupportednews.org/opinion2/279-82/7312-inequality-has-wrecked-the-economy.

18. Diane Sweet, "3.5 Million Homeless and 18.5 Million Vacant Homes in US," *Occupy America* (December 30, 2011), online at: http://occupyamerica.crooksandliars.com/diane-sweet/35-million-homeless-and-185-million-va.

19. Warren Buffett, "Stop Coddling the Super Rich," *New York Times* (August 14, 2011), p. A21.

20. Michelle Alexander cited in Dick Price, "More Black Men Now in Prison System Than Enslaved in 1850," *LA Progressive* (March 31, 2011), online at: http://www.zcommunications.org/more-black-men-now-in-prison-system-than-enslaved-in-1850-by-dick-price.

21. Ibid.

22. Erica Goode, "Many in U.S. Are Arrested by Age 23, Study Finds," *New York Times* (December 19, 2011), online at: http://www.nytimes.com/2011/12/19/us/nearly-a-third-of-americans-are-arrested-by-23-study-says.html?_r=1&pagewanted=print.

23. Jonathan Schell, "Cruel America," *Nation* (September 28, 2011), online at: http://www.thenation.com/article/163690/cruel-america.

24. Marian Wright Edelman, "Is Our Nation on the Titanic?" *Children's Defense Fund* (September 23, 2011), online at: http://cdf

.childrensdefense.org/site/MessageViewer?em_id=25042.0&dlv
_id=24881.

25. Elizabeth Warren, "Nobody Gets Rich on Their Own" (video), *Truthout*, online at http://www.truth-out.org/elizabeth-warren
-nobody-gets-rich-their-own/1316697977.

26. Robert Weiner and John Horton, "End Trickle-Down Economics to Pay off Debt," *Truthout* (July 11, 2011), online at: http://truth-out.org/index.php?option=com_k2&view=item&id=2104:end
-trickledown-economics-to-pay-off-debt.

27. See, for instance, Zygmunt Bauman, *Collateral Damage: Social Inequalities in a Global Age* (Cambridge: Polity, 2011).

28. See Jacob S. Hacker and Paul Pierson, *Winner-Take-All Politics* (New York: Simon and Schuster, 2010).

29. Chris Bowers, "First Official Statement from Occupy Wall Street," *Daily Kos* (October 1, 2011), online at: http://www.dailykos
.com/story/2011/10/01/1021956/-First-official-statement-from
-Occupy-Wall-Street.

30. Cited in Esther Vivas, "M15: A Look toward the Future," *Bullet* (May 14, 2012), online at: http://www.socialistproject.ca/bullet/633
.php.

Notes for Chapter Seven

1. Bernard E. Harcourt, "Occupy Wall Street's 'Political Disobedience,'" *New York Times* (October 13, 2011), online at: http://opinionator.blogs.nytimes.com/2011/10/13/occupy-wall-streets
-political-disobedience.

2. Glenn Greenwald, "The Roots of the UC-Davis Pepper-Spraying," *Salon* (November 20, 2011), online at: http://www.salon
.com/2011/11/20/the_roots_of_the_uc_davis_pepper_spraying/
singleton.

3. For further discussion of the criminalization of young people, especially poor minority youths, by schools and the justice system, see Henry A. Giroux, *Youth in a Suspect Society: Democracy of Disposability?* (New York: Palgrave Macmillan, 2009).

4. Juan Cole, "How Students Landed on the Front Lines of Class War," *Truthdig* (November 22, 2011), online at: http://www.truthdig
.com/report/item/how_students_landed_on_the_front_lines_of_class
_war_20111122.

5. Bryan Farrell, "College Campuses Now a Hotbed for Developing Frightening New Weapons," *Alternet* (March 4, 2012), online at: http://www.alternet.org/module/printversion/101020.

6. Anthony Grafton, "Can the Colleges Be Saved?" *New York*

Review of Books (May 24, 2012), online at: http://www.nybooks.com/articles/archives/2012/may/24/can-colleges-be-saved/?pagination=false.

7. Robert Reich, "The Decline of the Public Good," *Reader Supported News* (January 12, 2012), online at: http://www.readersupportednews.org/opinion2/287-124/9283-focus-the-decline-of-the-public-good. This issue has been taken up in great detail by David Harvey, Zygmunt Bauman, Michel Foucault, Colin Ley, Naomi Klein, myself, and a host of other writers.

8. Jacques Rancière, *Hatred of Democracy* (London: Verso, 2006).

9. Michael Collins, "Universities Need Reform—But the Market Is Not the Answer," *OpenDemocracy* (November 23, 2010), online at: http://www.opendemocracy.net/ourkingdom/michael-collins/universities-need-reform-but-market-is-not-answer.

10. See for instance, David H. Price, *Weaponizing Anthropology* (Oakland, CA: AK Press, 2011); and Henry A. Giroux, *The University in Chains: Confronting the Military-Industrial-Academic Complex* (Boulder, CO: Paradigm Publishers, 2007).

11. Scott Jaschik, "New Tactic to Kill Faculty Unions," *Inside Higher Ed* (March 3, 2011), online at: http://www.insidehighered.com/news/2011/03/03/ohio_bill_would_kill_faculty_unions_in_unexpected_way.

12. Ellen Schrecker, *The Lost Soul of Higher Education* (New York: The New Press, 2010), pp. 206–215.

13. I take up these attacks in great detail in Giroux, *The University in Chains*.

14. Zygmunt Bauman, *Does Ethics Have a Chance in a World of Consumers?* (Cambridge, MA: Harvard University Press, 2008), p. 159.

15. John Pilger, "The Revolt in Egypt Is Coming Home," *Truthout* (February 10, 2011), online at: http://www.truth-out.org/the-revolt-egypt-is-coming-home67624.

16. Zygmunt Bauman, *The Individualized Society* (London: Polity, 2001), p. 55.

17. Alex Honneth, *Pathologies of Reason: On the Legacy of Critical Theory* (New York: Columbia University Press, 2009), p. 188.

18. Zygmunt Bauman, "Youth Unemployment—the Precariat Is Welcoming Generation Y," *Social Europe Journal* (May 22, 2012), online at: http://www.social-europe.eu/2012/05/youth-unemployment-the-precariat-is-welcoming-generation-y.

19. Ibid.

20. Chris Hedges, "Northern Light," *Truthdig* (June 4, 2012), online at: http://www.truthdig.com/report/item/northern_light_20120603.

21. Half an hour after the police raid on Liberty Square in Zuccotti

Park, the Occupy Wall Street media team issued a statement saying, "Some politicians may physically remove us from public spaces—our spaces—and, physically, they may succeed. But we are engaged in a battle of ideas." Online at: http://occupywallst.org/article/you-cant-evict-idea-whose-time-has-come. The issue of space is also taken up brilliantly on Peter Marcuse's blog. See Peter Marcuse, "The Purpose of the Occupation Movement and the Danger of Fetishizing Space" (November 15, 2011), online at: http://pmarcuse.wordpress.com/2011/11/15/the-purpose-of-the-occupation-movement-and-the-danger-of-fetishizing-space. Marcuse is especially helpful in rejecting the fetishization of Zuccotti Park while distinguishing among seven functions of the movement: (1) a *confrontation function*, "taking the struggle to the enemy's territory, confronting, potentially disrupting, the operations at the center of the problem"; (2) a *symbolic function*, which registers a collective and "deeply felt unhappiness about things as they are and the direction in which they are going"; (3) an *educational function*, "provoking questioning, exploration, juxtaposition of differing viewpoints and issues, seeking clarification and sources of commonality within difference"; (4) a *glue function*, "creating a community of trust and commitment to the pursuit of common goals; [providing] a way of coming together in a community for those who are deeply affected and concerned"; (5) an *umbrella function*, "creating a space ... in which quite disparate groups can work together in pursuit of ultimately consistent and mutually reinforcing goals ... a political umbrella, an organizing base for an on-going alliance, not just a temporary coalition, of the deprived and discontented"; (6) an *activation function*, "inspiring others to greater militancy and sharper focus on common goals and specific demands ... providing space for ... cross discussions among supporting groups and interests, organizing ... events in support of ... reforms that [suggest] Occupy's own ultimate goals of change"; and (7) a *model function*, "showing, by its internal organization and methods of proceeding, that an alternative form of democracy is possible."

22. Robert Scheer, "If a Republican Were President," *Truthdig* (October 13, 2011), online at: http://www.truthdig.com/report/item/if_a_republican_were_president_20111013.

23. Zygmunt Bauman, *Collateral Damage: Social Inequalities in a Global Age* (Cambridge: Polity Press, 2011), p. 14.

◇

Index

◆

About the Author

Henry A. Giroux, a prominent social critic who writes regularly for the media, currently holds the Global TV Network Chair Professorship at McMaster University, Canada, in the English and Cultural Studies Department. His recent books include *Twilight of the Social* (Paradigm 2012) and *Hearts of Darkness: Torturing Children in the War on Terror* (Paradigm 2010).